Jonathan H. Jellett

Pacific Coast Collection Laws

A summary of the laws of California, Nevada, Oregon, Washington, Idaho,

Montana, Utah, Wyoming, Arizona, British Columbia, Colorado, New Mexico, and

Texas. Including insolvency laws, also the jurisdiction of U. S. court

Jonathan H. Jellett

Pacific Coast Collection Laws
A summary of the laws of California, Nevada, Oregon, Washington, Idaho, Montana, Utah, Wyoming, Arizona, British Columbia, Colorado, New Mexico, and Texas. Including insolvency laws, also the jurisdiction of U. S. court

ISBN/EAN: 9783337218973

Printed in Europe, USA, Canada, Australia, Japan

Cover: Foto ©Suzi / pixelio.de

More available books at **www.hansebooks.com**

Pacific Coast

COLLECTION LAWS

A SUMMARY OF THE

LAWS OF CALIFORNIA, NEVADA, OREGON, WASHINGTON
TERRITORY, IDAHO, MONTANA, UTAH, WYOMING, ARI-
ZONA, AND BRITISH COLUMBIA, AND OF THE UNITED
STATES, IN RELATION TO BANKRUPTCY;

ALSO,

THE JURISDICTION OF U. S. COURTS,

WITH

THE NAMES OF RELIABLE ATTORNEYS IN THE PRINCIPAL
CITIES AND TOWNS THROUGHOUT THE PACIFIC COAST.

BY

J. H. JELLETT,

Attorney at Law.

SAN FRANCISCO:

BACON & COMPANY, BOOK AND JOB PRINTERS,

Corner of Clay and Sansome Streets.

1876.

PREFACE.

Having for upwards of six years been in charge of the Law and Collection Department of "The Mercantile Agency" of R. G. DUN & Co., San Francisco, the compiling of this work has suggested itself to me as important to Bankers, Merchants, and Manufacturers having business transactions in the Pacific States and Territories, including British Columbia. Further, it has been prepared with a view to aid Attorneys and Notaries in matters arising outside of their own State or Territory.

I have endeavored to give a concise statement of the laws relating to the collection of debts, together with the names of carefully selected attorneys ; and in compiling the work have been assisted by the following named practicing attorneys :

DOLPH, BRONOUGH, DOLPH & SIMON........ Portland, Oregon.
BISHOP & SABIN.........................Pioche, Nevada.
LEWIS BURNES.....................Salt Lake City, Utah.
HON. JAMES K. KENNEDY..Walla Walla, Washington Territory.
D. E. CULLEN.........................Helena, Montana.
E. P. JOHNSON.....................Cheyenne, Wyoming.
JONAS W. BROWN.................. ....Idaho City, Idaho.
M. W. T. DRAKE, of Drake & Jackson........Victoria, B. C.

J. H. JELLETT.

SAN FRANCISCO, January, 1876.

CONTENTS.

PART I.

ATTORNEYS.

PART II.

JURISDICTION OF U. S. COURTS AND BANKRUPTCY PROCEEDINGS.

PART III.

CALIFORNIA.

PART IV.

NEVADA.

6 CONTENTS.

PART V.

OREGON.

Part VI.

UTAH.

Part VII.

IDAHO.

PART VIII.

WYOMING.

PART IX.

MONTANA.

PART X.

WASHINGTON TERRITORY.

Part XI
ARIZONA.

Part XII.
BRITISH COLUMBIA.

PART I.

ATTORNEYS.

THE FOLLOWING ARE RECOMMENDED AS RELIABLE.

CALIFORNIA.

COUNTY.	RESIDENCE.	NAME.
Alameda	Oakland	J. C. Plunkett.
	Livermore	E. Aubury.
	Pleasanton . . .	J. R. Palmer. Also Notary Public.
Amador	Jackson . . . : . .	J. M. Porter.
Butte	Oroville	John C. Gray.
	Chico	Park Henshaw.
Colusa	Colusa	John T. Harrington.
Contra Costa . .	Martinez	Mills & Jones.
	Antioch	James T. Cruikshank.
Del Norte	Crescent City .	W. A. Hamilton.
El Dorado	Placerville	George G. Blanchard.
Fresno	Fresno	H. S. Dixon.
Humboldt	Eureka	James Hanna.

CALIFORNIA—*Continued.*

COUNTY.	RESIDENCE.	NAME.
Inyo.........	Independence.	Reddy & Conklin.
Kern	Bakersfield ...	J. W. Freeman.
Lake	Lakeport.....	A. P. McCarty.
Lassen.......	Susanville	J. S. Chapman.
Los Angeles..	Los Angeles..	Henry T. Hazard.
Marin........	San Rafael....	Hepburn Wilkins.
Mariposa.....	Mariposa.....	John M. Corcoran.
Mendocino ...	Ukiah	Thos. L. Carothers.
Merced	Merced	Samuel C. Bates, Collector.
Modoc	Dorris Bridge.	Geo. F. Harris. ·
Monterey....	Salinas.......	M. Farley.
Napa	Napa	R. Burnell.
Nevada	Nevada City.. Grass Valley.. Truckee	Jno. I. Caldwell. A. J. Ridge. C. F. McGlashan.
Placer	Ophir, (Near Auburn.)	James Moore.
Plumas.......	Quincy ...... La ·Porte.....	J. D. Goodwin. G. G. Clough.
Sacramento...	Sacramento ...	Edgerton, Tubbs & Cole, Successors to Beatty & Denson.

CALIFORNIA—*Continued.*

COUNTY.	RESIDENCE.	NAME.
San Benito....	Hollister.....	N. C. Briggs.
San Bernardino	San Bernardino	H. C. Rolfe.
San Diego....	San Diego....	Chase & Leach.
San Francisco.	San Francisco.	Campbell, Fox & Campbell. E. H. Rixford.
San Joaquin ..	Stockton.....	Jos. M. Cavis.
San Luis Obispo.........	San Luis Obispo.........	Harrison & McMurtry.
San Mateo....	Redwood City.	Geo. W. Fox.
Santa Barbara.	Santa Barbara	Jarrett T. Richards.
Santa Clara...	San Jose..... Gilroy.......	C. D. Wright. W. W. Hoover.
Santa Cruz ...	Santa Cruz.... Watsonville...	E. L. Williams. J. A. Barham.
Shasta.......	Shasta.......	Ephraim Garter.
Sierra........	Downieville...	E. Barry.
Siskiyou.....	Yreka........	E. Steele.
Solano.......	Suisun....... Vallejo.......	Joseph McKenna. S. G. Hilborn.
Sonoma......	Santa Rosa ... Healdsburg ...	James H. McGee. H. C. Firebaugh.

CALIFORNIA—*Continued*.

COUNTY.	RESIDENCE.	NAME.
Sonoma	Petaluma	W. D. Bliss.
Stanislaus	Modesto	A. Hewel.
Sutter	Yuba City	Stabler & Bayne.
Tehama	Red Bluff	W. Henry Jones.
Tulare	Visalia	Brown & Daggett.
Tuolumne	Sonora	C. L. Street.
Ventura	San Buenaventura	Henry Robinson.
Yolo	Woodland	C. S. Frost.
Yuba	Marysville	Van Clief & Cowden.

NEVADA.

COUNTY.	RESIDENCE.	NAME.
Douglas	Genoa	D. W. Virgin.
Elko	Elko	R. R. Bigelow.
Esmeralda	Aurora	A. L. Greeley.
Eureka	Eureka	Geo. W. Baker.
Humboldt	Winnemucca	W. L. French, Collector.
Lander	Austin	Henry Mayenbaum.
Lincoln	Pioche	Bishop & Sabin.

NEVADA—*Continued.*

COUNTY.	RESIDENCE.	NAME.
Lyon	Dayton	Geo. W. Keith.
Nye	Belmont......	Williams & Owen.
Ormsby	Carson City...	Wm. Patterson.
Storey	Virginia City..	W. E. F. Deal.
Washoe	Reno	C. W. Jones, Collector.

OREGON.

COUNTY.	RESIDENCE.	NAME.
Baker........	Baker City....	L. O. Sterns. Also Notary Public.
Benton.......	Corvallis.......	F. A. Chenoweth.
Clackamas....	Oregon City ..	Johnson & Cowan.
Coos.........	Empire City ..	D. L. Watson.
Douglas......	Roseburg.....	J. F. Watson.
Jackson	Jacksonville...	H. K. Hanna.
Lane	Eugene City ..	George B. Dorris.
Linn	Albany.......	Powell & Flinn.
Marion.......	Salem........	Knight & Lord.
Multnomah ...	Portland......	Dolph, Bronough, Dolph & Simon.

OREGON—*Continued.*

COUNTY.	RESIDENCE.	NAME.
Polk	Dallas	J. L. Collins.
Umatilla.	Pendleton	J. H. Turner.
Union	La Grande . . .	B. W. Lichtenthaler.
Wasco	The Dalles . . .	J. B. Condon.
Washington. . .	Hillsboro	Thos. H. Tongue.
Yam Hill.	La Fayette . . .	H. Hurley.

UTAH TERRITORY.

COUNTY.	RESIDENCE.	NAME.
Salt Lake	Salt Lake City.	Lewis Burnes.
Box Elder	Corinne	E. P. Johnson.

WASHINGTON TERRITORY.

COUNTY.	RESIDENCE.	NAME.
Clarke	Vancouver. . . .	Charles Brown, Collector.
Jefferson	Port Townsend	Judson & Kuhn.
King.	Seattle	Leary & McNaught.

WASHINGTON TERRITORY—*Continued.*

COUNTY.	RESIDENCE.	NAME.
Pierce	Steilacoom ...	Jacob Hoover.
Thurston.....	Olympia	John P. Judson.
Walla Walla..	Walla Walla..	Kennedy & George.
		James K. Kennedy, Late Judge District Court, First Judicial District. Wyatt A. George.

MONTANA TERRITORY.

COUNTY.	RESIDENCE.	NAME.
Gallatin'......	Bozeman	Sharp & Napton.
Lewis & Clarke	Helena	W. E. Cullen.
Madison	Virginia City..	Theo. Muffly.

IDAHO TERRITORY.

COUNTY.	RESIDENCE.	NAME.
Ada	Boise City....	H. E. Prickett.
Boise	Idaho City....	Jonas W. Brown.
Nez Perces ...	Lewiston	J. M. Howe.

2

ARIZONA TERRITORY.

COUNTY.	RESIDENCE.	NAME.
Pima	Tucson	Farley & Pomroy.

WYOMING TERRITORY.

COUNTY.	RESIDENCE.	NAME.
Laramie......	Cheyenne.....	E. P. Johnson.

BRITISH COLUMBIA.

DISTRICT.	RESIDENCE.	NAME.
Victoria	Victoria......	Drake & Jackson.

PART II.

JURISDICTION OF U. S. COURTS AND BANK-RUPTCY PROCEEDINGS.

CHAPTER I.

COURTS AND THEIR JURISDICTION.

The CIRCUIT COURTS of the United States have jurisdiction—

Of all suits of a civil nature at common law or in equity, where the matter in dispute, exclusive of costs, exceeds the sum or value of five hundred dollars, and an alien is a party, or the suit is between a citizen of the State where it is brought and a citizen of another State: *Provided*, that no Circuit Court shall have cognizance of any suit to recover the contents of any promissory note or other chose in action in favor of an assignee, unless a suit might have been prosecuted in such Court to recover the said contents if no assignment had been made, except in case of foreign bills of exchange.

In all suits at law or in equity arising under the patent or copyright laws of the United States.

Of all suits by or against any banking association established in the district for which the Court is held, under any law providing for national banking associations.

In matters of bankruptcy, a general superintendence and jurisdiction.

Any suit commenced in a State Court, when the amount in dispute, exclusive of costs, exceeds the sum or value of five hundred dollars, to be made to appear to the satisfaction of said Court, may be removed, for trial, into the Circuit Court for the district where such suit is pending, next to be held after the filing of the petition for such removal, in the cases following :

1. When the suit is against an alien, or is by a citizen of the State wherein it is brought, and against a citizen of another State, on the petition of the defendant.

2. When the suit is against an alien and a citizen of the State where it is brought, or is by a citizen of such State against a citizen of the same and the citizen of another State, it may be so removed, as against said alien or citizen of another State, upon the petition of such defendant. But such removal shall not take away or prejudice the right of the plaintiff to proceed at the same time with the suit in the State Court, as against the other defendants.

3. When a suit is between a citizen of the State in which it is brought and a citizen of another State, it may be removed on the petition of the latter, whether he be plaintiff or defendant, if he makes and files in said State Court an affidavit, stating that he has reason to believe, and does believe, that, from prejudice or local influence, he will not be able to obtain justice in such State Court.

The DISTRICT COURTS of the United States have jurisdiction—

In all suits by or against any association established under any law providing for national banking associations, within the district for which the Court is held.

The District Courts are constituted Courts of Bankruptcy, and shall have, in their respective districts, original jurisdiction in all matters and proceedings in Bankruptcy.

It also has jurisdiction of suits for the collection of the Internal Revenue, and is the Court of Admiralty.

CHAPTER II.

BANKRUPTCY.

INVOLUNTARY BANKRUPTCY—ACTS OF BANKRUPTCY.

When any person departs from the State, district, or territory of which he is an inhabitant, with intent to defraud his creditors; or, being absent, shall, with such intent, remain absent; or shall conceal himself to avoid the service of legal process in any action for the recovery of a debt or demand provable under the bankruptcy act; or shall conceal or remove any of his property to avoid its being attached, taken, or sequestered on legal process; or shall make any assignment, gift, sale, conveyance, or transfer of his estate, property, rights, or credits, either within the United States or elsewhere, with intent to delay, defraud, or hinder his creditors; or who has been arrested and held in custody under, or by virtue of, mesne process or execution, issued out of any Court of the United States, or of any State, district, or territory within which such debtor resides or has property, founded upon a demand in its nature provable against a bankrupt's estate under this act, and for a sum exceeding one hundred dollars, and such process is remaining in force and not discharged by payment, or in any other manner provided by the law of the United States or of such State, district, or territory, applicable thereto, for a period of twenty days, or has been actually imprisoned for more than twenty days in a civil action founded on contract for the sum of one hundred dollars or upwards; or who, being bankrupt or insolvent, or in contemplation of bankruptcy or insolvency, shall make any payment, gift, grant, sale, conveyance, or transfer of money, or other property, estate, rights, or credits, or confess judgment, or give any warrant to confess judgment, or procure his property to be taken on legal process, with intent to give a preference to one or more of his creditors, or to any person or persons who are or may be liable for him as indorsers, bail, sureties, or otherwise; or with the intent by such disposition of his property to defeat or delay the operation of the bankruptcy act;

or who, being a bank, banker, broker, merchant, trader, manufacturer, or miner, has fraudulently stopped payment, or being a bank, banker, broker, merchant, trader, manufacturer, or miner, has stopped or suspended and not resumed payment, within a period of forty days, of his commercial paper, (made or passed in the course of his business as such) or who, being a bank or banker, shall fail for forty days to pay any depositor upon demand of payment lawfully made, shall be deemed to have committed an act of bankruptcy, and shall be adjudged a bankrupt on the petition of one or more of his creditors, who shall constitute one-fourth thereof, at least, in number, and the aggregate of whose debts, provable under this act, amounts to at least one-third of the debts so provable: *Provided,* that such petition is brought within six months after such act of bankruptcy.

The petition of creditors may be sufficiently verified by the oaths of the first five signers thereof, if so many there be, and if any of the first five signers shall not reside in the district in which such petition is to be filed, the same may be signed and verified by the oath or oaths of the attorney or attorneys, agent or agents, of such signers; and in computing the number of creditors, as aforesaid, who shall join in such petition, creditors whose respective debts do not exceed two hundred and fifty dollars shall not be received. But if there be no creditors whose debts exceed said sum of two hundred and fifty dollars, or if the requisite number of creditors holding debts exceeding two hundred and fifty dollars fail to sign the petition, the creditors having debts of a less amount shall be received for the purposes aforesaid.

Voluntary Bankruptcy.

Any person residing within the jurisdiction of the United States, owing debts provable under the bankruptcy act, exceeding the amount of three hundred dollars, may file his petition in bankruptcy.

Preferences and Fraudulent Conveyances.

If any person, being insolvent, or in contemplation of insolvency, within two months before the filing of the petition by or against

him, with a view to give a preference to any creditor or person
having a claim against him, or who is under any liability for him,
procures any part of his property to be attached, sequestered,·or
seized on execution, or makes any payment, pledge, assignment,
transfer, or conveyance of any part of his property, either directly
or indirectly, absolutely or conditionally, the person receiving such
payment, pledge, assignment, transfer, or conveyance, or to be
benefited thereby, or by such attachment, having reasonable cause
to believe such person is insolvent, and knowing that such attachment, sequestration, seizure, payment, pledge, assignment, or conveyance, is made in fraud of the provisions of the act, the same shall
be void, and the assignee may recover the property, or the value
of it, from the person so receiving it, or so to be benefited ; and if
any person being insolvent, or in contemplation of insolvency or
bankruptcy, within three months before the filing of the petition
by or against him, makes any payment, sale, assignment, transfer,
conveyance, or other disposition of any part of his property to any
person who then has reasonable cause to believe him to be insolvent,
or to be acting in contemplation of insolvency, and knowing that
such payment, sale, assignment, transfer, or other conveyance is
made with a view to prevent his property from coming to his assignee in bankruptcy, or to prevent the same from being distributed
under the bankruptcy act, or to defeat the object of, or in any way
impair, hinder, impede, or delay the operation and effect of, or to
evade any of the provisions of, the bankruptcy act, the sale, assignment, transfer, or conveyance shall be void, and the assignee may
recover the property or the value thereof, as assets of the bankrupt
—and if such sale, assignment, transfer or conveyance is not made
in the usual and ordinary course of business of the debtor, the
fact shall be prima facie evidence of fraud.

PER CENT. TO BE PAID BY BANKRUPT.

In cases of involuntary bankruptcy, the bankrupt is not required to pay a percentage of the claims proved against the estate
in order to entitle him to a discharge.

In cases of voluntary bankruptcy, no discharge shall be granted
to a debtor whose assets shall not be equal to thirty per centum of

the claims proved against his estate, upon which he shall be liable as principal debtor, without the assent of at least one-fourth of his creditors in number, and one-third in value.

Proofs of Debts.

Proofs of debts against the estate of the bankrupt, by or on behalf of creditors residing within the judicial district where the proceedings in bankruptcy are pending, shall be made before one of the registers of the Court in said district, or before a notary public ; such proof to be certified by the notary and attested by his signature and official seal ; and by or on behalf of non-resident creditors, before any register in bankruptcy in the judicial district where such creditors, or either of them, reside, or before any commissioner of the Circuit Court authorized to administer oaths in any district, or before a notary public ; certified and attested as aforesaid.

The affidavit in proof of claim shall be made by the claimant, unless he be absent from the United States, or is prevented by some other good cause from testifying, in which case the demand may be verified by the attorney or authorized agent of the claimant.

When a claim is presented for proof before the election of the assignee, and the judge entertains doubts of its validity, or of the right of the creditor to prove it, and is of opinion that such validity or right ought to be investigated by the assignee, he may postpone the proof of the claim until the assignee is chosen—any person who, after the approval of the act, shall have accepted any preference, having reasonable cause to believe that the same was made or given by the debtor, contrary to any provision of the act, shall not prove the debt or claim on account of which the preference was made or given ; nor shall he receive any dividend therefrom until he shall first have surrendered to the assignee all property, money, benefit or advantage received by him under such preference.

When any person who, being bankrupt or insolvent, or in contemplation of bankruptcy or insolvency, shall make any payment, gift, grant, sale, conveyance or transfer of money or other property, estate, rights or credits, with intent to give a preference, and upon being adjudged a bankrupt, the assignee may recover back the money or property so paid, conveyed, sold, assigned, or transferred, contrary to the act; provided, that the person receiving such payment or conveyance had reasonable cause to believe that the debtor was insolvent, and knew that a fraud on the act was intended; and such person, if a creditor, shall not, in case of actual fraud on his part, be allowed to prove for more than a moiety of his debt.

LIENS.

The lien of a levy made under an execution, issued under a final judgment, obtained in good faith and without collusion, is preserved, provided such lien attached before petition in bankruptcy is filed; but the lien is not preserved when it does not attach until after petition filed.

DISCHARGE.

At any time after the expiration of six months from the adjudication of bankruptcy, or if no debts have been proved against the bankrupt, or if no assets have come to the hands of the assignee, at any time after the expiration of sixty days, and within one year from the adjudication of bankruptcy, the bankrupt may apply to the Court for a discharge from his debts, and the Court shall thereupon order notice to be given by mail to all creditors who have proved their debts, and by publication at least once a week in such newspapers as the Court shall designate, to appear on a day appointed for that purpose, and show cause why a discharge should not be granted to the bankrupt. No discharge shall be granted, or, if granted, be valid, if the bankrupt has willfully sworn falsely in his affidavit attached to his petition, schedule, or inventory, or upon any examination in the course of the proceedings in bankruptcy, in relation to any material fact concerning his estate or his debts, or to any other material fact; or if he has concealed any part of his estate or effects, or any books or writings relating thereto; or if he has been guilty of any fraud or negligence in the care, custody, or delivery to the assignee of the property belonging to him at the time of the presentation to him of his petition and inventory, excepting such property as he is permitted to retain under the provisions of the act ; or if he has caused, permitted, or suffered any loss, waste, or destruction thereof ; or if within four months before the commencement of such proceedings, he has procured his lands, goods, moneys, or chattels to be attached, sequestered, or seized on execution ; or if he has destroyed, mutilated, altered, or falsified any of his books, documents, papers, writings, or securities, or has made or been privy to the making of any false or fraudulent entry in any book of account or other document, with intent to defraud his creditors ; or has removed or caused to be removed any part of his property from the district, with intent to defraud his creditors ; or if he has given any fraudulent preference contrary to the provisions of this act, or made any fraudulent payment, gift, transfer, conveyance, or assignment of any part of his property, or has lost any part thereof in gaming, or has admitted a false or fictitious debt against his estate ; or if, having knowledge that any person has proved such false or fictitious debt, he has not disclosed the same to his assignee within one month after such knowledge ; or if, being a merchant or tradesman, he has not, subsequently to the passage of the act, kept proper books of account ; or if he, or any person in his behalf, has procured the assent of any creditor to the discharge, or influenced the action of any creditor at any stage of the proceedings, by any pecuniary consideration or obligation ; or if he has, in contemplation of becoming bankrupt, made any pledge, payment, transfer, assignment, or conveyance of any part of his property, directly or indirectly, absolutely or conditionally, for the purpose of preferring any creditor or person having a claim against him, or who is or may be under liability for him, or for the purpose of preventing the property from coming into the hands of the assignee, or of being distributed under the act in satisfaction of his debts ; or if he has been convicted of any misdemeanor under this act, or has been guilty of any fraud whatever, contrary to the true intent of the act : and before any discharge is granted, the bankrupt shall take and subscribe an oath to the effect that he has not done, suffered, or been privy to any act, matter, or thing specified in the act as a ground for withholding such discharge, or as invalidating such discharge, if granted.

COMPOSITION.

A meeting of creditors may be called under the direction of the Court, and the creditors resolve that a composition proposed by the debtor shall be accepted in satisfaction of the debts due to them from the debtor. And such resolution shall, to be operative, have been passed by a majority in number, and three-fourths in value of the creditors of the debtor assembled at such meeting, either in person or by proxy, and shall be confirmed by the signatures thereto of the debtor and two-thirds in number and one-half in value of all the creditors of the debtor. And in calculating a majority for the purposes of a composition, creditors whose debts amount to sums not exceeding fifty dollars shall be reckoned in the majority in value, but not in the majority in number; and the value of the debts of secured creditors above the amount of such security, to be determined by the Court, shall, as nearly as circumstances admit, be estimated in the same way. And creditors whose debts are fully secured shall not be entitled to vote upon or to sign such resolution, without first relinquishing such security for the benefit of the estate.

The resolution must be approved by the Court and recorded, and until so approved and recorded shall be of no validity.

The provisions of a composition accepted by such a resolution shall be binding on all the creditors whose names and addresses, and the amounts of the debts due to whom, are shown in the statement of the debtor, produced at the meeting at which the resolution shall have been passed; but shall not affect or prejudice the rights of any other creditors.

PART III.

STATE OF CALIFORNIA.

CHAPTER I.

COURTS AND THEIR JURISDICTION.

THE SUPREME COURT OF THE STATE OF CALIFORNIA has original and appellate jurisdiction. *Its original jurisdiction* extends—

To the issuance of writs of mandamus, certiorari, prohibition, and habeas corpus, and all other writs necessary or proper to the complete exercise of its appellate jurisdiction.

Its appellate jurisdiction extends—

1. To all civil actions for relief formerly given in courts of equity.

2. To all civil actions in which the subject of litigation is not capable of pecuniary estimation.

3. To all civil actions in which the subject of litigation is capable of pecuniary estimation, which involve the title or possession of real estate, or the legality of any tax, impost, assessment, toll or municipal fine, or in which the demand exclusive of interest, or the value of the property in controversy, amounts to three hundred dollars.

4. To all special proceedings.

5. To all cases arising in the Probate Courts.

DISTRICT COURTS.

The jurisdiction of these Courts extends—

1. To all civil actions for relief formerly given in courts of equity.

2. To all civil actions in which the subject of litigation is not capable of pecuniary estimation.

3. To all civil actions (except actions of forcible-entry and detainer) in which the subject of litigation is capable of pecuniary estimation, which involve the title of possession of real estate, or the legality of any tax, impost, assessment, toll or municipal fine, or in which the demand, exclusive of interest, or the value of the property in controversy, amounts to three hundred dollars.

4. To special proceedings not within the jurisdiction of the County and Probate Courts.

5. To the issuance of writs of mandamus, certiorari, prohibition, habeas corpus, and all writs necessary to the exercise of its powers.

COUNTY COURTS

Have original and appellate jurisdiction. *Their original jurisdiction* extends—

1. To actions to prevent or abate a nuisance.

2. To actions of forcible entry and detainer.

3. To proceedings in insolvency.

4. To all special cases or proceedings in which the law, giving the remedy or authorizing the proceedings, confers the jurisdiction upon it.

5. To the issuance of writs of habeas corpus, and all writs necessary to the exercise of its powers.

6. To inquire, by the intervention of a grand jury, of all public offenses committed, or triable in the county.

7. *Their appellate jurisdiction* extends to all cases arising in Justices' or Police Courts.

PROBATE COURTS.

Probate Courts have jurisdiction—

1. To open and receive proof of last wills and testaments, and to admit them to probate.

2. To grant letters testamentary, of administration and of guardianship, and to revoke the same.

3. To appoint appraisers of estates of deceased persons.

4. To compel executors, administrators and guardians to render accounts.

5. To order the sale of property of estates, or belonging to minors.

6. To order the payment of debts due from estates.

7. To order and regulate all distributions and partitions of property, or estates of deceased persons.

8. To compel the attendance of witnesses, and the production of title deeds, papers, and other property of an estate, or of a minor.

9. To make such orders as may be necessary to the exercise of the powers conferred upon it.

10. To exercise jurisdiction in all matters of probate and guardianship.

JUSTICES' COURTS.

The civil jurisdiction of these Courts within their respective townships or cities extends—

1. To an action arising on contract, for the recovery of money only, if the sum claimed, exclusive of interest, does not amount to three hundred dollars.

2. To an action for damages for injury to the person, or for taking or detaining personal property, or for injuring personal property, or for an injury to real property, where no issue is raised by the answer involving the plaintiff's title or possession of the same, if the damages claimed do not amount to three hundred dollars.

3. To all actions for a fine, penalty, or forfeiture, not amounting to three hundred dollars, given by statute or the ordinance of an incorporated city or town.

4. To an action upon a bond or undertaking conditioned for the

payment of money, not amounting to three hundred dollars, though the penalty exceed that sum; the judgment to be given for the sum actually due. When the payments are to be made by installments, an action may be brought for each installment as it falls due.

5. To an action to recover the possession of personal property, when the value of such property does not amount to three hundred dollars.

6. To take and enter judgment on the confession of a defendant, when the amount confessed, exclusive of interest, does not amount to three hundred dollars.

The jurisdiction above does not extend, however—

1. To a civil action in which the title or possession of real property is put in issue.

2. Nor to an action or proceeding against ships, vessels, or boats, when the suit or proceeding is for the recovery of seamen's wages for a voyage performed in whole or in part without the waters of this State.

CHAPTER II.

TERMS OF COURTS, WHEN AND WHERE HELD.

SUPREME COURT.

There must be four terms in each year for the hearing of causes, to commence on the second Monday of January, April, July, and October. The January and July terms are held at the city of San Francisco. The April and October terms are held at the city of Sacramento. Additional terms may be held by order of the Court.

DISTRICT COURTS.

The State is divided into twenty judicial districts.

There is a District Court in each of the judicial districts, and Court is held at the county seat of each county, as follows :

COUNTY.	DISTRICT.	WHEN HELD.
Alameda	Third	3d Monday February, June, and October.
Alpine	Sixteenth	1st Monday April and October.
Amador	Eleventh	2d Monday March, June, September, and December.
Butte	Second	1st Monday March; 3d Monday November; 2d Monday July.
Calaveras	Eleventh	2d Monday January, April, July, and October.
Colusa	Tenth	4th Monday April; 2d Monday August; 1st Monday December.
Contra Costa	Fifteenth	3d Tuesday April, July, and November.
Del Norte	Eighth	2d Monday May, August, and November.
El Dorado	Eleventh	2d Monday February, and May; 3d Monday August, and November.
Fresno	Thirteenth	3d Monday February, June, and October.
Humboldt	Eighth	2d Monday March, June, September, and December.
Inyo	Sixteenth	1st Monday May and November.
Kern	Sixteenth	3d Monday May and November.
Klamath	Eighth	2d Monday April, July, and October.
Lake	Seventh	3d Monday April; 2d Monday November.
Lassen	Second	2d Monday June; 2d Monday September.
Los Angeles	Seventeenth	1st Monday February, May, August, and November.
Marin	Seventh	1st Monday March and July; 3d Monday November.
Mariposa	Thirteenth	3d Monday April; 3d Monday August; 2d Monday December.
Mendocino	Seventh	2d Monday April; 3d Monday July; 1st Monday November.
Merced	Thirteenth	3d Monday March, July, and November.
Modoc	Ninth	2d Monday July; 3d Monday October.
Mono	Sixteenth	3d Monday April and October.
Monterey	Twentieth	3d Monday March, July, and November.
Napa	Seventh	1st Monday February, June, and October.
Nevada	Fourteenth	2d Monday March, June, September, and December.
Placer	Fourteenth	1st Monday February, May, August, and November.
Plumas	Second	4th Monday May; 1st Monday October.
Sacramento	Sixth	1st Monday February, April, June, August, October, and December.
San Benito	Twentieth	1st Monday April, August, and December.
San Bernardino	Eighteenth	2d Monday March, June, September, and December.
San Diego	Eighteenth	2d Monday January, April, July, and October.
San Francisco		3d D. C.—3d Monday April, August, December. 4th—1st Monday February, May, August, December. 12th—1st Monday January, April, July, October. 15th—1st Monday March, June, September, December. 19th—1st Monday April, August, and December.
San Joaquin	Fifth	1st Monday February, May, August; 3d Monday October.
San Luis Obispo	First	2d Monday May, September, and January.
San Mateo	Twelfth	2d Monday February; 4th Monday May, August, and November.
Santa Barbara	First	3d Monday March, July, and November.
Santa Clara	Twentieth	1st Monday January, May, and September.
Santa Cruz	Twentieth	2d Monday February, June, and October.
Shasta	Ninth	2d Monday March, June, and November.
Sierra	Tenth	1st Monday April; 2d Monday July; 4th Monday October.
Siskiyou	Ninth	3d Monday January, May, and September. At Lake City—2d Monday July.
Solano	Seventh	3d Monday January, May, and September.
Sonoma	Seventh	3d Monday February, June, and October.
Stanislaus	Fifth	2d Monday January, April, and September.
Sutter	Tenth	4th Monday February; 3d Monday June; 2d Monday November.
Tehama	Second	4th Monday October; 4th Monday January; 1st Monday May.
Trinity	Ninth	2d Monday April, August, and December.
Tulare	Thirteenth	3d Monday January, May, and December.
Tuolumne	Fifth	1st Monday March and July; 3d Monday November.
Ventura	First	1st Monday March, July, and November.
Yolo	Sixth	3d Monday January, May, and September.
Yuba	Tenth	3d Monday January; 3d Monday May; 1st Monday October.

COUNTY AND PROBATE COURTS.

The terms of these Courts are held at the county seat of each county, as follows:

COUNTY.	COUNTY COURTS.	PROBATE COURTS.
Alameda	1st Monday Jan., Apr., July ; 3d Monday Sept.	Same as County Court.
Alpine	1st Monday February, June, October	Same as County Court.
Amador	1st Monday February, May, August, November	Same as County Court.
Butte	1st Monday Jan., Mch., May, July, Sept., Nov.	Same as County Court.
Calaveras	1st Monday March, June, September, Dec	Same as County Court.
Colusa	1st Monday Jan., April ; 3d Monday July, Oct.	Same as County Court.
Contra Costa	1st Monday March, August, November.,	Same as County Court.
Del Norte	1st Monday April, July, October	Same as County Court.
El Dorado	2d Monday March, June, September, Dec. ...	2d Jan., April, July, Oct.
Fresno	1st Monday Jan., Mch., May, July, Sept., Nov.	Same as County Court.
Humboldt	1st Monday Jan., Mch., May, July, Sept., Nov.	Same as County Court.
Inyo.	1st Monday Jan., Mch., May, July, Sept., Nov.	Same as County Court.
Kern	1st Monday Jan., Mch , May, July, Sept., Nov.	Same as County Court.
Klamath	1st Monday April, July, October	Same as County Court.
Lake	1st Monday January, April, July, October.....	Same as County Court.
Lassen	1st Monday February, May, August, November	Same as County Court.
Los Angeles	1st Monday Jan., Mch., May, July, Sept., Nov.	Same as County Court.
Marin	3d Monday March, June, September, December	Same as County Court.
Mariposa	1st Monday Jan., Mch., May, July, Sept., Nov.	Same as County Court.
Mendocino	1st Monday March, June, September, December	Same as County Court.
Merced	1st Monday Jan., Mch., May, July, Sept., Nov.	Same as County Court.
Modoc	1st Monday February, June, October	When necessity requires.
Mono	1st Monday January, May, September	Same as County Court.
Monterey	1st Monday March, May, July, Sept., Nov	1st Monday each month.
Napa	1st Monday Mch., Sept., Dec. ; 3d Monday June	Same as County Court.
Nevada	1st Monday February, May, August, November Sessions may be held at Truckee at the discretion of the Judge.	1st Monday each month.
Placer	1st Monday Jan., Mch., May, July, Sept., Nov.	Same as County Court.
Plumas	1st Monday March, June, September, Dec.	Same as County Court.
Sacramento	1st Monday January, April, July, October	Same as County Court.
San Benito	1st Monday February, May ; 3d Monday August ; 1st Monday November	1st Monday of each month.
San Bernardino	1st Monday Jan., Mch., May, July, Sept., Nov.	4th Monday of each month.
San Diego	1st Monday Jan.. Mch., May, July, Sept., Nov.	Same as County Court.
San Francisco	1st Monday Jan., Mch., May, July, Sept., Nov.	1st Monday of each month.
San Joaquin	1st Monday Jan., Mch., May, July, Sept., Nov.	Same as County Court.
San Luis Obispo	1st Monday March, June ; 3d Monday August ; 1st Monday December	Same as County Court.
San Mateo	2d Monday March, June, September, Dec	Same as County Court.
Santa Barbara	1st Monday March, June, September, Dec	Same as County Court.
Santa Clara	3d Monday February, May, August, November	1st Monday of each month.
Santa Cruz	1st Monday Jan., Mch., May, July, Sept., Nov.	Same as County Court.
Shasta	1st Monday January, May, September	1st Monday February, April, June, August, Oct., Dec.
Sierra	3d Monday April, June. Sept.; 2d Monday Dec.	1st Monday of each month.
Siskiyou	1st Monday Jan., Mch., May, July, Sept., Nov.	Same as County Court.
Siskiyou	At Lake City 2d Monday of July	
Solano	3d Monday April, August, December	Same as County Court.
Sonoma	1st Monday January, April, July, October	1st Monday of each month.
Stanislaus	1st Monday Jan., Mch., May, July, Sept., Nov.	Same as County Court.
Sutter	1st Monday January, April, July, October	1st Monday of each month.
Tehama	1st Monday Jan., Mch., May, July, Sept., Nov.	Same as County Court.
Trinity	1st Monday Jan., Mch., May, July, Sept., Nov.	Same as County Court.
Tulare	1st Monday Mch., June, September, December	Same as County Court.
Tuolumne	1st Monday January, May, September	4th Monday of each month.
Ventura	1st Monday February, July, October	When necessity requires.
Yolo	1st Monday January, April, July, October	Same as County Court.
Yuba	1st Monday Jan., April, July ; 2d Monday Oct.	1st Monday of each month.

JUSTICES' COURTS.

These Courts may be held at any place selected by the justice holding the same, in the township or city for which he is elected, and they are always open for the transaction of business.

THE CIRCUIT COURT OF THE UNITED STATES—DISTRICT OF CALIFORNIA.

The regular terms shall be held at San Francisco as follows:

On the second Monday in February, July, and December of each year.

The circuit judge may appoint special sessions of the Circuit Court, to be held at the place where the regular session is held.

THE DISTRICT COURT OF THE UNITED STATES—DISTRICT OF CALIFORNIA.

The regular terms shall be held at San Francisco as follows:

On the first Monday in April, on the second Monday in August, and on the first Monday in December.

Whenever the judge fails to hold any regular term thereof, it shall be his duty, if it appears that the business of the Court requires it, to hold an intermediate term. The Court is always open for the transaction of business under the bankruptcy act.

CHAPTER III.

PLACE OF TRIAL OF CIVIL ACTIONS.

Actions for the following causes must be tried in the county in which the subject of the action, or some part thereof, is situated:

1. For the recovery of real property, or of an estate or interest

therein, or for the determination, in any form, of such right or interest, and for injuries to real property.

2. For the partition of real property.

3. For the foreclosure of a mortgage of real property.

Where the real property is situated partly in one county and partly in another, the plaintiff may select either of the counties, and the county so selected is the proper county for the trial of such action.

Actions for the following causes must be tried in the county where the cause or some part thereof arose.

1. For the recovery of a penalty or forfeiture imposed by statute, except that when it is imposed for an offense committed on a lake, river, or other stream of water situated in two or more counties, the action may be brought in any county bordering on such lake, river, or stream, and opposite to the place where the offense was committed.

2. Against a public officer or person especially appointed to execute his duties, for an act done by him in virtue of his office, or against a person who, by his command, or in his aid, does anything touching the duties of such officer.

Actions against counties may be commenced and tried in any county in the judicial district in which such county is situated, unless such actions are between counties, in which case they may be commenced and tried in any county not a party thereto.

All other actions must be tried in the county in which the defendants, or some of them, reside at the commencement of the action; or if none of the defendants reside in the State, or if residing in this State, the county in which they reside is unknown to the plaintiff, the same may be tried in any county which the plaintiff may designate in his complaint; and if the defendant is about to depart from the State, such action may be tried in any county where either of the parties reside, or where service is had.

If the county in which the action is commenced is not the proper county for the trial thereof, the action may, notwithstanding, be tried therein, unless the defendant, at the time he appears and answers or demurs, files an affidavit of merits, and demands in writing that the trial be had in the proper county.

The place of trial may be changed in the following cases:

1. When the county designated in the complaint is not the proper county.

2. When there is reason to believe that an impartial trial cannot be had therein.

3. When the convenience of witnesses and the ends of justice would be promoted by the change.

4. When from any cause the judge is disqualified for acting.

Place of Trial of Actions in Justices' Courts.

1. If there be no Justices' Courts for the township or city in which the defendant resides : in any city or township of the county in which he resides.

2. When two or more persons are jointly, or jointly and severally, bound in any debt or contract, or otherwise jointly liable in the same action, and reside in different townships or different cities of the same county, or in different counties : in the township or city in which any of the persons liable may reside.

3. In case of injury to the person or property : in the township or city where the injury was committed, or where the defendant resides.

4. If for the recovery of personal property, or the value thereof, or damages for taking or detaining the same : in the township or city in which the property may be found, or in which the property was taken, or in which the defendant resides.

5. When the defendant is a non-resident of the county : in any township or city wherein he may be found.

6. When the defendant is a non-resident of the State : in any township or city in the State.

7. When a person has contracted to perform an obligation at a particular place, and resides in another county, township or city ; in the township or city in which such obligation is to be performed, or in which he resides ; and the township or city in which the obligation is incurred shall be deemed to be the township or city in which it is to be performed, unless there is a special contract to the contrary.

· 8. When the parties voluntarily appear and plead without summons : in any township or city in the State.

9. In all other cases: in the township or city in which the defendant resides.

The place of trial may be changed in the following cases :

1. When it appears to the satisfaction of the justice before whom the action is pending, by affidavit of either party, that such justice is a material witness for either party.

2. When either party makes and files an affidavit that he believes that he cannot have a fair and impartial trial before such justice, by reason of the interest, prejudice, or bias of the justice.

3. When a jury has been demanded, and either party makes and files an affidavit that he cannot have a fair and impartial trial on account of the bias or prejudice of the citizens of the township or city against him.

4. When from any cause the justice is disqualified from acting.

5. When the justice is sick or unable to act.

PROBATE COURT.

In what county wills must be proved and letters testamentary or of administration granted:

1. In the county of which the deceased was a resident at the time of his death, in whatever place he may have died.

2. In the county in which the deceased may have died, leaving estate therein, he not being a resident of the State.

3. In the county in which any part of the estate may be, the deceased having died out of the State and not resident therein at the time of his death.

4. In the county in which any part of the estate may be, the deceased not being a resident of the State, and not leaving estate in the county in which he died.

5. In all other cases, in the county where application for letters is first made.

Chapter IV.

LIMITATION OF CIVIL ACTIONS.

The periods prescribed for the commencement of civil actions are as follows:

Within five years:

1. An action upon a judgment or decree of any Court of the United States or of any State within the United States.

2. An action for mesne profits of real property.

Within four years:

An action upon any contract, obligation, or liability founded upon an instrument in writing executed in this State, (promissory notes included).

Within three years:

1. An action upon a liability created by statute, other than a penalty or forfeiture.

2. An action for trespass upon real property.

3. An action for taking, detaining, or injuring any goods or chattels, including actions for the specific recovery of personal property.

4. An action for relief on the ground of fraud or mistake. In this case the time begins to run from the discovery, by the aggrieved party, of the facts constituting the fraud or mistake.

Within two years:

1. An action upon a contract, obligation, or liability, not founded upon an instrument of writing, made within or out of this State, (accounts included).

2. An action founded upon an instrument of writing executed out of this State, (promissory notes included).

3. An action against a sheriff, coroner, or constable, upon a liability incurred by the doing of an act in his official capacity, and in virtue of his office, or by the omission of an official duty, including the non-payment of money collected upon an execution—except for an escape.

4. An action to recover damages for the death of one caused by the wrongful act or neglect of another.

Within one year:

1. An action upon a statute for a penalty or forfeiture, where the action is given to an individual, or to an individual and the State, except where the statute imposing it prescribes a different limitation.

2. An action for libel, slander, assault, battery, false imprisonment, or seduction.

3. An action against a sheriff or other officer for the escape of a prisoner arrested or imprisoned on civil process.

4. An action against a municipal corporation for damages for injuries to property caused by a mob or riot.

Within six months:

An action against an officer, or officer *de facto*—

1. To recover any goods, wares, merchandise, or other property, seized by such officer in his official capacity as tax collector, or to recover the price or value of any goods, wares, merchandise, or other personal property so seized, or for damages for the seizure, detention, sale of, or injury to any goods, wares, merchandise, or other personal property seized, or for damages done to any person or property in making any such seizure.

2. To recover stock sold for a delinquent assessment, upon the ground of irregularity in the assessment, or irregularity or defect of the notice of sale, or defect or irregularity in the sale.

No limitation:

To actions for the recovery of money or other property deposited with any bank, banker, trust company, or savings and loan society.

General provisions:

The period of limitation begins to run from the time the cause of action accrues, or in other words, from the time when suit can be brought.

A partial payment of an amount due under an agreement in writing, (promissory notes included) or under an agreement not in writing, (book accounts included) does not prevent the statute

running; but where a balance is due upon a mutual, open, and cur
rent account, where there have been reciprocal demands between
the parties, the statute begins to run from the last item proved in
the account on either side.

If when the cause of action accrues against a person, he is out
of the State, the action may be commenced within the time above
limited, after his return to the State, and if, after the cause of
action accrues, he departs from the State, the time of his absence is
not part of the time limited for the commencement of the action.

If a person entitled to bring an action be, at the time the cause
of action accrues, either within the age of majority, insane, imprisoned on a criminal charge, or in execution under the sentence
of a Criminal Court for a term less than for life, or a married
woman, and her husband be a necessary party with her in commencing such action, the time of such disability is not a part of
the time limited.

If a person entitled to bring an action die before the expiration
of the time limited for the commencement thereof, and the cause
of action survive, an action may be commenced by his representatives, after the expiration of that time, and within six months from
his death. If a person, against whom an action may be brought,
die before the expiration of the time, limited for the commencement thereof, and the cause of action survive, an action may be
commenced against his representatives after the expiration of that
time, and within one year after the issuing of letters testamentary.
or of administration.

When a person is an alien subject, or citizen of a country at
war with the United States, the time of the continuance of the
war is not part of the period limited for the commencement of the
action.

When the commencement of an action is stayed by injunction
or statutory prohibition, the time of the continuance of the injunction or prohibition is not part of the time limited for the commencement of the action.

When a cause of action has arisen in another State, or in a foreign country, and by the laws thereof an action thereon cannot
there be maintained against a person by reason of the lapse of

time, an action thereon shall not be maintained against him in this State, except in favor of one who has been a citizen of this State, and who has held the cause of action from the time it accrued.

No acknowledgment or promise is sufficient evidence of a new or continuing contract, by which to take the case out of the operation of the statute, unless the same is contained in some writing, signed by the party to be charged thereby. ˘

Chapter V.

PARTIES TO SUITS—COMMENCEMENT OF ACTIONS.

Every action must be prosecuted in the name of the real party in interest, except in the case of an executor, or administrator, or trustee of an express trust, (including a person with whom, or in whose name, a contract is made for the benefit of another) or a person expressly authorized by statute, who may sue without joining with him the person or persons for whose benefit the action is brought.

In the case of an assignment of a right to recover money or other personal property by a judicial proceeding, the action by the assignee is without prejudice to any set-off or other defense existing at the time of, or before notice of, the assignment; but this does not apply to a negotiable promissory note or bill of exchange, transferred, in good faith and upon good consideration, before maturity.

Persons severally liable upon the same obligation or instrument, including the parties to bills of exchange and promissory notes, and sureties on the same or separate instruments, may all or any of them be included in the same action, at the option of the plaintiff.

Civil actions in the Courts of this State are commenced by filing a complaint. In the Justices' Courts, by filing a complaint and issuing a summons thereon, or by the voluntary appearance and pleading of the parties.

The plaintiff may have summons issued any time within one year after the complaint is filed with the clerk or justice.

In the District Courts the defendant is allowed ten days after the service of summons and complaint to appear and answer the complaint, where service is made within the county in which the action is brought; twenty days if served out of the county but in the district in which the action is brought, and forty days if served elsewhere.

In the District Courts, the summons and copy of complaint may be served by the sheriff of the county where defendant may be found, or by any other person over the age of eighteen, not a party to the action.

On whom summons to be served:

1. If the suit is against a corporation formed under the laws of this State : the president or other head of the corporation, secretary, cashier, or managing agent thereof.

2. If against a foreign corporation, or a non-resident joint-stock company or association, doing business and having a managing or business agent, cashier, or secretary within this State : the agent, cashier, or secretary.

3. If against a minor under the age of fourteen years, residing within this State: such minor personally, and also his father, mother, or guardian; or if there be none within this State, then any person having the care or control of such minor, or with whom he resides, or in whose service he is emploped.

4. If against a person, residing within this State, who has been judicially declared to be of unsound mind, or incapable of conducting his own affairs, and for whom a guardian has been appointed : such person, and also his guardian.

5. If against a county, city, or town: the president of the board of supervisors, president of the council, or trustees, or other head of the legislative department thereof.

6. In all other cases the defendant must be served personally.

Service by publication:

When the person on whom the service is to be made resides out of the State, or has departed from the State, or cannot, after due diligence, be found within the State, or conceals himself to avoid service, or is a foreign corporation having no managing or business agent, cashier, or secretary within the State, and the fact appears by affidavit to the satisfaction of the Court, or a judge thereof, or a county judge, and it also appears by such affidavit, or by the verified complaint on file, that a cause of action exists against the defendant in respect to whom the service is to be made, or that he is a necessary or proper party to the action, such Court or judge may make an order that the service be made by the publication of the summons.

The order must direct the publication to be made in a newspaper, to be designated as most likely to give notice to the person to be served, and for such length of time as may be deemed reasonable, at least once a week ; but publication against a defendant residing out of the State, or absent therefrom, must not be less than two months.   In case of publication, where the residence of a nonresident or absent defendant is known, the Court or a judge must direct a copy of the summons and complaint to be forthwith deposited in the postoffice, directed to the person to be served, at his place of residence.   When publication is ordered, personal service of a copy of the summons and complaint out of the State is equivalent to publication and deposit in the postoffice.   In either case, the service of the summons is complete at the expiration of the time prescribed by the order for publication.

PROVISIONS IN JUSTICES' COURTS.

In Justices' Courts, the time for the appearance of the defendant must be set forth in the summons, and must be as follows :—

1. Forthwith, if an order of arrest is indorsed upon the summons.

2. Not less than twenty nor more than thirty days from its date, if the defendant is not a resident of the county in which the action is brought.

3. In all other cases, not less than three nor more than twelve days from its date.

On whom summons to be served in Justice Court actions: see rule for service in District Courts.

Service by publication:
Rule in District Courts applicable to Justices' Courts.

In Justice Court actions the summons cannot be served out of the county of the justice before whom the action is brought, except when the action is brought upon a joint contract or obligation of two or more persons who reside in different counties, and the summons has been served upon the defendant resident of the county, in which case the summons may be served upon the other defendants out of the county; and except also when an action is brought against a party who has contracted to perform an obligation at a particular place, and resides in a different county, in which case summons may be served in the county where he resides. When the defendant resides in the county, the summons cannot be served within two days of the time fixed for the appearance of the defendant; and when he resides out of the county and the summons is served out of the county, the summons cannot be served within twenty days of such time.

The justice may, within a year from the date of filing the complaint, issue as many alias summons as may be demanded by the plaintiff.

The summons in a Justice Court action may be served by a sheriff or constable of any of the counties of this State, or by any male resident over the age of twenty-one years, not a party to the suit, and within the county where the action is brought, or it may be served by publication. When a summons is issued by a justice of the peace for service out of the county in which it was issued, the summons shall have attached to it a certificate, under seal by the county clerk of such county, to the effect that the person issuing the same was an acting justice of the peace at the date of the summons.

CHAPTER VI.

FORM OF CIVIL ACTIONS—PLEADINGS.

There is in this State but one form of civil actions for the enforcement or protection of private rights and the redress or prevention of private wrongs.

In such action the party complaining is known as the plaintiff, and the adverse party as the defendant.

PLEADINGS.

Pleadings are the formal allegations by the parties of their respective claims and defenses, for the judgment of the Court.

The only pleadings allowed on the part of the plaintiff are—

1. The complaint.
2. The demurrer to the answer.
3. Demurrer and answer to a cross-complaint.

Those allowed on the part of the defendant are—

1. The demurrer to the complaint.
2. The answer.
3. Cross-complaint.

A demurrer raises an issue of law.

An answer raises an issue of fact.

An issue of law is tried by the Court.

An issue of fact is tried by a jury, unless a jury trial is waived.

The complaint must contain a concise statement, in writing, of the facts constituting the cause of action.

In the Justice Court a copy of the account, note, bill, bond, or instrument upon which the action is based, is sufficient.

The plaintiff may unite several causes of action in the same complaint where they all arise out of—

1. Contracts, express or implied.
2. Claims to recover specific real property, with or without damages for the withholding thereof, or for waste committed thereon, and the rents and profits of the same

3. Claims to recover specific personal property, with or without damages for the withholding thereof.

4. Claims against a trustee by virtue of a contract or by operation of law.

5. Injuries to character.

6. Injuries to person.

7. Injuries to property.

The causes of action so united must all belong to one only of these classes, and must affect all the parties to the action, and not require different places of trial, and must be separately stated.

The defendant may demur to the complaint within the time required in the summons to answer, when it appears upon the face thereof, either—

1. That the Court has no jurisdiction of the person of the defendant, or the subject of the action ; or,

2. That the plaintiff has not legal capacity to sue ; or,

3. That there is another action pending between the same parties for the same cause ; or,

4. That there is a defect or misjoinder of parties plaintiff or defendant ; or,

5. That several causes of action have been improperly united ; or

6. That the complaint does not state facts sufficient to constitute a cause of action ; or,

7. That the complaint is ambiguous, unintelligible, or uncertain.

Unless the demurrer distinctly specify the grounds upon which any of the objections to the complaint are taken, it may be disregarded.

The defendant may demur and answer at the same time.

The answer of the defendant shall contain—

1. A general or specific denial of the material allegations of the complaint controverted by the defendant.

2. A statement of any new matter constituting a defense or counter claim. If the complaint be verified, the denial of each allegation controverted must be specific, and be made positively, or according to the information and belief of the defendant. If the defendant has no information or belief upon the subject sufficient to enable him to answer an allegation of the complaint, he may so

state in his answer, and place his denial on that ground. If the complaint be not verified, a general denial is sufficient, but only puts in issue the material allegations of the complaint.

The counter-claim above mentioned must be one existing in favor of a defendant, and against a plaintiff, between whom a several judgment might be had in the action, and arising out of one of the following causes of action :

1. A cause of action arising out of the transaction set forth in the complaint as the foundation of the plaintiff's claim, or connected with the subject of the action.

2. In an action arising upon contract ; any other cause of action arising upon contract, and existing at the commencement of the action.

If the defendant omit to set up a counter-claim arising out of the transaction set forth in the complaint as the foundation of the plaintiff's claim, or connected with the subject of the action, neither he nor his assignee can afterwards maintain an action against the plaintiff therefor.

When cross-demands have existed between persons under such circumstances that, if one had brought an action against the other, a counter-claim could have been set up, the two demands shall be deemed compensated, so far as they equal each other, and neither can be deprived of the benefit thereof by the assignment or death of the other.

The plaintiff may, within the same length of time after the service of the answer as the defendant is allowed to answer after service of summons, demur to the answer of the defendant, or to one or more of the several defenses or counter-claims set up in the answer.

The demurrer may be taken upon one or more of the following grounds :

1. That several causes of counter-claim have been improperly joined.

2. That the answer does not state facts sufficient to constitute a defense or counter claim.

3. That the answer is ambiguous, unintelligible, or uncertain.

Verification of Pleadings.

Every pleading must be subscribed by the party or his attorney ; and when the complaint is verified, the answer must be verified, unless an admission of the truth of the complaint might subject the party to a criminal prosecution, or unless an officer of the State in his official capacity is defendant. In all cases of the verification of a pleading, the affidavit of the party must state that the same is true of his own knowledge, except as to the matters which are therein stated on his information or belief, and as to those matters that he believes it to be true ; and where a pleading is verified it must be by the affidavit of a party, unless the parties are absent from the county where the attorney resides, or from some cause unable to verify it, or the facts are within the knowledge of his attorney or other person verifying the same. When the pleading is verified by the attorney, or any other person except one of the parties, he must set forth in the affidavit the reasons why it is not made by one of the parties. When a corporation is a party the verification can be made by an officer thereof.

Provisions in Justices' Courts.

Pleadings in Justices' Courts are not required to be in any particular form, but must be such as to enable a person of common understanding to know what is intended.

May—except the complaint—be oral or in writing.

Not to be verified.

If in writing, must be filed with the justice.

If oral, an entry of their substance must be made in the docket.

The defendant may, at any time before answering, demur to the complaint.

The answer may contain a denial of any or all of the material facts stated in the complaint, which the defendant believes to be untrue, and also a statement, in a plain and direct manner, of any other facts constituting a defense or counter claim, upon which an action might be brought by the defendant against the plaintiff in a Justice's Court.

4

If the defendant omit to set up a counter claim in the cases just mentioned, neither he nor his assignee can afterwards maintain an action against the plaintiff therefor.

When the answer contains new matter in avoidance, or constituting a defense or a counter claim, the plaintiff may, at any time before the trial, demur to the same for insufficiency, stating therein the grounds of such demurrer.

The proceedings on demurrer are as follows:

1. If the demurrer to the complaint is sustained, the plaintiff may within such time, not exceeding two days, as the Court allows, amend his complaint.

2. If the demurrer to the complaint is overruled, the defendant may answer forthwith.

3. If the demurrer to an answer is sustained, the defendant may amend his answer within such time, not exceeding two days, as the Court may allow.

4. If the demurrer to an answer is overruled, the action must proceed as if no demurrer had been interposed.

Either party may, at any time before the conclusion of the trial, amend any pleading; but if the amendment is made after the issue, and it appears to the satisfaction of the Court, by oath, that an adjournment is necessary to the adverse party in consequence of such amendment, an adjournment must be granted. The Court may also, in its discretion, when an adjournment be rendered necessary, require as a condition to the allowance of such amendment, made after issue joined, the payment of costs to the adverse party, to be fixed by the Court, not exceeding twenty dollars. The Court may also, on such terms as may be just, and on payment of costs, relieve a party from a judgment by default taken against him by his mistake, inadvertence, surprise, or excusable neglect; but the application for such relief must be made within ten days after the entry of the judgment, and upon an affidavit showing good cause therefor.

When a pleading is amended, the adverse party may answer or demur to it within such time, not exceeding two days, as the Court may allow.

CHAPTER VII.

ATTACHMENTS.

The plaintiff, at the time of issuing the summons, or at any time afterwards, may have the property of the defendant attached as security for the satisfaction of any judgment that may be recovered, unless the defendant gives security to pay such judgment, in the following cases :

1. In an action upon a contract, express or implied, for the direct payment of money, where the contract is made or is payable in this State, and is not secured by any mortgage or lien upon real or personal property, or any pledge of personal property ; or if originally so secured, such security has, without any act of the plaintiff, or the person to whom the security was given, become valueless.

2. In an action upon a contract, express or implied, against a defendant not residing in this State.

In Justices' Courts, the writ to attach the property of the defendant must be issued at the time of or after issuing summons, and before answer.

Before issuing the writ of attachment, the clerk of the Court or justice must require an affidavit by or on behalf of the plaintiff, showing :

1. That the defendant is indebted to the plaintiff (specifying the amount of such indebtedness, over and above all legal set-offs or counter-claims) upon a contract, express or implied, for the direct payment of money, and that such contract was made or is payable in this State, and that the payment of the same has not been secured by any mortgage or lien upon real or personal property, or any pledge of personal property ; or if originally so secured, that such security has, without any act of the plaintiff, or the person to whom the security was given, become valueless ; or,

2. That the defendant is indebted to the plaintiff (specifying the amount of such indebtedness over and above all legal set-offs, or

counter-claims) and that the defendant is a non-resident of the State ; and,

3. That the attachment is not sought and the action is not prosecuted to hinder, delay, or defraud any creditor of the defendant.

The clerk or justice must also require, before issuing the writ, a written undertaking on the part of the plaintiff, (in the District Court, in a sum not less than two hundred dollars, and not exceeding the amount claimed by the plaintiff; and in the Justice's Court, in a sum not less than fifty dollars, and not more than three hundred dollars) by two or more sufficient sureties, to the effect that if the defendant recover judgment, the plaintiff will pay all costs that may be awarded to the defendant, and all damages which he may sustain by reason of the attachment, not exceeding the sum specified in the undertaking.

The defendant may except to the sufficiency of the sureties.

The writ of attachment in District Court actions must be directed to the sheriff of any county in which property of such defendant may be; in Justice Court actions to the sheriff of any county in which property of the defendant may be, or to the sheriff or constable in the county where the suit is brought, and must require him to attach and safely keep all the property of the defendant within his county, not exempt from execution, or so much thereof as may be sufficient to satisfy the plaintiff's demand, the amount of which must be stated in conformity with the complaint, unless the defendant give him security by the undertaking of at least two sufficient sureties, in an amount sufficient to satisfy such demand, besides costs, or in an amount equal to the value of the property which has been, or is about to be, attached. Several writs may be issued at the same time, to the sheriffs of different counties.

The writ of attachment must be executed, without delay, by the sheriff to whom it is directed :

1. Real property, standing upon the records of the county in the name of the defendant, must be attached by filing with the recorder of the county a copy of the writ, together with a description of the property attached, and a notice that it is attached, and by leaving a similar copy of the writ, description and notice with an occupant of the property, if there is one; if not, then by posting the same in a conspicuous place on the property attached.

2. Real property, or an interest therein, belonging to the defendant, and held by any other person, or standing on the records of the county in the name of any other person, must be attached by filing with the recorder of the county a copy of the writ, together with a description of the property, and a notice that such real property and any interest of the defendant therein, held by or standing in the name of such other person, (naming him) are attached ; and by leaving with the occupant, if any, and with such other person or his agent, if known and within the county, or at the residence of either, if within the county, a copy of the writ, with a similar description and notice. If there is no occupant of the property, a copy of the writ, together with such description and notice, must be posted in a conspicuous place upon the property. The recorder must index such attachment when filed, in the names both of the defendant and of the person by whom the property is held, or in whose name it stands on the records.

3. Personal property, capable of manual delivery, must be attached by taking it into custody.

4. Stocks or shares, or interest in stocks or shares of any corporation or company, must be attached by leaving with the president or other head of the same, or the secretary, cashier, or other managing agent thereof, a copy of the writ, and a notice stating that the stock or interest of the defendant is attached, in pursuance of such writ.

5. Debts and credits, and other personal property not capable of manual delivery, must be attached by leaving with the person owning such debts, or having in his possession, or under his control, such credits and other personal property, or with his agent, a copy of the writ, and a notice that the debts owing by him to the defendant, or the credits and other personal property in his possession or under his control, belonging to the defendant, are attached in pursuance of such writ..

Upon receiving information, in writing, from the plaintiff or his attorney, that any person has in his possession, or under his control, any credits or other personal property belonging to the defendant, or is owing any debt to the defendant, the sheriff must serve upon such person a copy of the writ, and a notice that such credits or other property or debts, as the case may be, are attached in pursuance of such writ.

All persons having in their possession, or under their control, any credits or other personal property belonging to the defendant, or owing any debts to the defendant at the time of service upon them of a copy of the writ and notice, as above directed, shall be, unless such property be delivered up or transferred, or such debts be paid to the sheriff, liable to the plaintiff for the amount of such credits, property, or debts, until the attachment be discharged, or any judgment recovered by him be satisfied.

Any person owing debts to the defendant, or having in his possession, or under his control, any credits or other personal property belonging to the defendant, may be required to attend before the Court or judge, or a referee appointed by the Court or judge, and be examined on oath respecting the same. The defendant may also be required to attend for the purpose of giving information respecting his property, and may be examined on oath. The Court or judge may, after such examination, order personal property, capable of manual delivery, to be delivered to the sheriff on such terms as may be just, having reference to any liens thereon, or any claims against the same, and a memorandum to be given of all other personal property, containing the amount and description thereof.

Perishable property attached must be sold by the sheriff. The proceeds, and other property attached, must be retained by him to answer any judgment that may be recovered in the action, unless sooner subjected to execution upon another judgment recovered previous to the issuing of the attachment. Debts and credits attached may be collected by him, if the same can be done without suit. The sheriff's receipt is a sufficient discharge for the amount paid.

Whenever property has been taken by an officer under a writ of attachment, and it is made to appear satisfactorily to the Court, or a judge thereof, or a county judge, that the interest of the parties to the action will be subserved by a sale thereof, the Court or a judge may order such property to be sold in the same manner as property is sold under an execution, and the proceeds to be deposited in the Court, to abide the judgment in the action.

If any personal property attached be claimed by a third person as his property, the sheriff may summon a jury of six men to try the validity of such claim.

Whenever the defendant has appeared in the action, he may, upon reasonable notice to the plaintiff, apply to the Court in which the action is pending, or to the judge thereof, or to a county judge, for an order to discharge the attachment, wholly or in part ; and, upon the execution of the undertaking mentioned hereafter, an order may be made, releasing from the operation of the attachment any or all of the property attached ; and all the property so released, and all of the proceeds of the sales thereof, must be delivered to the defendant, upon the justification of the sureties on the undertaking, if required by the plaintiff.

Before making such order, the Court or judge must require an undertaking on behalf of the defendant, by at least two sureties, residents and freeholders, or householders, in the State, to the effect that, in case the plaintiff recover judgment in the action, the defendant will, on demand, re-deliver the attached property so released to the proper officer, to be applied to the payment of the judgment ; or, in default thereof, that the defendant and sureties will, on demand, pay to the plaintiff the full value of the property released. The Court or judge making such order may fix the sum for which the undertaking must be executed, and if necessary, in fixing such sum, to know the value of the property released, the same may be appraised by one or more disinterested persons, to be appointed for that purpose. The sureties may be required to justify before the Court or judge, and the property cannot be released without their justification, if the same be required.

The defendant may also, at any time, either before or after the release of the attached property, or before any attachment shall have been actually levied, apply on motion, upon reasonable notice to the plaintiff, to the Court in which the action is brought, or to the judge thereof, or to a county judge, that the writ of attachment be discharged, on the ground that the same was improperly or irregularly issued.

If, upon such application, it satisfactorily appears that the writ of attachment was improperly or irregularly issued, it must be discharged.

CHAPTER VIII.

CLAIM AND DELIVERY OF PERSONAL PROPERTY.

The plaintiff in an action to recover the possession of personal property may, at the time of issuing the summons, or at any time before answer, claim the delivery of such property to him.

Where a delivery is claimed, an affidavit must be made by the plaintiff, or by some one on his behalf, showing—

1. That the plaintiff is the owner of the property claimed, (particularly describing it) or is entitled to the possession thereof.

2. That the property is wrongfully detained by the defendant.

3. The alleged cause of the detention thereof, according to his best knowledge, information, and belief.

4. That it has not been taken for a tax, assessment or fine, pursuant to a statute ; or seized under an execution or an attachment against the property of the plaintiff; or if so seized, that it is by statute exempt from seizure.

5. The actual value of the property.

The plaintiff or his attorney may, thereupon, by an endorsement in writing upon the affidavit, require the sheriff of the . county where the property claimed may be, to take the same from the defendant.

Upon a receipt of the affidavit and notice with a written undertaking, executed by two or more sufficient sureties, approved by the sheriff, to the effect that they are bound to the defendant in double the value of the property as stated in the affidavit for the prosecution of the action, for the return of the property to the defendant, if return thereof be adjudged, and for the payment to him of such sum as may from any cause be recovered against the plaintiff, the sheriff must forthwith take the property described in the affidavit, if it be in the possession of the defendant or his agent, and retain it in his custody. The Sheriff must, without delay, serve on the defendant a copy of the affidavit, notice, and undertaking.

The defendant may within two days after the service of a copy of the affidavit and undertaking give notice to the sheriff that he excepts to the sufficiency of the sureties. If he fails to do so, he is deemed to have waived all objections to them. When the defendant excepts, the sureties must justify on notice before the judge or county clerk ; and the sheriff is responsible for the sufficiency of the sureties until the objection to them is either waived or until they justify.

At any time before the delivery of the property to the plaintiff, the defendant may, if he do not except to the sureties of the plaintiff, require the return thereof, upon giving to the sheriff a written undertaking, executed by two or more sufficient sureties, to the effect that they are bound in double the value of the property, as stated in the affidavit of the plaintiff, for the delivery thereof to the plaintiff, if such delivery be adjudged ; and for the payment to him of such sum as may, for any cause, be recovered against the defendant. If a return of the property be not so required within five days after the taking and service of notice to the defendant, it must be delivered to the plaintiff, unless claimed by a third party, as hereafter set forth. The defendant's sureties, upon notice to the plaintiff of not less than two or more than five days, must justify before a judge or county clerk ; and, upon such justification, the sheriff must deliver the property to the defendant. The sheriff is responsible for the defendant's sureties until they justify, or until the justification is completed or waived, and may retain the property until that time ; if they, or others in their place, fail to justify at the time and place appointed, he must deliver the property to the plaintiff.

If the property taken be claimed by any other person than the defendant or his agent, and such person make affidavit of his title thereto, or right to the possession thereof, stating the grounds of such title or right, and serve the same upon the sheriff, the sheriff is not bound to keep the property or deliver it to the plaintiff, unless the plaintiff, on demand of him, or his agent, indemnify the sheriff against such claim, by an undertaking, by two sufficient sureties ; and no claim to such property by any other person than the defendant or his agent is valid against the sheriff, unless so made.

The provisions contained in this chapter are applicable to cases in Justices' Courts, the word "constable" being substituted for "sheriff," and "justice" for "judge."

CHAPTER IX.

ARREST AND BAIL.

The defendant may be arrested in a civil action in the following cases:

1. In an action for the recovery of money or damages on a cause of action arising upon contract, express or implied, when the defendant is about to depart from the State, with intent to defraud his creditors.

2. In an action for a fine or penalty, or for money or property embezzled, or fraudulently misapplied, or converted to his own use, by a public officer, or an officer of a corporation, or an attorney, factor, broker, agent, or clerk, in the course of his employment as such, or by any other person in a fiduciary capacity; or for misconduct or neglect in office, or in a professional employment, or for a willful violation of duty.

3. In an action to recover the possession of personal property unjustly detained, when the property or any part thereof has been concealed, removed, or disposed of, to prevent its being found or taken by the sheriff.

4. When the defendant has been guilty of a fraud in contracting the debt, or incurring the obligation for which the action is brought; or in concealing or disposing of the property, for the taking, detention, or conversion of which the action is brought.

5. When the defendant has removed or disposed of his property, or is about to do so, with intent to defraud his creditors.

The order of arrest is made upon affidavit of the plaintiff, or some other person, that a sufficient cause of action exists, and the case is one of those mentioned above.

Before making the order of arrest, the judge must require a written undertaking on the part of the plaintiff, with sureties in an amount to be fixed by the judge, which must be at least five hundred dollars, to the effect that the plaintiff will pay all costs which may be adjudged to the defendant, and all damages which he may sustain by reason of the arrest, if the same be wrongful, or without sufficient cause, not exceeding the sum specified in the undertaking.

In the Justice's Court, the defendant may be arrested in a civil action, in the following cases:

1. In an action for the recovery of money or damages, on a cause of action arising upon contract, express or implied, when the defendant is about to depart from the State, with intent to defraud his creditors.

2. In an action for a fine or penalty, or for money or property embezzled or fraudulently misapplied, or converted to his own use, by one who received it in a fiduciary capacity.

3. When the defendant has been guilty of a fraud in contracting the debt or incurring the obligation for which the action is brought.

4. When the defendant has removed, concealed, or disposed of his property, or is about to do so, with intent to defraud his creditors.

No female can be arrested in an action in the Justice's Court. Before an order of arrest can be made, the party applying must prove to the satisfaction of the justice, by the affidavit of himself, or some other person, the facts upon which the application is founded, and the plaintiff must execute and deliver to the justice a written undertaking in the sum of three hundred dollars, with sufficient sureties, to the effect that the plaintiff will pay all costs that may be adjudged to the defendant, and all damages which he may sustain by reason of the arrest, if the same be wrongful or without sufficient cause, not exceeding the sum specified in the undertaking.

Chapter X.

INJUNCTIONS.

An injunction is a writ or order requiring a person to refrain from a particular act. It may be granted in the following cases:

1. When it appears by the complaint that the plaintiff is entitled to the relief demanded, and such relief, or any proof thereof, consists in restraining the commission or continuance of the act complained of, either for a limited period or perpetually.

2. When it appears by the complaint or affidavit, that the commission or continuance of some act during the litigation would produce waste, great or irreparable injury to the plaintiff.

3. When it appears, during the litigation, that the defendant is doing or threatens, or is about to do, or is procuring or suffering to be done, some act in violation of the plaintiff's rights respecting the subject of the action, and tending to render the judgment ineffectual.

Chapter XI.

JUDGMENTS AND JUDGMENT LIENS.

A judgment is the final determination of the rights of the parties in an action or proceeding.

A judgment may be given for or against one or more of several plaintiffs, and for or against one or more of several defendants; and it may, when the justice of the case requires it, determine the ultimate rights of the parties on each side, as between themselves.

In an action against several defendants, the Court may, in its discretion, render judgment against one or more of them, leaving the action to proceed against the others, whenever a several judgment is proper.—

The relief granted to the plaintiff, if there be no answer, cannot exceed that which he shall have demanded in his complaint; but in any other case, the Court may grant him any relief consistent with the case made by the complaint and embraced within the issue.

An action may be dismissed or a judgment of non-suit entered in the following cases:

1. By the plaintiff himself, at any time before trial, upon the payment of costs, if a counter-claim has not been made.

2. By either party, upon the written consent of the other.

3. By the Court, when the plaintiff fails to appear on the trial, and the defendant appears and asks for the dismissal.

4. By the Court, when, upon the trial, and before the final submission of the case, the plaintiff abandons it.

5. By the Court, upon motion of the defendant, when, upon the trial, the plaintiff fails to prove a sufficient case for the jury.

In all other cases, judgment must be rendered on the merits.

JUDGMENT UPON FAILURE TO ANSWER.

Judgment may be had if the defendant fail to answer or demur to the complaint within the time specified in the summons, or within such further time as may have been granted, as follows:

1. In an action arising upon contract for the recovery of money or damages only, the clerk, upon application of the plaintiff, must enter the default of the defendant, and immediately thereafter enter judgment for the amount specified in the summons, including the costs, against the defendant, or against one or more of several defendants, when the action is against two or more defendants, jointly or severally liable on a contract, and the summons is served on one or more, and not on all of them, in which case the plaintiff may proceed against the defendants served in the same manner as if they were the only defendants.

2. In other actions, the clerk must enter the default of the de-

fendant; and thereafter the plaintiff may apply at the first or any subsequent term of the Court for the relief demanded in the complaint. If the taking of an account, or the proof of any fact, is necessary to enable the Court to give judgment, or to carry the judgment into effect, the Court may take the account or hear the proof; or may, in its discretion, order a reference for that purpose. And when the action is for damages, in whole or in part, the Court may order the damages to be assessed by a jury ; or if, to determine the amount of damages, the examination of a long account be involved, by a reference as above provided.

3. In an action where the service of summons was by publication, the plaintiff, upon the expiration of the time for answering, may, upon proof of the publication, and that no answer has been filed, apply for judgment ; and the Court must thereupon require proof to be made of the demand mentioned in the complaint; and if the defendant be not a resident of the State, must require the plaintiff or his agent to be examined on oath respecting any payments that have been made to the plaintiff, or to any one for his use, on account of such demand, and may render judgment for the amount which he is entitled to recover.

JUDGMENT BY CONFESSION.

A judgment by confession may be entered without action, either for money due or to become due, or to secure any person against contingent liability on behalf of the defendant, or both.

A statement in writing must be made, signed by the defendant and verified by his oath, to the following effect :

1. It must authorize the entry of judgment for a specified sum.

2. If it be for money due, or to become due, it must state concisely the facts out of which it arose, and show that the sum confessed therefor is justly due, or to become due.

3. If it be for the purpose of securing the plaintiff against a contingent liability, it must state concisely the facts constituting the liability, and show that the sum confessed therefor does not exceed the same.

Judgment on Proceedings Without Action by Submission of a Controversy.

Parties to a question in difference, which might be the subject of a civil action, may, without action, agree upon a case containing the facts upon which the controversy depends, and present a submission of the same to any Court which would have jurisdiction, if an action had been brought; but it must appear by affidavit that the controversy is real, and the proceedings in good faith to determine the rights of the parties. The Court must, thereupon, hear and determine the case, and render judgment thereon, as if an action were pending.

Judgment after Verdict.

When trial by jury has been had, judgment must be entered by the Clerk in conformity to the verdict, within twenty-four hours after the rendition of the verdict, unless the Court order the case to be reserved for argument for further consideration, or grant a stay of proceedings.

Upon the trial of a question of fact by the Court, its decision must be given in writing, and filed with the clerk, within thirty days after the cause is submitted for decision.

Judgment upon the decision must be entered accordingly.

On a judgment for the plaintiff upon an issue of law, he may proceed as in the case of judgment upon failure to answer. If judgment be for the defendant upon an issue of law, and the taking of an account or the proof of any fact be necessary to enable the Court to complete the judgment, a reference may be ordered.

Proceedings against Joint Debtors.

When a judgment is recovered against one or more of several persons, jointly indebted upon an obligation, those who were not originally served with the summons, and did not appear to the action, may be summoned to show cause why they should not be bound by the judgment in the same manner as though they had been originally served with the summons.

Proceedings on Offer of Defendant to Compromise.

The defendant may, at any time before the trial or judgment, serve upon the plaintiff an offer to allow judgment to be taken against him for the sum or property, or to the effect therein specified. If the plaintiff accept the offer, and give notice thereof within five days, he may file the offer, with proof of notice of acceptance, and the clerk must thereupon enter judgment accordingly. If the notice of acceptance be not given, the offer is to be deemed withdrawn, and cannot be given in evidence upon the trial; and if the plaintiff fail to obtain a more favorable judgment, he cannot recover costs, but must pay the defendant's costs from the time of the offer.

Gold Coin or Currency Judgment.

In an action on a contract or obligation in writing, for the direct payment of money, made payable in a specified kind of money or currency, judgment for the plaintiff, whether it be by default or after verdict, may follow the contract or obligation, and be made payable in the kind of money or currency specified therein; and in all actions for the recovery of money, if the plaintiff allege in his complaint that the same was understood and agreed by the respective parties to be payable in a specified kind of money or currency, and this fact is admitted by the default of the defendant or established by evidence, the judgment for the plaintiff must be made payable in the kind of money or currency so alleged in the complaint; and in an action against any person for the recovery of money received by such person in a fiduciary capacity, or to the use of another, judgment for the plaintiff must be made payable in the kind of money or currency so received by such person.

Judgment in Replevin.

In an action to recover the possession of personal property, judgment for the plaintiff may be for the possession or value thereof, in case a delivery cannot be had, and damages for the detention. If the property has been delivered to the plaintiff, and the defendant claim a return thereof, judgment for the defendant may be for a return of the property, or the value thereof, in case a return cannot be had, and damages for taking and withholding the same.

JUDGMENT LIEN.

From the time the judgment is docketed it becomes a lien upon all the real property of the judgment debtor, not exempt from execution in the county, owned by him at the time, or which he may afterwards acquire, until the lien ceases. The lien continues for two years, unless the enforcement of the judgment be stayed on appeal by execution of a sufficient undertaking, in which case the lien of the judgment ceases. See elsewhere, how judgments in Justices' Courts are made a lien on real property.

A transcript of the original docket, certified by the clerk, may be filed with the recorder of any other county; and from the time of the filing the judgment becomes a lien upon all the real property of the judgment debtor, not exempt from execution, in such county, owned by him at the time, or which he may afterwards, and before the lien expires, acquire. The lien continues for two years.

PROVISIONS IN JUSTICES' COURTS.

Judgment by default.

When the defendant fails to appear and answer or demur at the time specified in the summons, or within one hour thereafter, then, upon proof of service of the summons, the following proceedings must be had :

1. If the action is based upon a contract, and is for the recovery of money or damages only, the Court must render judgment in favor of plaintiff for the sum specified in the summons.

2. In all other actions, the Court must hear the evidence offered by the plaintiff, and must render judgment for such a sum (not exceeding the amount stated in the summons) as appears by such evidence to be just.

In the following cases the same proceedings must be had, and

5

judgment must be rendered in like manner, as if the defendant had failed to appear and answer or demur:

1. If the complaint has been amended, and the defendant fails to answer it as amended, within the time allowed by the Court.

2. If the demurrer to the complaint is overruled, and the defendant fails to answer at once.

3. If the demurrer to the answer is sustained, and the defendant fails to amend the answer within the time allowed by the Court.

Judgments other than by default:

Judgments upon confession may be entered up in any Justice's Court specified in the confession.

Judgment that the action be dismissed without prejudice to a new action, may be entered with costs in the following cases:

1. When the plaintiff voluntarily dismisses the action before it is finally submitted.

2. When he fails to appear at the time specified in the summons, or at the time to which the action has been postponed, or within one hour thereafter.

3. When after a demurrer to the complaint has been sustained, the plaintiff fails to amend it within the time allowed by the Court.

4. When it is objected at the trial, and appears by the evidence, that the action is brought in the wrong county, or township, or city; but if the objection is taken and overruled, it is cause only of reversal on appeal, and does not otherwise invalidate the judgment; if not taken at the trial, it is waived.

When a trial by a jury has been had, judgment must be entered by the justice, at once, in conformity with the verdict.

When the trial is by the Court, judgment must be entered at the end of the trial.

When the amount found due to either party exceeds the sum for which the justice is authorized to enter judgment, such party may remit the excess, and judgment may be entered for the residue.

If the defendant, at any time before the trial, offer in writing to allow judgment to be taken against him for a specific sum, the plaintiff may immediately have judgment therefor, with the costs then accrued; but if he do not accept such offer before the trial, and fail to recover in the action a sum equal to the offer, he cannot recover costs, but costs must be adjudged against him, and if he recover, be deducted from his recovery.   The offer and failure to accept it cannot be given in evidence, nor affect the recovery otherwise than as to costs.

The justice must tax and include in the judgment the costs allowed by law to the prevailing party.

An abstract of the judgment may be filed and docketed in the office of the county clerk of the county in which the judgment was rendered, and must be docketed in the judgment docket of the county court.

A judgment rendered in a Justice's Court creates no lien upon any land of the defendant, unless an abstract of the judgment is filed and recorded in the office of the recorder of the county in which the lands are situated ; when so filed and recorded, such a judgment is a lien upon the lands of the judgment debtor situated in that county.

CHAPTER XII.

EXECUTION—SALE AND REDEMPTION.

The party in whose favor judgment is given may at any time, within five years after the entry thereof, have a writ of execution issued for its enforcement—same in Justice Court actions.   The execution may be made returnable at any time not less than ten nor more than sixty days after its receipt by the sheriff or constable.

Executions may at the same time be issued to different counties.

In Justices' Courts, the justice before whom the action is brought may issue an execution directed to the sheriff or constable of the county in which judgment is obtained ; when it is desired to issue execution directed to the sheriff of another county, it is necessary

to file an abstract of the judgment with the county clerk of the
county within which the judgment is obtained, and have him issue
the execution.

Notwithstanding the death of a party after the judgment, execution thereon may be issued, or it may be enforced as follows :

1. In the case of the death of the judgment creditor, upon the
application of his executor or administrator, or successor in interest.

2. In the case of the judgment debtor, if the judgment be for
the recovery of real or personal property, or the enforcement of a
lien thereon.

When any judgment has been rendered for or against the testator or intestate in his lifetime, no execution shall issue thereon after
his death, except as above provided. If execution is actually levied upon any property of the decedent before his death, the same
may be sold for the satisfaction thereof; and the officer making the
sale must account to the executor or administrator for any surplus
in his hands.

The following property is exempt from execution except upon a
judgment recovered for its price, or upon a mortgage thereon :

1. Chairs, tables, desks and books, to the value of two hundred
dollars.

2. Necessary household, table and kitchen furniture, including
one sewing machine and one piano, in actual use in a family, or
belonging to a womam; stoves, stove-pipes and stove furniture,
wearing apparel, beds, bedding and bedsteads, and provisions
actually provided for individual or family use, sufficient for one
month.

3. The farming utensils or implements of husbandry of the
judgment debtor ; also, two oxen or two horses, or two mules and
their harness, one cart or wagon, and food for such oxen, horses,
or mules for one month ; also, all seed grain or vegetables actually
provided, reserved or on hand, for the purpose of planting or sowing at any time within the ensuing six months, not exceeding in
value the sum of two hundred dollars.

4. Tools or implements of a mechanic or artisan, necessary to
carry on trade ; the notarial seal and records of a notary public ;
the instruments and chest of a surgeon, physician, surveyor and

dentist, necessary to the exercise of their profession, with their scientific and professional libraries; the law professional libraries and office furniture of attorneys, counselors, and judges, and the libraries of ministers of the gospel.

5. The cabin or dwelling of a miner, not exceeding in value the sum of five hundred dollars; also his sluices, pipes, hose, windlass, derrick, cars, pumps, tools, implements and appliances necessary for carrying on any kind of mining operations, not exceeding in value the aggregate sum of five hundred dollars; and two horses, mules or oxen, with their harness; and food for such horses, mules or oxen for one month, when necessary to be used in any whim, windlass, derrick, car, pump or hoisting gear.

6. Two oxen, two horses or two mules, and their harness; one cart or wagon, one dray or truck, one coupee, one hack or carriage for one or two horses, by the use of which a cartman, drayman, truckman, huckster, peddler, hackman, teamster or other laborer habitually earns his living; and one horse, with vehicle and harness, or other equipments, used by a physician, surgeon or minister of the gospel in making his professional visits, with food for such oxen, horses or mules, for one month.

7. Four cows with their sucking calves, and four hogs with their sucking pigs.

8. Poultry, not exceeding in value fifty dollars.

9. The earnings of the judgment debtor for his personal services rendered at any time within thirty days next preceding the levy of execution or levy of attachment, when it appears by the debtor's affidavit or otherwise that such earnings are necessary for the use of his family residing in this State, supported wholly or in part by his labor.

10. The shares held by a member of a homestead association duly incorporated, not exceeding in value one thousand dollars—if the person holding the shares is not the owner of a homestead under the law of this State.

11. All moneys, benefits, privileges, or immunities accruing, or in any manner growing out of any life insurance on the life of the debtor, made in any company incorporated under the laws of this State, if the annual premiums paid do not exceed five hundred dollars.

12. All fire engines, hooks, and ladders, with the carts, trucks, and carriages, hose, buckets, implements, and apparatus thereto appertaining, and all furniture and uniform of any fire company or department organized under any law of this State.

13. All arms, uniforms, and accoutrements required by law to be kept by any person.

14. All court-houses, jails, public offices and buildings, lots, grounds and personal property, the fixtures, furniture, books, papers, and appurtenances belonging and pertaining to the court-house, jail, and public offices belonging to any county of this State; and all cemeteries, public squares, parks and places, public buildings, town halls, markets, buildings for the use of fire departments and military organizations, and the lots and grounds thereto belonging and appertaining, owned or held by any town or incorporated city, or dedicated by such town or city to health, ornament, or public use, or for the use of any fire or military company organized under the laws of this State.

For exemption of homesteads, see " Homesteads."

NOTICE OF SALE.

Before the sale of property on execution, notice thereof must be given as follows: [Same in Justice Court actions.]

1. In the case of perishable property ; by posting written notice of the time and place of sale in three public places of the township or city where the sale is to take place, for such time as may be reasonable, considering the character and condition of the property.

2. In case of other personal property ; by posting a similar notice in three public places in the township or city where the sale is to take place, for not less than five nor more than ten days.

3. In case of real property ; by posting a similar notice particularly describing the property, for twenty days, in three public places of the township or city where the property is situated, and also where the property is to be sold, and publishing a copy thereof once a week for the same period, in some newspaper published in the county, if there be one.

SALE OF REAL PROPERTY—WHEN ABSOLUTE OR NOT.

Upon a sale of real property, the purchaser is substituted to and acquires all the right, title, and interest, and claim of the judgment debtor thereto ; and when the estate is less than a leasehold of two years' unexpired term, the sale is absolute. In other cases the property is subject to redemption.

CERTIFICATE OF SALE OF REAL ESTATE.

The officer must give the purchaser a certificate of sale, and a duplicate of such certificate must be filed by the officer in the office of the recorder of the county.

BY WHOM PROPERTY MAY BE REDEEMED, AND WHEN.

Property sold, subject to redemption, as above provided, or any part sold separately, may be redeemed in the manner hereinafter provided, by the following persons or their successors in interest :

1.   The judgment debtor, or his successor in interest, in the whole or any part of the property.

2. A creditor, having a lien by judgment or mortgage on the property sold, or on some share or part thereof subsequent to that on which the property was sold.

The judgment debtor or redemptioner may redeem the property from the purchaser within six months after the sale, on paying the purchaser the amount of the purchase, with twelve per cent. thereon in addition, together with the amount of any assessment or taxes which the purchaser may have paid thereon after the purchase, and interest on such amount; and if the purchaser be also a creditor, having a prior lien to that of the redemptioner, other than the judgment under which such purchase was made, the amount of such lien, with interest.

If property be so redeemed by a redemptioner, another redemptioner may, within sixty days after the last redemption, again redeem it from the last redemptioner, on paying the sum paid on such last redemption, with four per cent. thereon in addition, and the amount of any assessment or taxes which the last redemptioner may have paid thereon after the redemption by him, with interest on such amount ; and, in addition, the amount of any liens held by said last redemptioner prior to his own, with interest ; but the judgment under which the property was sold need not be so paid as a lien.   The property may be again, and as often as a redemptioner is so disposed, redeemed from any previous redemptioner within sixty days after the last redemption, on paying the sum paid on the last previous redemption, with four per cent. thereon in addition, and the amount of any assessments or taxes which the last previous redemptioner paid after the redemption by him, with interest thereon ; and the amount of any liens, other than the judgment under which the property was sold, held by the last redemptioner previous to his own, with interest.   Written notice of redemption must be given to the sheriff, and a duplicate filed with the recorder of the county ; and if any taxes or assessments are paid by the redemptioner, or if he has or acquires any lien other than that upon which the redemption was made, notice thereof must in like manner be given to the sheriff, and filed with the recorder ; and if such notice be not filed, the property may be redeemed without paying such tax, assessment, or lien.   If no redemption be made within six months after the sale, the purchaser or his assignee is entitled to a conveyance ; or, if so redeemed, whenever sixty days have elapsed, and no other redemption has been made, and notice thereof given, and the time for redemption has expired, the last redemptioner or his assignee is entitled to a sheriff's deed ; but in all cases the judgment debtor shall have the entire period of six months from the date of the sale to redeem the property.   If the judgment debtor redeem, he must make the same payments as are required to effect a redemption by a redemptioner.   If the debtor redeem, the effect of the sale is terminated, and he is restored to his estate.   Upon a redemption by the debtor, the person to whom the payment is made must execute and deliver to him a certificate of redemption, acknowledged or proved before an officer authorized to take acknowledgments of conveyances of real property.   Such certificate must be filed and recorded in the office of the recorder of the county in which the property is situated.

Payment may be made to the purchaser or redemptioner, or for him, to the officer who made the sale.

A redemptioner must produce to the officer or person from whom he seeks to redeem, and serve with his notice to the sheriff—

1. A copy of the docket of the judgment under which he claims the right to redeem, certified by the clerk of the Court, or of the county where the judgment is docketed; or if he redeem upon a mortgage or other lien, a note of the record thereof certified by the recorder.

2. A copy of any assignment necessary to establish his claims, verified by the affidavit of himself or of a subscribing witness thereto.

3. An affidavit by himself or his agent, showing the amount then actually due on the lien.

Until the expiration of the time allowed for redemption, the Court may restrain the commission of waste on the property.

The purchaser from the time of the sale until a redemption, and a redemptioner, from the time of his redemption until another redemption, is entitled to receive from the tenant in possession the rents of the property sold, or the value of the use and occupation thereof. But when any rents or profits have been received by the judgment creditor or purchaser, or his or their assigns, from the property thus sold preceding such redemption, the amounts of such rents and profits shall be a credit upon the redemption money to be paid.

Chapter XIII.

PROCEEDINGS SUPPLEMENTARY TO EXECUTION.

When an execution against property of the judgment debtor, or any one of several debtors in the same judgment, issued to the sheriff of the county where he resides, or if he do not reside in this State, to the sheriff of the county where the judgment roll is filed, is returned unsatisfied, in whole or in part, the judgment creditor, at any time after such return is made, is entitled to an order from the judge of the Court, or a county judge, requiring such judgment debtor to appear and answer concerning his property, before such judge, or a referee appointed by him, at a time and place specified in the order; but no judgment debtor must be required to attend before a judge or referee out of the county in which he resides.

After the issuing of an execution against property, and upon proof by affidavit of a party or otherwise, to the satisfaction of the Court, or of a judge thereof, or county judge, that any judgment debter has property which he unjustly refuses to apply towards the satisfaction of the judgment, such Court or judge may, by an order, require the judgment debtor to appear at a specified time and place before such judge, or a referee appointed by him, to answer concerning the same; and such proceedings may thereupon be had for the application of the property of the judgment debtor toward the satisfaction of the judgment as are provided upon the return of an execution. Instead of the order requiring the attendance of the judgment debtor, the judge may, upon affidavit of the judgment creditor, his agent or attorney, if it appears to him that there is danger of the debtor absconding, order the sheriff to arrest the debtor and bring him before such judge. Upon being brought before the judge, he may be ordered to enter into an undertaking, with sufficient surety, that he will attend from time to time before the judge or referee, as may be directed, during the pendency of proceedings and until the final termination thereof, and will not in the meantime dispose of any portion of his property, not exempt from execution. In default of entering into such undertaking he may be committed to prison.

After the issuing of an execution against property, and before its return, any person indebted to the judgment debtor may pay to the sheriff the amount of his debt, or so much thereof as may be necessary to satisfy the execution; and the sheriff's receipt is a sufficient discharge for the amount so paid.

After the issuing or return of an execution against property of the judgment debtor, or of any one of several debtors in the same judgment, or upon proof, by affidavit or otherwise, to the satisfaction of the judge, that any person or corporation has property of such judgment debtor, or is indebted to him in an amount exceeding fifty dollars, the judge may, by an order, require such person or corporation, or any officer or member thereof, to appear at a specified time and place before him, or a referee appointed by him, and answer concerning the same.

Witnesses may be required to appear and testify before the judge or referee. The judge or referee may order any property of a judgment debtor, not exempt from execution, in the hands of such debtor or any other person, or due to the judgment debtor, to be applied towards the satisfaction of the judgment.

If it appear that a person or corporation, alleged to have property of the judgment debtor, or to be indebted to him, claims an interest in the property adverse to him, or denies the debt, the Court or a judge may authorize, by an order made to that effect, the judgment creditor to institute an action against such person or corporation for the recovery of such interest or debt; and the Court or judge may, by order, forbid a transfer or other disposition of such interest or debt, until an action can be commenced and prosecuted to judgment.

If any person, party, or witness disobey an order of the referee, properly made, in proceedings before him, he may be punished by the Court or judge ordering the reference, for a contempt.

Chapter XIV.

COSTS.

The general rule is, that judgment carries costs.

When, in an action for the recovery of money only, the defendant alleges in his answer that before the commencement of the action he tendered to the plaintiff the full amount to which he was entitled, and thereupon deposits in Court for the plaintiff the amount so tendered, and the allegation be found to be true, the plaintiff cannot recover costs, but must pay costs to the defendant.

When several actions are brought on one bond, undertaking, promissory note, bill of exchange, or other instrument in writing, or in any other case for the same cause of action, against several parties who might have been joined as defendants in the same action, no costs can be allowed to the plaintiff in more than one of such actions, which may be at his election, if the parties proceeded against in the other actions were, at the commencement of the previous action, openly within this State; but the disbursements of the plaintiff must be allowed to him in each action.

Security for Costs.

When the plaintiff in an action resides out of the State, or is a foreign corporation, security for the costs and charges, which may be awarded against such plaintiff, may be required by the defendant. When required, all proceedings in the action must be stayed until an undertaking, executed by two or more persons, is filed with the clerk, to the effect that they will pay such costs and charges as may be awarded against the plaintiff by judgment, or in the progress of the action, not exceeding the sum of three hundred dollars. A new or additional undertaking may be ordered by the Court or judge, upon proof that the original undertaking is insufficient security, and proceedings in the action stayed until such new or additional undertaking is executed and filed. If such security is

not given by the plaintiff within thirty days after notice that security is required, the Court or judge may order the action dismissed.

CHAPTER XV.

APPEALS IN CIVIL ACTIONS.

APPEALS IN GENERAL.

Within what time appeals may be taken:

1. From a final judgment in an action or special proceeding
commenced in the Court in which the same is rendered, within one
year after the entry of judgment. But an exception to the decision
or verdict, on the ground that it is not supported by the evidence,
cannot be reviewed on an appeal from the judgment, unless the
appeal is taken within sixty days after the rendition of the judgment.

2. From a judgment rendered on an appeal from an inferior
Court, within ninety days after the entry of such judgment.

3. From an order granting or refusing a new trial; from an order
granting or dissolving an injunction; from an order refusing to
grant or dissolve an injunction; from an order dissolving or refusing to dissolve an attachment; from an order granting or refusing
to grant a change of the place of trial; from any special order
made after the final judgment, and from an interlocutory judgment
in actions for partition of real property, within sixty days after the
order or interlocutory judgment is made and entered in the minutes
of the Court, or filed with the clerk.

An appeal is taken by filing with the clerk of the Court in which
the judgment or order appealed from is entered, a notice stating
the appeal from the same, or some specific part thereof, and serving
a similar notice on the adverse party or his attorney. The order of

service is immaterial, but the appeal is ineffectual for any purpose
unless within five days after service of the notice of appeal, an undertaking be filed, or a deposit of money be made with the clerk,
as hereinafter provided, or the undertaking be waived by the adverse party in writing.

The undertaking on appeal·must be in writing, and must be executed on the part of the appellant by at least two sureties, to the
effect that the appellant will pay all damages and costs which may
be·awarded against him on the appeal, or on a dismissal thereof,
not exceeding three hundred dollars ; or that sum must be deposited with the clerk with whom the judgment or order was entered,
to abide the event of the appeal.

If the appeal be from a judgment or order directing the payment
of money, it does not stay the execution of the judgment or order,
unless a written undertaking be executed on the part òf the appellant, by two or more sureties, to the effect that they are bound in
double the amount named in the judgment or order, that if the
judgment or order appealed fròm, or any part thereof, be affirmed,
or the appeal be dismissed. the appellant will pay the amount
directed to be paid by the judgment or order, or the part of such
amount as to which the judgment or order is affirmed, if affirmed
only in part, and all damages and costs which may be awarded
against the appellant upon the appeal ; and that if the appellant
does not make such payment within thirty days after the filing of
the remittitur from the Supreme Court, in the Court from which
the appeal is taken, judgment may be entered on motion of the re-
spondent in his favor against the sureties, for such amount, together
with the interest that may be due thereon, and the damages and
costs which may be awarded against the appellant upon the appeal.
If the judgment or order appealed from be for a greater amount
than two thousand dollars, and the sureties do not state in their
affidavits of justification accompanying the undertaking, that they
are each worth the sum specified in the undertaking, the stipulation
may be that the judgment·to be entered against the sureties shall
be for such amounts only as in their affidavits they may state
that they are severally worth, and judgment may be entered
against the sureties by the Court from which the appeal is taken,

pursuant to the stipulations therein designated. When the judgment, or order, appealed from is made payable in a specified kind
of money or currency, the judgment entered against the sureties
upon the undertaking must be made payable in the same kind of
money or currency.

When an appeal is perfected, it stays all further proceedings in
the Court below, upon the judgment or order appealed from, or
upon the matters embraced therein, and releases from levy property
which has been levied upon under execution issued upon such judgment.

The adverse party may except to the sufficiency of the sureties
to the undertakings on appeal.

The foregoing provisions in regard to appeals do not apply to appeals to the County Court from Justices' or Police Courts.

APPEALS FROM DISTRICT COURTS.

An appeal may be taken to the Supreme Court from the District Courts in the following cases:

1. From a final judgment entered in an action or special proceeding commenced in those Courts, or brought into those Courts
from other Courts.

2. From an order granting or refusing a new trial ; from an order granting or dissolving an injunction ; from an order refusing to
grant or dissolve an injunction ; from an order dissolving, or refusing to dissolve, an attachment; from an order changing, or refusing
to change, the place of trial; from any special order made after
final judgment, and from such interlocutory judgment in actions for
partition as determines the rights and interests of the respective
parties, and directs partition to be made.

APPEALS FROM COUNTY COURTS.

An appeal may be taken to the Supreme Court from the County
Courts in the following cases:

1. From a final judgment in an action of forcible entry and detainer ; in an action to prevent or abate a nuisance ; in a proceeding in insolvency ; and in any special cases and proceedings ; and

in cases which involve the legality of any tax, impost, assessment, toll, or municipal fine, or in which the demand, exclusive of interest, or the value of the property in controversy, amounts to three hundred dollars.

2. From an order granting or refusing a new trial in the cases herein designated, and from any special order made after final judgment in such cases.

APPEALS FROM PROBATE COURTS.

An appeal may be taken to the Supreme Court from a judgment or order of the Probate Court as follows :

1. Granting, or refusing, or revoking letters testamentary, or of administration, or of guardianship.

2. Admitting, or refusing to admit, a will to probate.

. 3. Against or in favor of the validity of a will, or revoking the probate thereof.

4. Against or in favor of setting apart property, or making an allowance for a widow or child.

5. Against or in favor of directing the partition, sale, or conveyance of real property.

6. Settling an account of an executor, or administrator, or guardian.

7. Refusing, allowing, or directing the distribution or partition of an estate, or any part thereof, or the payment of a debt, claim, legacy, or distributive share.

8. Overruling a motion for new trial.

9. Confirming a report of an appraiser setting apart the homestead.

APPEALS FROM JUSTICES' OR POLICE COURTS.

Any party dissatisfied with a judgment rendered in a civil action in a Police or Justice's Court may appeal therefrom to the County Court of the county, at any time within thirty days after the rendition of the judgment.

Parties appealing on questions of law alone, must prepare a statement for the justice or judge. When the appeal is taken on questions of fact, or questions of both law and fact, no statement need be made, but the action must be tried anew in the County Court.

An appeal from a Justice's or Police Court is not effectual for any purpose, unless an undertaking be filed, with two or more sureties. in the sum of one hundred dollars, for the payment of the costs on the appeal; or if a stay of the proceedings be claimed, in a sum equal to twice the amount of the judgment, including costs, when the judgment is for the payment of money; or twice the value of the property, including costs, when the judgment is for the recovery of specific personal property; and must be conditioned, when the action is for the recovery of money, that the appellant will pay the amount of the judgment appealed from, and all costs, if the appeal be withdrawn or dismissed, or the amount of any judgment and all costs that may be recovered against him in the County Court. When the action is for the recovery of specific personal property, the undertaking must be conditioned that the appellant will pay the judgment and costs appealed from, and obey the order of the Court made therein, if the appeal be withdrawn or dismissed, or any judgment and costs that may be recovered against him in said action in the County Court, and will obey any order made by the Court therein. A deposit of the amount of the judgment, including all costs, appealed from, or of the value of the property, including all costs, in actions for the recovery of specific personal property, with the justice or judge, is equivalent to the filing of the undertaking. The adverse party may except to the sufficiency of the sureties within five days after the filing of the undertaking, and unless they or other sureties justify before the justice or judge before whom the appeal is taken, within five days thereafter, upon notice to the adverse party, to the amounts stated in their affidavits, the appeal must be regarded as if no such undertaking had been given.

On filing the above undertaking, execution must be stayed. For a failure to prosecute an appeal, or unnecessary delay in bringing it to a hearing, the County Court, after notice, may order the appeal to be dismissed.

6

Chapter XVI.

NEW TRIALS.

A new trial may be granted for any of the following causes, materially affecting the substantial rights of the party aggrieved : •

1. Irregularity in the proceedings of the Court, jury, or adverse party, or any order of the Court, or abuse of discretion, by which either party was prevented from having a fair trial.

2. Misconduct of the jury; and whenever any one or more of the jurors have been induced to assent to any general or special verdict, or to finding on any question submitted to them by the Court, by a resort to the determination of chance, such misconduct may be proved by the affidavit of any one of the jurors.

3. Accident or surprise, which ordinary prudence could not have guarded against.

4. Newly discovered evidence, material for the party making the application, which he could not, with reasonable diligence, have discovered and produced at the trial.

5. Excessive damages, appearing to have been given under the influence of passion or prejudice.

6. Insufficiency of the evidence to justify the verdict or other decision, or that it is against law.

7. Error in law occurring at the trial and excepted to by the party making the application.

The party intending to move for a new trial must, within ten days after the verdict, if the action were tried by a jury, or after notice of the decision of the Court or referee, if the action were tried without a jury, file with the Clerk and serve upon the adverse party a notice of his intention, designating the ground upon which the motion will be made.

Chapter XVII.

ESTATES OF DECEASED PERSONS.

Order of persons entitled to administer:

· 1. The surviving husband or wife, or some competent person whom he or she may request to have appointed.

2. The children.

3. The father or mother.

4. The brothers.

5. The sisters.

6. The grandchildren.

7. The next of kin entitled to share in the distribution of the estate.

8. The creditors.

9. The public administrator.

10. Any person legally competent.

If the deceased was a member of a partnership at the time of his decease, the surviving partner must in no case be appointed administrator of his estate.

A married woman must not be appointed administratrix.

When a creditor is claiming letters, the Court may, in its discretion, at the request of another creditor, grant letters to any other person legally competent.

Letters of administration must be granted to any applicant, though it appears that there are other persons having better rights to the administration, when such persons fail to appear and claim the issuing of letters to themselves.

The administrator must give bonds, with two or more sufficient sureties, to be approved by the probate judge, the penalty to be not less than twice the value of the personal property, and twice the probable value of the annual rents, profits, and issues of the real property: additional bonds may be required, when a sale of real estate is ordered.

When a person dies leaving a widow or minor children, until letters are granted and the inventory is returned, they are entitled to remain in possession of the homestead, of the wearing apparel of the family, and of all the household furniture of the decedent, and are also entitled to a reasonable provision for their support, to be allowed by the probate judge.

The Court or probate judge may set apart for the use of the surviving husband or wife, or the minor children of the decedent, all property exempt from execution, including the homestead selected, designated and recorded. If no homestead has been selected, designated and recorded, the judge or the Court must select, designate, set apart and cause to be recorded, a homestead for the use of the persons before named.

If the amount set apart be insufficient for the support of the widow and children, or either, the Probate Court or judge must make such reasonable allowance out of the estate as shall be necessary for the maintenance of the family, according to their circumstances, during the progress of the settlement of the estate ; which, in case of an insolvent estate, must not be longer than one year after granting of letters.

If on the return of the inventory of the estate of an intestate, it appears that the value of the whole estate does not exceed the sum of fifteen hundred dollars, it must be assigned for the use of the widow and minor child or children, after the payment of the expenses of his last illness, funeral charges, and the expenses of the administration.

If it appear that the value of the whole estate does not exceed the sum of three thousand dollars, there may by a summary administration of the estate, and an order of distribution at the end of six months after the issuing of letters.

Claims against the estate must be presented to the executor or administrator within the time specified in the notice to creditors, requesting them to present their claims ; when the value of the estate exceeds ten thousand dollars, the time expressed in the notice must be ten months ; when it does not exceed ten thousand dollars, four months. If a claim be not presented within the time limited in the notice, it is barred forever ; except where it is made to appear, by the affidavit of the claimant, to the satisfaction of the executor or administrator, and the probate judge, that the claimant had no notice, by reason of being out of the State, it may be presented at any time before a decree of distribution is entered. A claim for a deficiency remaining unpaid after a sale of property of the estate, mortgaged or pledged, must be presented within one month after such deficiency is ascertained.

Every claim which is due when presented to the administrator must be supported by the affidavit of the claimant, or some one in his behalf, that the amount is justly due, that no payments have been made thereon which are not credited, and that there are no offsets to the same, to the knowledge of the claimant or affiant. If the claim be not due when presented, or be contingent, the particulars of such claim must be stated. When the affidavit is made by a person other than the claimant, he must set forth in the affidavit the reasons why it is not made by the claimant. The oath may be taken by any officer authorized to administer oaths. The executor or administrator may also require satisfactory vouchers or proofs to be produced in support of the claim. If the estate be insolvent, no greater rate of interest shall be allowed upon any claim, after the first publication of notice to creditors, than seven per cent.

When a claim, accompanied by the affidavit required as aforesaid, is presented to the executor or administrator, he must endorse thereon his allowance or rejection, with the day and date thereof. If he allows the claim, it must be presented to the probate judge for his approval, who must, in the same manner, indorse upon it his allowance or rejection. If the executor, or administrator, or judge, refuse or neglect to endorse such allowance or rejection, for ten days after the claim has been presented to him, such refusal or neglect is equivalent to a rejection on the tenth day; and if the presentation be made by a notary, the certificate of such notary, under seal, is prima facie evidence of such presentation and rejection. If the claim be presented to the executor or administrator before the expiration of the time limited for the presentation of claims, the same is presented in time, though acted upon by the executor or administrator, and by the judge, after the expiration of such time. If a claim be payable in a particular kind of money or currency, it shall, if allowed, be payable only in such money or currency.

Every claim allowed by the executor or administrator, and approved by the probate judge, or a copy thereof, must, within thirty days thereafter, be filed in the Probate Court.

If the claim is founded on a bond, bill, note, or any other instrument, a copy of such instrument must accompany the claim, and the original instrument must be exhibited if demanded, unless it be lost or destroyed ; in which case the claimant must accompany his claim by his affidavit, containing a copy or particular description of such instrument, and state its loss or destruction. Book accounts should be made out in detail, and attached to the affidavit in proof of claim. If the claim, or any part thereof, is secured by a mortgage or other lien which has been recorded in the office of the recorder of the county in which the land affected by it lies, it is sufficient to describe the mortgage or lien, and refer to the date, volume, and page of its record. A judgment for the recovery of money must be presented to the executor or administrator like any other claim. A rejected claim must be sued for within three months from date of its rejection, if it be then due, or within two months after it becomes due ; otherwise the claim is forever barred.

Claims barred by the statute of limitations must not be allowed. No holder of any claim against an estate shall maintain any action thereon, unless the claim is first presented to the executor or administrator.

A judgment rendered against a decedent dying after verdict or decision on an issue of fact, but before judgment is rendered thereon, is not a lien on the real property of the decedent, but is payable in due course of administration.

A judgment rendered against an executor or administrator, upon any claim for money against the estate, only establishes the claim in the same manner as if it had been duly allowed, and the judgment must be that the executor or administrator pay in due course of administration the amount ascertained to be due. A certified copy of the judgment must be filed in the Probate Court. No execution must issue upon such judgment, and no lien is created.

Every executor or administrator must render a full account and a report of his administration at the expiration of one year from the time of his appointment.

Upon the settlement of the accounts at the end of the year, as required, the Court must make an order for the payment of the debts, as the circumstances of the estate require.

In case of the death of any employer, the wages of each miner, mechanic, salesman, clerk, servant and laborer, for services rendered within the sixty days next preceding the death of the employer, not exceeding one hundred dollars, rank in priority next after the funeral expenses, expenses of the last sickness, the charges and expenses of administering upon the estate, and the allowance to the widow and infant children, and must be paid before other claims against the estate of the deceased person.

The debts of the estate subject to the foregoing provision must be paid in the following order :

1. Funeral expenses.

2. The expenses of the last sickness.

3. Debts having preference by the laws of the United States.

4. Judgments rendered against the decedent in his lifetime, and mortgages in the order of their date.

5. All other demands against the estate.

The preference in the case of a mortgage only extends to the proceeds of the property mortgaged. The deficiency, if any, must be classed with the other demands against the estate.

CHAPTER XVIII.

DESCENTS.

The property, both real and personal, of one who dies without disposing of it by will, passes to the heirs of the intestate, subject to the control of the Probate Court, and to the possession of any administrator appointed by that Court for the purposes of administration.

When any person having title to any estate not otherwise limited by marriage contract dies without disposing of the estate by will, the rule of distribution is as follows, subject to the payment of his debts:

1. If the decedent leave a surviving husband or wife, and only one child, or the lawful issue of one child, in equal shares to the surviving husband, or wife and child, or issue of such child. If the decedent leave a surviving husband or wife, and more than one child living, or one child living and the lawful issue of one or more deceased children, one third to the surviving husband or wife, and the remainder in equal shares to his children, and to the lawful issue of any deceased child, by right of representation; but if there be no child of the decedent living at his death, the remainder goes to all of his lineal descendants; and if all of the descendants are in the same degree of kindred to the decedent, they share equally, otherwise they take according to the right of representation. If the decedent leave no surviving husband or wife, but leave issue, the whole estate goes to such issue; and if such issue consists of more than one child living, or one child living, and the lawful issue of one or more deceased children, then the estate goes in equal shares to the children living, or to the child living, and the issue of the deceased child or children by right of representation.

2. If the decedent leave no issue the estate goes in equal shares to the surviving husband or wife, and to the decedent's father. If there be no father, then one-half goes in equal shares to the brothers and sisters of the decedent, and to the children of

any deceased brother or sister, by right of representation ; if he leave a mother also, she takes an equal share with the brothers and sisters. If the decedent leave no issue, nor husband nor wife, the estate must go to his father.

3. If there be no issue, nor husband, nor wife, nor father, then in equal shares to the brothers and sisters of the decedent, and to the children of any deceased brother or sister, by right of representation ; if a mother survive, she takes an equal share with the brothers and sisters.

4. If the decedent leave no issue, nor husband, nor wife, nor father, and no brother nor sister is living at the time of his death, the estate goes to his mother, to the exclusion of the issue, if any, of deceased brothers or sisters.

5. If the decedent leave a surviving husband or wife, and no issue, and no father, nor mother, nor brother, nor sister, the whole estate goes to the surviving husband.

6. If the decedent leave no issue, nor husband, nor wife, and no father, nor mother, nor brother, nor sister, the estate must go to the next of kin, in equal degree, excepting that when there are two or more collateral kindred, in equal degree, but claiming through different ancestors, those who claimed through the nearest ancestors must be preferred to those claiming through an ancestor more remote ; however,

7. If the decedent leave several children, or one child and the issue of one or more children, and any such surviving child dies under age, and not having been married, all the estate that came to the deceased child by inheritance from such decedent descends in equal shares to the other children of the same parent, and to the issue of any such other children who are dead, by right of representation.

8. If, at the death of such child, who dies under age, not having been married, all the other children of his parents are also dead, and any of them have left issue, the estate that came to such child, by inheritance from his parent, descends to the issue of all other children of the same parent ; and if all the issue are in the same degree of kindred to the child, they share the estate equally, otherwise they take according to the right of representation.

9. If the decedent leave no husband, wife, or kindred, the estate escheats to the State for the support of common schools.

The above provisions, as to the inheritance of the husband and wife from each other, apply only to the separate property of the decedents.

Upon the death of the wife, the entire community property, without administration, belongs to the surviving husband, except such portion thereof as may have been set apart to her by judicial decree, for her support and maintenance, which portion is subject to her testamentary disposition, and in the absence of such disposition goes to her descendants or heirs, exclusive of her husband.

Upon the death of the husband, one-half of the community property goes to the surviving wife, and the other half is subject to the testamentary disposition of the husband, and in the absence of such disposition goes to his descendants, equally, if such descendants are in the same degree of kindred to the decedent; otherwise, according to the right of representation; and in the absence of both such dispositions, and such descendants, is subject to distribution in the same manner as the separate property of the husband. In case of the dissolution of the community by the death of the husband, the entire community property is equally subject to his debts, the family allowance, and the charges and expenses of administration.

Every illegitimate child is an heir of the person who, in writing, signed in the presence of a competent witness, acknowledges himself to be the father of such child; and in all cases is an heir of his mother; and inherits his or her estate, in whole or in part, as the case may be, in the same manner as if he had been born in lawful wedlock; but he does not represent his father or mother by inheriting any part of the estate of his or her kindred, either lineal or collateral, unless, before his death, his parents shall have intermarried, and his father, after such marriage, acknowledges him as his child, or adopts him into his family; in which case such child and all the legitimate children are considered brothers and sisters, and on the death of either of them intestate, and without issue, the others inherit his estate, and are heirs as hereinbefore provided, in like manner as if all the children had been legitimate; saving to the father and mother respectively their rights in the estates of all the children in like manner as if all had been legitimate. The issue of all marriages null in law, or dissolved by divorce, are legitimate.

If an illegitimate child, who has not been acknowledged or adopted by his father, dies intestate, without lawful issue, his estate goes to his mother, or in case of her decease, to her heirs at law.

CHAPTER XIX.

LIENS OF MECHANICS AND OTHERS UPON REAL PROPERTY.

Every person performing labor upon, or furnishing materials to be used in the construction, alteration, or repair of any mining claim, building, wharf, bridge, ditch, flume, tunnel, fence, machinery, railroad, wagon-road, aqueduct to create hydraulic power, or any other structure, or who performs labor in any mining claim, has a lien upon the same for his work or labor done or materials furnished by each, respectively, whether done or furnished at the instance of the owner of the building or other improvement, or his agent ; and every contractor, sub-contractor, architect, builder, or other person having charge of any mining, or of the construction, alteration, or repair, either in whole or in part, of any building or other improvement, as aforesaid, shall be held to be the agent of the owner.

The land upon which any building, improvement, or structure is constructed, together with a convenient space about the same, or so much as may be required for the convenient use and occupation thereof, to be determined by the Court on rendering judgment, is also subject to the lien, if, at the commencement of the work, or of the furnishing of the materials for the same, the land belonged to the person who caused said building, improvement, or structure to be constructed, altered, or repaired; but if such person owned less than a fee simple estate in such land, then only his interest therein is subject to such lien.

Improvements are held to be constructed at the instance of the owner of the lands, unless he, within three days after he shall have received knowledge of the construction, alteration, or repair, or intended construction, alteration, or repair, give notice that he will not be responsible for the same, by posting a notice in writing on the premises in a conspicuous place to that effect.

Such liens are preferred to any lien, mortgage or other incumbrance which may have attached subsequent to the time when the building, improvement or structure was commenced, work done, or materials were commenced to be furnished; also, to any lien, mortgage or other incumbrance, of which the lien-holder had no notice, and which was unrecorded at the time the building, improvement or structure was commenced, work done, or the materials were commenced to be furnished.

Every original contractor, within sixty days after the completion of his contract, and every person, save the original contractor, claiming the benefit of this chapter, must, within thirty days after the completion of any building, improvement or structure, or after the completion of the alteration or repair thereof, or the performance of any labor in a mining claim, file for record with the county recorder of the county in which such property, or some part thereof, is situated, a claim containing a statement of his demand, after deducting all just credits and offsets, with the name of the owner or reputed owner, if known, and also the name of the person by whom he was employed, or to whom he furnished the materials, with a statement of the terms, time given, and conditions of his contract, and also a description of the property to be charged with the lien, sufficient for identification, which claim must be verified by the oath of himself or of some other person.

The lien does not bind any building, mining claim, improvement or structure, for a longer period than ninety days after the same has been filed, unless proceedings be commenced in a proper Court within that time to enforce the same ; or if a credit be given, then ninety days after the expiration of such credit ; but no lien continues in force for a longer time than two years from the time the work is completed, by any agreement to give credit.

In every case in which different liens are asserted against any property, the Court in the judgment must declare the rank of each lien or class of liens, which shall be in the following order, viz : First. All persons other than the original contractors and sub-contractors. Second. The sub-contractors. Third. The original contractors. And the proceeds of the sale of the property must be applied to each lien or class of liens in the order of its rank ; and whenever, on the sale of the property subject to the lien, there is a deficiency of proceeds, judgment may be docketed for the deficiency.

Any number of persons claiming liens may join in the same action, and when separate actions are commenced, the Court may consolidate them. The Court may also allow as part of the costs, the moneys paid for filing and recording the lien, and reasonable attorney's fees in the District and Supreme Courts. Whenever materials shall have been furnished for use in the construction, alteration, or repair of any building or other improvement, such materials shall not be subject to attachment, execution, or other legal process, to enforce any debt due by the purchaser of such materials, except a debt due for the purchase money thereof, so long as in good faith the same are about to be applied to the construction, alteration, or repair of such building, mining claim, or other improvement.

In a judgment enforcing a mechanic's lien, a personal judgment cannot be rendered against those defendants against whom no personal claim is established.

Chapter XX.

LIENS FOR SALARIES AND WAGES.

In all assignments of property, made by any person to trustees or assignees, on account of the inability of the person, at the time of the assignment, to pay his debts, or in proceedings in insolvency, the wages of the miners, mechanics, salesmen, servants, clerks or laborers employed by such person, to the amount of one hundred dollars each, and for services rendered within sixty days previously, are preferred claims, and must be paid by such trustees or assignees before any other creditor or creditors of the assignor.

In case of the death of any employer, the wages of each miner, mechanic, salesman, clerk, servant and laborer, for services rendered within the sixty days next preceding the death of the employer, not exceeding one hundred dollars, rank in priority next after the funeral expenses, expenses of the last sickness, the charges, and expenses of administering upon the estate, and the allowance to the widow and infant children, and must be paid before other claims against the estate of the deceased person.

In cases of executions, attachments, and writs of a similar nature, issued against any person, except for claims for labor done, any miners, mechanics, salesmen, servants, clerks and laborers, who have claims against the defendant for labor done, may give notice of their claims and the amount thereof, sworn to by the person making the claim, to the creditor and the officer executing either of such writs, at any time before the actual sale of the property levied upon ; and unless such claim is disputed by the debtor or a creditor, such officer must pay to such person, out of the proceeds of the sale, the amount each is entitled to receive for such services rendered within the sixty days next preceding the levy of the writ, not exceeding one hundred dollars. If any or all of the claims so presented, and claiming preference, are disputed by either the debtor or a creditor, the person presenting the same must commence an action within ten days for the recovery thereof, and must prosecute his action with due diligence, or be forever barred from any claim of priority of payment thereof; and the officer shall retain possession of so much of the proceeds of the sale as may be necessary to satisfy such claim, until the determination of such action; and in case judgment be had for the claim, or any part thereof, carrying costs, the costs taxable therein shall likewise be a preferred claim, with the same rank as the original claim.

CHAPTER XXI.

ARBITRATIONS.

Persons capable of contracting may submit to arbitration any controversy which might be the subject of a civil action between them, except a question of title to real property in fee or for life.

The submission to arbitration must be in writing, and may be made to one or more persons.

CHAPTER XXII.

HOMESTEADS.

The homestead consists of the dwelling-house in which the claimant resides, and the land on which the same is situated, selected as hereinafter provided. It may be used as a place of business, but actual residence is essential.

Homesteads may be selected and claimed:

1. Not exceeding five thousand dollars in value, by any head of a family.

2. Not exceeding one thousand dollars in value by any other person.

The phrase " head of a family," includes within its meaning:

1. The husband, when the claimant is a married person.

2. Every person who has residing on the premises with him or her, and under his or her care and maintenance, either:

(1.) His or her minor child, or the minor child of his or her deceased wife or husband.

(2.) A minor brother or sister, or the minor child of a deceased brother or sister.

(3.) A father, mother, grandfather, or grandmother.

(4.) The father, mother, grandfather, or grandmother of a deceased husband or wife.

(5.) An unmarried sister, or any other of the relatives mentioned who have attained the age of majority, and are unable to support themselves.

The declaration of homestead must be executed, acknowledged, and duly recorded in the office of the recorder of the county in which the land is situated. From and after the time the declaration is filed for record, the premises therein described constitute a homestead.

The homestead is exempt from execution or forced sale, except in satisfaction of judgments obtained:

1. Before the declaration of homestead was filed for record, and which constitute liens upon the premises.

2. On debts secured by mechanics', laborers' or vendors' liens upon the premises.

3. On debts secured by mortgages upon the premises, executed and acknowledged by the husband and wife, or an unmarried claimant.

4. On debts secured by mortgages upon the premises, executed and recorded before the declaration of homestead was filed for record. .

The homestead of a married person cannot be conveyed or incumbered, unless the instrument is executed and acknowledged by both husband and wife.

If the homestead exceed in value the amount of the homestead exemption, the excess may be reached on execution, but the property must first be appraised, upon application to the county judge.

The homestead may be abandoned by filing in the office where the declaration is filed a declaration of abandonment, duly executed.

CHAPTER XXIII.

CORPORATIONS.

Corporations are either public or private. Public corporations are formed or organized for the government of a portion of the State ; all other corporations are private.

Private corporations may be formed by the voluntary association of any five or more persons. A majority of such persons must be residents of this State. They may be formed for any purpose for which individuals may lawfully associate themselves.

The owners of shares in a corporation which has a capital stock are called stockholders. If a corporation has no capital stock, the corporators and their successors are called members.

Each stockholder of a corporation is individually and personally liable for such proportion of its debts and liabilities as the amount of stock or shares owned by him bears to the whole of the subscribed capital stock or shares of the corporation, and for a like proportion only of each debt or claim against the corporation. Any creditor of the corporation may institute joint or several actions against any of its stockholders, for the proportion of his claim payable by each, and in such action the Court must ascertain the proportion of the claim or debt for which each defendant is liable, and a several judgment must be rendered against each, in conformity therewith. If any stockholder pays his proportion of any debt

7

due from the corporation, incurred while he was such stockholder, he is relieved from any further personal liability for such debt; and if an action has been brought against him upon such debt, it shall be dismissed as to him upon his paying the costs, or such proportion thereof as may be properly chargeable against him. The liability of each stockholder is determined by the amount of stock or shares owned by him at the time the debt or liability was incurred; and such liability is not released by any subsequent transfer of stock. The term "stockholder" shall apply not only to such persons as appear by the books of the corporation to be such, but also to every equitable owner of stock, although the same appear on the books in the name of another, and also to every person who has advanced the installments or purchase-money of stock in the name of a minor, so long as the latter remains a minor; and also to every guardian or other trustee who voluntarily invests any trust funds in the stock. Trust funds in the hands of a guardian or trustee shall not be liable under the provisions of this section by reason of any such investment, nor shall the person for whose benefit the investment is made be responsible in respect to the stock, until he becomes competent and able to control the same; but the responsibility in the guardian or trustee making the investment shall continue until that period. Stock held as collateral security, or by a trustee, or in any other representative capacity, does not make the holder thereof a stockholder within the meaning of this section, except in the cases above mentioned, so as to charge him with any proportion of the debts or liabilities of the corporation; but the pledgor, or person, or estate represented, is to be deemed the stockholder as respects such liability. In corporations having no capital stock, each member is individually and personally liable for his proportion of its debts and liabilities, and similar actions may be brought against him, either alone or jointly with other members, to enforce such liability, as may be brought against one or more stockholders, and similar judgments may be rendered.

Chapter XXIV.

MODE OF TAKING TESTIMONY OF WITNESSES.

The testimony of witnesses is taken in three modes, viz:

1. By affidavit.
2. By deposition.
3. By oral examination.

An affidavit is a written declaration, under oath, made without notice to the adverse party.

A deposition is a written declaration, under oath, made upon notice to the adverse party, for the purpose of enabling him to attend and cross-examine.

An oral examination is an examination in presence of the jury or tribunal which is to decide the fact, or act upon it; the testimony being heard by the jury or tribunal from the lips of the witness.

Depositions must be taken in the form of question and answer, and the words of the witness must be written down, unless the parties agree to a different mode.

Affidavits are used to verify pleadings, or to prove service of papers, and such like.

Testimony of witnesses out of this State may be taken by deposition, at any time after service of summons, or the appearance of the defendant.

Testimony of witnesses in this State may be taken by deposition, in any action, at any time after the service of the summons, or the appearance of the defendant, in the following cases:

1. When the witness is a party to the action or proceeding, or a person for whose immediate benefit the action or proceeding is prosecuted or defended.

2. When the witness resides out of the county in which the testimony is to be used.

3. When the witness is about to leave the county where the action is to be tried, and will probably continue absent when the testimony is required.

4. When the witness, otherwise liable to attend the trial, is nevertheless too infirm to attend.

5. When the testimony is required upon a motion, or in any other case where the oral examination of the witness is not required.

The deposition of a witness out of this State may be taken upon commission issued from the Court, under the seal of the Court, upon an order of the judge or Court, or county judge, on the application of either party, upon five days previous notice to the other. If issued to any place within the United States, it may be directed to a person agreed upon by the parties; or if they do not agree, to any judge or justice of the peace, or commissioner, selected by the officer issuing it. If issued to any country out of the United States, it may be directed to a minister, embassador, consul, vice-consul, or consular agent of the United States, in such country, or to any person agreed upon by the parties.

The deposition of a witness in this State may be taken by either party before a judge or officer authorized to administer oaths, on serving upon the adverse party previous notice of the time and place of examination, together with a copy of an affidavit, showing that it is a case wherein deposition may be used. Such notice must be at least five days, adding also one day for every twenty-five miles of the distance of the place of examination from the residence of the person to whom the notice is given, unless, for a cause shown, a judge, by order, prescribe a shorter time. When a shorter time is prescribed, a copy of the order must be served with the notice.

CHAPTER XXV.

JUDICIAL RECORDS, HOW PROVED.

A judicial record is the record or official entry of the proceedings in a Court of justice, or of the official act of a judicial officer, in an action or special proceeding.

A judicial record of this State, or of the United States, may be proved by the production of the original, or of a copy thereof certified by the clerk or other person having the legal custody thereof. That of a sister State may be proved by the attestation of the clerk and the seal of the Court annexed, if there be a clerk and seal, together with a certificate of the chief judge or presiding magistrate, that the attestation is in due form.

A judicial record of a foreign country may be proved by the attestation of the clerk, with the seal of the Court annexed, if there be a clerk and seal, or of the legal keeper of the record, with the seal of his office annexed, if there be a seal, together with a certificate of the chief judge or presiding magistrate, that the person making the attestation is the clerk of the Court or the legal keeper of the record; and in either case, that the signature of such person is genuine, and that the attestation is in due form. The signature of the chief judge or presiding magistrate must be authenticated by the certificate of the minister or embassador, or a consul, vice-consul, or consular agent of the United States in such foreign country.

A copy of the judicial record of a foreign country is also admissible in evidence, upon proof:

1. That the copy offered has been compared by the witness with the original, and is an exact transcript of the whole of it.

2. That such original was in the custody of the clerk of the Court or other legal keeper of the same; and,

3. That the copy is duly attested by a seal which is proved to be the seal of the Court where the record remains, if it be the record of a Court; or if there be no such seal, or if it be not a record of a Court, by the signature of the legal keeper of the original.

CHAPTER XXVI.

ACKNOWLEDGMENTS.

The proof or acknowledgment of an instrument may be made at any place within this State, before a justice or clerk of the Supreme Court.

The proof or acknowledgment of an instrument may be made in this State within the city, county or district for which the officer was elected or appointed, before either :

1. A judge or clerk of a Court of record; or,
2. A mayor or recorder of a city ; or,
3. A court commissioner ; or,
4. A county recorder ; or,
5. A notary public ; or,
6. A justice of the peace.

The proof or acknowledgment of an instrument may be made without this State, but within the United States, and within the jurisdiction of the officer, before either :

1. A justice, judge, or clerk of any Court of record of the United States ; or,
2. A justice, judge, or clerk of any Court of record of any State ; or,
3. A commissioner appointed by the Governor of this State for that purpose ; or,
4. A notary public ; or,
5. Any other officer of the State where the acknowledgment is made, authorized by its laws to take such proof or acknowledgment.

A proof or acknowledgment of an instrument may be made without the United States, before either :

1. A minister, commissioner, or *charge d'affaires* of the United States, resident and accredited in the country where the proof or acknowledgment is made ; or,
2. A consul, vice-consul, or consular agent of the United States, resident in the country where the proof or acknowledgment is made ; or,

3. A judge of a Court of record of the county where the proof or acknowledgment is made; or,

4. Commissioners appointed for such purposes by the governor of the State, pursuant to special statutes; or,

5. A notary public.

If any of the above named officers are authorized by law to appoint a deputy, the acknowledgment or proof may be taken by such deputy in the name of his principal.

The acknowledgment of an instrument must not be taken, unless the officer taking it knows, or has satisfactory evidence, on the oath or affirmation of a credible witness, that the person making such acknowledgment is the individual who is described in and who executed the instrument; or if executed by a corporation, that the person making such acknowledgment is the president or secretary of such corporation.

The acknowledgment of a married woman to an instrument purporting to be executed by her must not be taken, unless she is made acquainted by the officer with the contents of the instrument on an examination without the hearing of her husband; nor certified, unless she thereupon acknowledges to the officer that she executed the instrument, and that she does not wish to retract such execution.

GENERAL FORM OF CERTIFICATE.

STATE OF——— }
　　COUNTY OF——— } ss.

On this——day of———, in the year———, before me, [here insert the name and quality of the officer] personally appeared ———, known to me [or proved to me on the oath of———] to be the person whose name is subscribed to the within instrument, and acknowledged to me that he [or they] executed the same.

FORM OF CERTIFICATE OF ACKNOWLEDGMENT BY MARRIED WOMAN.

STATE OF——— }
　　COUNTY OF——— } ss.

On this——day of———, in the year———, before me, [here

insert the name and quality of the officer] personally appeared
———, known to me [or proved to me on the oath of———] to
be the person whose name is subscribed to the within instrument,
described as a married woman; and upon an examination without
the hearing of her husband, I made her acquainted with the contents of the instrument; and thereupon she acknowledged to me
that she executed the same, and that she does not wish to retract
such execution.

FORM OF CERTIFICATE OF ACKNOWLEDGMENT BY A CORPORATION.

STATE OF———
    COUNTY OF——— } ss.

On this——day of———, in the year———, before me [here
insert the name and quality of the officer] personally appeared
—————known to me [or proved to me on the oath of————]
to be the president [or the secretary] of the corporation that executed the written instrument, and acknowledged to me that such
corporation executed the same.

FORM OF CERTIFICATE OF ACKNOWLEDGMENT BY ATTORNEY IN
FACT. ·

STATE OF———
    COUNTY OF——— } ss.

On this——day of————, in the year———, before me [here
insert the name and quality of the officer] personally appeared
———, known to me [or proved to me on the oath of———]
to be the person whose name is subscribed to the within instrument
as the attorney in fact of———, and acknowledged to me that he
subscribed the name of———thereto, as principal, and his own
name as attorney in fact.

Officers must authenticate their certificates by affixing thereto
their signatures, followed by the names of their offices; also their
seals of office, if by the laws of the State or country where the
acknowledgment or proof is taken, or by authority of which they
are acting, they are required to have official seals.

The certificate of proof or acknowledgment, if made before a justice of the peace, when used in any county other than that in which he residés, must be accompanied by a certificate under the hand and seal of the clerk of the county in which the justice resides, setting forth that such justice, at the time of taking such proof or acknowledgment, was authorized to take the same, and that the clerk is acquainted with his hand-writing, and believes that the signature to the original certificate is genuine.

Chapter XXVII.

PARTNERSHIPS.

Partnership is the association of two or more persons for the purpose of carrying on business together, and dividing its profits between them.

Every partnership that is not formed in accordance with the law concerning mining or special partnerships, and every special partnership, so far only as the general partners are concerned, is a general partnership.

Every general partner is agent for the partnership in the transaction of its business, and has authority to do whatever is necessary to carry on such business in the ordinary manner, and for this purpose may bind his copartners by an agreement in writing.

A partner, as such, has not authority to do any of the following acts, unless his copartners have wholly abandoned the business to him, or are incapable of acting:

1. To make an assignment of the partnership property or any portion thereof to a creditor, or to a third person in trust, for the benefit of a creditor or of all creditors.

2. To dispose of the good will of the business.

3. To dispose of the whole of the partnership property at once, unless it consists entirely of merchandise.

4. To do any act which would make it impossible to carry on the ordinary business of the partnership.

5. To confess a judgment.

6. To submit a partnership claim to arbitration.

7. To do any act which is not necessary to carry on such business in the ordinary manner.

Every general partner is liable to third persons for all the obligations of the partnership, jointly with his copartners.

Any one permitting himself to be represented as a partner, general or special, is liable as such to third persons to whom such representation is communicated, and who, on the faith thereof, give credit to the partnership.

The liability of a general partner for the acts of his copartners continues, even after a dissolution of the copartnership, in favor of persons who have had dealings with and given credit to the partnership during its existence, until they have had personal notice of the dissolution ; and in favor of other persons until such dissolution has been advertised in a newspaper published in every county where the partnership, at the time of its dissolution, had a place of business, if a newspaper is there published, to the extent in either case to which such persons part with value in good faith, and in the belief that such partner is still a member of the firm.

After the dissolution of a partnership, any general partner may act in liquidation of its affairs, unless the liquidation is committed, by consent of all the partners, to one or more of them ; and in such case the others have no right to act therein, but their acts are valid in favor of persons parting with value, in good faith, upon credit thereof.

A partner authorized to act in liquidation may collect, compromise, or release any debts due to the partnership, pay or compromise any claims against it, and dispose of the partnership property ; and he may indorse, in the name of the firm, promissory notes or other obligations held by the partnership, for the purpose of collecting the same ; but he cannot create any new obligation in its name, or revive a debt against the firm by an acknowledgment, when an action thereon is barred.

Except as hereafter provided, every partnership transacting business in this State under a fictitious name, or a designation not showing the names of the persons interested as partners in such business, must file with the clerk of the county in which its principal place of business is situated a certificate stating the names in full of all the members of such partnership and their places of residence, and publish the same once a week for four successive weeks in a newspaper published in the county, if there be one, and if there be none in such county, then in a newspaper published in an adjoining county.

A commercial or banking partnership, established and transacting business in a place without the United States, may, without filing the certificate, or making the publication heretofore mentioned, use in this State the partnership name used by it there, although it be fictitious, or do not show the names of the persons interested as partners in such business.

The certificate filed with the clerk must be signed by the partners, and acknowledged before some officer authorized to take the acknowledgment of conveyances of real property. Where the partnership is formed after the first of July, eighteen hundred and seventy-four, the certificate must be filed and the publication made within one month after the formation of the partnership, or within one month from the time designated in the agreement of its members for the commencement of the partnership. Where the partnership has been formed prior to the first of July, eighteen hundred and seventy-four, the certificate must be filed and the publication made within six months after the first of July aforesaid.

On every change in the members of a partnership transacting business in this State under a fictitious name, or a designation which does not show the names of the persons interested as partners in its business; except in the case of a commercial or banking partnership, established and transacting business in a place without the United States, as well as in this State, a new certificate must be filed and a new publication made, as is required on the formation of such partnership.

Persons doing business as partners contrary to the aforesaid provisons, shall not maintain any action upon or on account of any contract made or transactions had in their partnership name, in any Court of this State, until they have first filed the certificate and made the publication required. Copies of the entries of a county clerk, when certified by him, and affidavits·of publication made by the printer, publisher, or chief clerk of a newspaper, are presumptive evidence of the facts therein stated.

Special partnerships are formed by filing a certificate with the county clerk and recorder, severally signed, stating:

1. The name under which the partnership is to be conducted.

2. The general nature of the business intended to be transacted.

3. The names of all the partners, and their residences, specifying which are general and which are special partners.

4. The amount of capital which each special partner has contributed to the common stock.

5. The periods at which such partnerships shall begin and end.

Affidavits must be made and filed, setting forth the amount actually contributed by the special partners.

The certificate mentioned must be published in a newspaper in the county, once a week for four successive weeks.

The general partners in a special partnership are liable to the same extent as partners in a general partnership. The contribution of a special partner to the capital of the firm, and the increase thereof, is liable for its debts, but he is not otherwise liable therefor.

· Chapter XXVIII.

MARRIED WOMEN.

All property of the wife owned by her before marriage, and that acquired afterwards by gift, bequest, devise, or descent, with the rents, issues, and profits thereof, is her separate property. All property owned by the husband before marriage, and that acquired afterwards by gift, bequest, devise, or descent, with the rents, issues, and profits thereof, is his separate property. All other property acquired after marriage, by either husband or wife, or both, is community property. The earnings of the wife are not liable for the debts of the husband. The earnings and accumulations of the wife, and her minor children living with her and in her custody, while she is living separate from her husband, are the separate property of the wife.

The separate property of the wife is not liable for the debts of her husband, but is liable for her own debts, contracted before or after marriage. The separate property of the husband is not liable for the debts of the wife contracted before marriage. The property of the community is not liable for the contracts of the wife made after marriage, unless secured by a pledge or mortgage thereof executed by the husband.

The husband has the management and control of the community property, with the like absolute power of disposition (other than testamentary) as he has of his separate estate. No estate in dower is allotted to the wife upon the death of her husband.

If the husband neglects to make adequate provision for the support of his wife, any other person may, in good faith, supply her with articles necessary for her support, and recover the reasonable value thereof from the husband ; except that a husband abandoned by his wife is not liable for her support until she offers to return, unless she was justified, by his misconduct, in abandoning him ; nor is he liable for her support when she is living separate from him, by agreement, unless such support is stipulated in the agreement.

A married woman may become a sole trader by the judgment of the County Court of the county in which she has resided for six months next preceding the application.

A certified copy of the decree of the Court must be recorded in the office of the recorder of the county where the business is to be carried on.

A sole trader is entitled to carry on the business specified in her own name, and the property, revenues, moneys and credits so by her invested, and the profits thereof, belong exclusively to her, and are not liable for any debts of her husband. The husband of a sole trader is not liable for any debts contracted by her in the course of her sole trader's business, unless contracted upon his written consent.

Chapter XXIX.

MINORS.

Minors are males under twenty-one years of age, females under eighteen years of age.

A minor cannot give a delegation of power, nor, under the age of eighteen, make a contract relating to real property, or any interest therein, or relating to any personal property not in his immediate possession or control. A minor may make any other contract, in the same manner as an adult, subject to his power of disaffirmance. A minor cannot disaffirm a contract, otherwise valid, to pay the reasonable value of things necessary for his support, or that of his family, entered into by him when not under the care of a parent or guardian able to provide for him or them. Nor can a minor disaffirm an obligation, otherwise valid, entered into by him under the express authority or direction of a statute. In all other cases, the contract of a minor, if made whilst he is under the age of eighteen, may be disaffirmed by the minor himself, either before his majority, or within a reasonable time afterwards; or in case of his death within that period, by his heirs or personal representatives; and if the contract be made by the minor whilst he is over the age of eighteen, it may be disaffirmed in like manner, upon restoring the consideration to the party from whom it was received, or paying its equivalent.

If a parent neglect to provide articles necessary for his child, who is under his charge, according to his circumstances, a third person may in good faith supply such necessaries, and recover the reasonable value thereof from the parent.

A minor may enforce his rights by civil action, or other legal proceedings, in the same manner as a person of full age, except that a guardian must conduct the same.

CHAPTER XXX.

STOPPAGE IN TRANSIT.

A seller or consignor of property, whose claim for its price or proceeds has not been extinguished, may, upon the insolvency of the buyer or consignee becoming known to him after parting with the property, stop it while on its transit to the buyer or consignee, and resume possession thereof. A person is insolvent, within the meaning of the above term, when he ceases to pay his debts in the manner usual with persons of his business, or when he declares his inability or unwillingness to do so. The transit of property is at an end when it comes into the possession of the consignee, or into that of his agent, unless such agent is employed merely to forward the property to the consignee. Stoppage in transit can be effected only by notice to the carrier or depositary of the property, or by taking actual possession thereof.

Stoppage in transit does not, of itself, rescind a sale, but is a means of enforcing the lien of the seller.

A bona fide transfer of a bill of lading defeats the right of stoppage in transit, if such transfer is made before the right of stoppage has been actually exercised by the consignor.

CHAPTER XXXI.

BILLS OF LADING.

A bill of lading is an instrument in writing, signed by a carrier or his agent, describing the freight so as to identify it, stating the name of the consignor, the terms of the contract for carriage, and agreeing or directing that the freight be delivered to the order or assigns of a specified person, at a specified place.

The title to the freight which the first holder of a bill of lading had when he received it passes to every subsequent indorsee thereof, in good faith and for value, in the ordinary course of business, with like effect, and in like manner, as in the case of a bill of exchange. If a bill of lading is made payable to "bearer," it is transferable by delivery.

CHAPTER XXXII.

INTEREST.

Unless there is an express contract in writing fixing a different rate, interest is payable on all moneys at the rate of ten per cent. per annum, after they become due, on any instrument of writing except a judgment, and on moneys lent or due on any settlement of accounts from the day on which the balance is ascertained, and on moneys received to the use of another, and detained from him. In the computation of interest for a period less than a year, three hundred and sixty days are deemed to constitute a year.

Interest is payable on judgments recovered in the Courts of this

State at the rate of seven per cent. per annum, and no greater rate ; but such interest must not be compounded in any manner or form.

Parties may agree in writing for the payment of any rate of interest, and it shall be allowed, according to the terms of the agreement, until the entry of judgment; and they may, in any contract in writing whereby any debt is secured to be paid, agree that if the interest on such debt is not punctually paid, it shall become a part of the principal, and thereafter bear the same rate as the principal debt.

Open accounts do not bear interest.

CHAPTER XXXIII.

COMMON CARRIERS.

Unless the consignor accompanies the freight, and retains exclusive control thereof, an inland common carrier of property is liable, from the time that he accepts until he relieves himself from liability, for the loss or injury thereof, except:

1. An inherent defect, vice, or weakness, or a spontaneous action of the property itself.

2. The act of a public enemy of the United States, or of this State.

3. The act of the law ; or

4. Any irresistible superhuman cause.

He is liable, even in the cases above excepted, if his ordinary negligence exposes the property to the cause of the loss. A common carrier is liable for delay only when it is caused by his want of ordinary care and diligence.

A marine carrier is liable in like manner as an inland carrier, except for loss or injury caused by the perils of the sea or fire.

8

Chapter XXXIV.

MORTGAGES OF PERSONAL PROPERTY.

Mortgages may be made upon :

1. Locomotives, engines, and the other rolling stock of a railroad.

2. Steamboat machinery, and machinery used by machinists, foundrymen, and mechanics.

3. Steam engines and boilers.

4. Mining machinery.

5. Printing presses and material.

6. Professional libraries.

7. Instruments of a surgeon, physician, or dentist.

8. Upholstery and furniture used in hotels or boarding houses, when mortgaged to secure the purchase money of the articles mortgaged.

9. Growing crops.

10. Vessels of more than five tons' burden.

A mortgage of personal property is void as against creditors of the mortgagor, and subsequent purchasers and incumbrancers of the property in good faith and for value, unless—

1. It is accompanied by the affidavit of all the parties thereto that it is made in good faith, and without any design to hinder, delay, or defraud creditors.

2. It is acknowledged or proved, certified and recorded.

A mortgage of personal property must be recorded in the office of the county recorder of the county in which the mortgagor resides, and also of the county in which the property mortgaged is situated, or to which it may be removed.

A certified copy of a mortgage of personal property once recorded may be recorded in any other county, and when so recorded, the record thereof has the same force and effect as though it was of the original mortgage.

When property mortgaged is thereafter by the mortgagor removed from the county in which it is situated, it is, except as between the parties to the mortgage, exempt from the operation thereof, unless either :

1. The mortgagee, within thirty days after such removal, causes the mortgage to be recorded in the county to which the property has been removed ; or,

2. The mortgagee, within thirty days after such removal, takes possession of the property, as prescribed in the next paragraph.

If the mortgagor voluntarily removes or permits the removal of the mortgaged property from the county in which it was situated at the time it was mortgaged, the mortgagee may take possession and dispose of the property as a pledge for the payment of the debt, though the debt is not due.

Personal property mortgaged may be taken under attachment or execution issued at the suit of a creditor. Before the property is so taken, the officer must pay or tender to the mortgagee the amount of the mortgage debt and interest, or must deposit the amount thereof with the county clerk or treasurer, payable to the order of the mortgagee.

When the property thus taken is sold under process, the officer must apply the proceeds of sale as follows :

1. To the repayment of the sum paid to the mortgagee, with interest from the date of such payment ; and,

2. The balance, if any, in like manner as the proceeds of sales under execution are applied in other cases.

A mortgagee of personal property, when the debt to secure which the mortgage was executed becomes due, may foreclose the mortgagor's right of redemption by a sale of the property made in the manner prescribed in the chapter on "pledge," or may proceed by a judicial sale under the direction of a competent Court.

Chapter XXXV.

PLEDGE.

A pledge is a deposit of personal property by way of security for the performance of another act.

Where a debtor has obtained credit, or an extension of time, by a fraudulent misrepresentation of the value of property pledged by or for him, the creditor may demand a further pledge to correspond with the value represented ; and in default thereof may recover his debt immediately, though it be not actually due.

When performance of the act for which a pledge is given is due, in whole or in part, the pledgee may collect what is due to him by a sale of the property pledged.

Before property pledged can be sold, and after performance of the act for which it is security is due, the pledgee must demand performance thereof from the debtor, if the debtor can be found.

A pledgee must give actual notice to the pledgor of the time and place at which the property pledged will be sold, at such a reasonable time before the sale as will enable the pledgor to attend.

The sale by a pledgee of property pledged must be made by public auction, in the manner and upon the notice to the public usual at the place of sale, in respect to auction sales of similar property ; and must be for the highest obtainable price.

A pledgee cannot sell any evidence of debt pledged to him, except the obligations of governments, States, or corporations ; but he may collect the same when due.

The pledgor may require the property to be sold when it will bring a sufficient amount to satisfy the claim of the pledgee.

A pledgee or pledge holder cannot purchase the property pledged, except by direct dealings with the pledgor.

Instead of selling property pledged, as hereinbefore provided, a pledgee may foreclose the right of redemption by a judicial sale, under the directions of a competent Court ; and in that case may be authorized by the Court to purchase at the sale.

CHAPTER XXXVI.

GUARANTY AND SURETYSHIP.

A guaranty is a promise to answer for the debt, default, or miscarriage of another person.

Where a guaranty is entered into at the same time with the original obligation, or with the acceptance of the latter by the guarantee, and forms with that obligation a part of the consideration to him, no other consideration need exist. In all other cases there must be a consideration distinct from that of the original obligation.

Except as hereinafter described, a guaranty must be in writing, and signed by the guarantor; but the writing need not express a consideration.

A promise to answer for the obligation of another, in any of the following cases, is deemed an original obligation of the promisor, and need not be in writing:

1. Where the promise is made by one who has received property of another upon an undertaking to apply it pursuant to such promise; or by one who has received a discharge from an obligation in whole or in part, in consideration of such promise.

2. Where the creditor parts with value, or enters into an obligation in consideration of the obligation in respect to which the promise is made, in terms or under circumstances such as to render the party making the promise the principal debtor, and the person in whose behalf it is made his surety.

3. Where the promise, being for an antecedent obligation of another, is made upon the consideration that the party receiving it cancels the antecedent obligation, accepting the new promise as a substitute therefor; or upon the consideration that the party receiving it releases the property from a levy, or his person from imprisonment, under an execution on a judgment obtained upon the antecedent obligation; or upon a consideration beneficial to the promisor, whether moving from either party to the antecedent obligation, or from another person.

4. Where a factor undertakes, for a commission, to sell merchandise and guarantee the sale.

5. Where the holder of an instrument for the payment of money, upon which a third person is or may become liable to him, transfers it in payment of a precedent debt of his own, or for a new consideration, and in connection with such transfer enters into a promise respecting such instrument.

A guarantor is exonerated, exept so far as he may be indemnified by the principal, if by any act of the creditor without the consent of the guarantor the original obligation of the principal is altered in any respect, or the remedies or rights of the creditor against the principal in respect thereto are in any way impaired or suspended.

A surety is one who, at the request of another, and for the purpose of securing to him a benefit, becomes responsible for the performance, by the latter, of some act in favor of a third person, or hypothecates property as security therefor.

A surety is exonerated :

1. In like manner with a guarantor.

2. To the extent to which he is prejudiced by any act of the creditor which would naturally prove injurious to the remedies of the surety, or inconsistent with his rights, or which lessens his security ; or,

3. To the extent to which he is prejudiced by an omission of the creditor to do anything, when required by the surety, which it is his duty to do.

A surety has all the rights of a guarantor.

A surety may require his creditor to proceed against the principal, or to pursue any other remedy in his power which the surety cannot himself pursue, and which would lighten his burden ; and if in such case the creditor neglects to do so, the surety is exonerated to the extent to which he is thereby prejudiced.

A surety may compel his principal to perform the obligation when due.

A surety, upon satisfying the obligation of the principal, is entitled to enforce every remedy which the creditor then has against the principal, to the extent of reimbursing what he has expended, and also to require all his co-sureties to contribute thereto, without regard to the order of time in which they became such.

Whenever property of a surety is hypothecated with property of the principal, the surety is entitled to have the property of the principal first applied to the discharge of the obligation.

LETTER OF CREDIT.

A letter of credit is a written instrument, addressed by one person to another, requesting the latter to give credit to the person in whose favor it is drawn.

The writer of a letter of credit is, upon the default of the debtor, liable to those who gave credit in compliance with its terms.

CHAPTER XXXVII.

SALE.

No sale of personal property, or agreement to buy or sell it, for a price of two hundred dollars or more, is valid, unless:

1. The agreement, or some note or memorandum thereof, be in writing, and subscribed by the party to be charged, or by his agent; or,

2. The buyer accepts and receives part of the thing sold, or when it consists of a thing in action, part of the evidences thereof, or some of them; or,

3. The buyer, at the time of sale, pays a part of the price.

The foregoing provisions do not affect an agreement to manufacture a thing from materials furnished by the manufacturer or by another person.

No agreement for the sale of real property, or of an interest therein, is valid, unless the same, or some note or memorandum thereof, be in writing, and subscribed by the party to be charged, or his agent thereunto authorized in writing.

If a buyer of personal property does not pay for it according to contract, and it remains in the possession of the seller after payment is due, the seller may rescind the sale, or enforce his lien for the price.

In order to make a sale of personal property effectual as against creditors, there must be an immediate, actual, and continued change of possession.

CHAPTER XXXVIII.

CONTRACTS.

A contract is an agreement to do or not to do a certain thing. It is essential to the existence of a contract that there should be :

1. Parties capable of contracting.
2. Their consent.
3. A lawful object.
4. A sufficient cause of consideration.

A written instrument is presumptive evidence of consideration. Contracts are either express or implied.

An express contract is one, the terms of which are stated in words.

An implied contract is one, the existence and terms of which are manifested by conduct.

The following contracts are invalid, unless the same, or some note or memorandum thereof, be in writing, and subscribed by the party to be charged, or by his agent :

1. An agreement that by its terms is not to be performed within a year from the making thereof.

2. A special promise to answer for the debts, default or miscarriage of another, except in the cases mentioned in Chapter XXXVI.

3. An agreement made upon consideration of marriage, other than a mutual promise to marry.

4. An agreement for the sale of goods, chattels, or things in action, at a price not less than two hundred dollars, unless the buyer accept or receive part of such goods and chattels, or the evidences, or some of them, of such things in action, or pay at the time some part of the purchase money; but when a sale is made by auction, an entry by the auctioneer in his sale book, at the time of the sale, of the kind of property sold, the terms of sale, the price, and the names of the purchaser and person on whose account the sale is made, is a sufficient memorandum.

5. An agreement for the leasing for a longer period than one year, or for the sale of real property, or of an interest therein; and such agreement, if made by an agent of the party sought to be charged, is invalid, unless the authority of the agent be in writing, subscribed by the party sought to be charged.

All contracts may be oral, except such as are specially required by statute to be in writing.

Chapter XXXIX.

NEGOTIABLE INSTRUMENTS.

A bill of exchange is an instrument negotiable in form, by which one, who is called the drawer, requests another, called the drawee, to pay a specified sum of money.

A bill of exchange is payable :

1. At the place where, by its terms, it is made payable ; or,

2. If it specify no place of payment, then at the place to which it is addressed ; or,

3. If it is not addressed to any place, then at the place of residence or business of the drawee, or wherever he may be found. If the drawee has no place of business, or if his place of business or residence cannot, with reasonable diligence, be ascertained, presentment for payment is excused, and the bill may be protested for non-payment.

Presentment of a bill of exchange for acceptance must be made in the following manner, as nearly as by reasonable diligence it is practicable :

1. The bill must be presented by the holder or his agent.

2. It must be presented on a business day, and within reasonable hours.

3. It must be presented to the drawee, or if he be absent from his place of residence or business, to some person having charge thereof, or employed therein ; and,

4. The drawee, on such presentment, may postpone his acceptance or refusal until the next day. If the drawee have no place of business, or if his place of business or residence cannot, with reasonable diligence, be ascertained, presentment for acceptance is excused, and the bill may be protested for non-acceptance.

When a bill of exchange is payable at a specified time after sight, the drawer and endorsers are exonerated if it is not presented for acceptance within ten days after the time which would suffice, with ordinary diligence, to forward it for acceptance, unless presentment is excused.

An acceptance of a bill must be made in writing, and may be made by the acceptor writing his name across the face of the bill, with or without other words.

An unconditional promise, in writing, to accept a bill of exchange, is a sufficient acceptance thereof, in favor of every person who upon the faith thereof has taken the bill for value or other good consideration.

On the dishonor of a bill of exchange by the drawee, and in

case of a foreign bill, after it has been duly protested, it may be accepted or paid by any person, for the honor of any party thereto.

If a bill of exchange, payable at sight or on demand, without interest, is not duly presented for payment within ten days after the time in which it could, with reasonable diligence, be transmitted to the proper place for presentment, the drawer and endorsers are exonerated unless such presentment is excused.

The presentment of a bill of exchange for acceptance is excused if the drawee has not capacity to accept it.

Delay in the presentment of a bill of exchange for acceptance is excused, when caused by circumstances over which the owner has no control.

Presentment of a bill of exchange for acceptance or payment, and notice of its dishonor, are excused as to the drawer, if he forbids the drawee to accept, or the acceptor to pay the bill; or if, at the time of drawing, he had no reason to believe that the drawee would accept or pay the same.

An inland bill of exchange is one drawn and payable within this State. All others are foreign.

Notice of the dishonor of a foreign bill of exchange can be given only by notice of its protest, and the protest must be made by a notary public, if with reasonable diligence one can be obtained; and if not, then by any reputable person, in the presence of two witnesses. Protest for non-acceptance must be made in the city or town in which the bill is presented for acceptance, and a protest for non-payment in the city or town in which it is presented for payment.

One who pays a foreign bill for honor must declare, before payment, in the presence of a person authorized to make protest, for whose honor he pays the same, in order to entitle him to reimbursement.

Damages on foreign bills of exchange are allowed as hereinafter prescribed, as a full compensation for interest accrued before notice of dishonor, re-exchange, expenses, and all other damages, in favor of holders for value only, upon bills of exchange drawn or negotiated within this State, and protested for non-acceptance or non-payment.

Damages are allowed as follows :

1. If drawn upon any person in this State, two dollars upon each one hundred dollars of the principal sum specified in the bill.

2. If drawn upon any person out of this State, but in any other of the States west of the Rocky Mountains, five dollars upon each hundred dollars of the principal sum specified in the bill.

3. If drawn upon any person in any of the United States, east of the Rocky Mountains, ten dollars upon each hundred dollars of the principal sum specified in the bill.

4. If drawn upon any person in any place in a foreign country, fifteen dollars upon each hundred dollars of the principal sum specified in the bill.

From the time of notice of dishonor and demand of payment, lawful interest must be allowed upon the aggregate amount of the principal sum specified in the bill, and the damages above mentioned.

A promissory note is an instrument negotiable in form, whereby the signer promises to pay a specified sum of money.

If a promissory note, payable on demand, or at sight, without interest, is not duly presented for payment within six months from its date, the indorsers thereof are exonerated, unless such presentment is excused.

Days of grace are not allowed on bills of exchange and promissory notes.

A check is a bill of exchange drawn upon a bank or banker, or a person described as such upon the face thereof, and payable on demand without interest.

A check is subject to all the provisions herein mentioned concerning bills of exchange, except that:

1. The drawer and indorsers are exonerated by delay in presentation only to the extent of the injury they suffer thereby.

2. An indorsee, after its apparent maturity, but without actual notice of its dishonor, acquires a title equal to that of an indorsee before such period.

A negotiable instrument must be made payable in money only, and without any condition not certain of fulfillment.

A negotiable instrument may be with or without date, and with or without designation of the time or place of payment.

A negotiable instrument may contain a pledge of collateral security, with authority to dispose thereof.

A negotiable instrument which does not specify a place of payment is payable at the residence or place of business of the maker, or wherever he may be found.

A negotiable instrument, made payable to the order of the maker, or of a fictitious person, if issued by the maker for a valid consideration, without indorsement, has the same effect against him and all other persons having notice of the facts as if payable to the bearer.

An indorsement of a negotiable instrument may be general or special.

A general indorsement is one by which no indorsee is named. A special indorsement specifies the indorsee.

A negotiable instrument bearing a general indorsement cannot be afterwards specially indorsed; but any lawful holder may turn a general indorsement into a special one, by writing above it a direction for payment to a particular person.

A special indorsement may, by express words for that purpose, but not otherwise, be ·so made as to render the instrument not negotiable.

An indorser may qualify his indorsement with the words, "without recourse," or equivalent words; and upon such indorsement he is responsible only to the same extent as in the case of a transfer without indorsement.

An indorsee in due course is one who, in good faith, in the ordinary course of business, and for value, before its apparent maturity or presumptive dishonor, and without knowledge of its actual dishonor, acquires a negotiable instrument duly indorsed to him, or indorsed generally, or payable to the bearer.

An indorsee of a negotiable instrument, in due course, acquires an absolute title thereto, so that it is valid in his hands, notwithstanding any provision of law making it generally void or voidable, and notwithstanding any defect in the title of the person from whom he acquired it.

The want of consideration for the undertaking of a maker, acceptor, or indorser of a negotiable instrument does not exonerate him from liability thereon to an indorsee in good faith for a consideration.

It is not necessary to make a demand of payment upon the principal debtor in a negotiable instrument in order to charge him ; but if the instrument is, by its terms, payable at a specified place, and he is able and willing to pay it there at maturity, such ability and willingness are equivalent to an offer of payment on his part.

Presentment of a negotiable instrument for payment, when necessary, must be made as follows, as nearly as by reasonable diligence it is practicable :

1. The instrument must be presented by the holder.

2. The instrument must be presented to the principal debtor, if he can be found at the place where presentment should be made ; and if not, then it must be presented to some other person having charge thereof, or employed therein, if one can be found there.

3. An instrument which specifies a place for its payment must be presented there ; and if the place specified includes more than one house, then at the place of residence or business of the principal debtor, if it can be found therein.

4. An instrument which does not specify a place for its payment must be presented at the place of residence or business of the principal debtor, or wherever he may be found, at the option of the presentor ; and

5. The instrument must be presented upon the day of its maturity, or if it be payable on demand, it may be presented on any day. It must be presented within reasonable hours ; and if it be payable at a banking house, within the usual banking hours of the vicinity ; but by the consent of the person to whom it should be presented, it may be presented at any hour of the day.

6. If the principal debtor have no place of business, or if his place of business or residence cannot, with reasonable diligence, be ascertained, presentment for payment is excused.

The apparent maturity of a negotiable instrument, payable at a particular time, is the day on which, by its terms, it becomes due, or when that is a holiday, the next business day.

A bill of exchange, payable at a certain time after sight, which is not accepted within ten days after its date, in addition to the time which would suffice, with ordinary diligence, to forward it for acceptance, is presumed to have been dishonored.

The apparent maturity of a bill of exchange, payable at sight or on demand, is:

1. If it bears interest, one year after its date ; or,

2. If it does not bear interest, ten days after its date, in addition to the time which would suffice, with ordinary diligence, to forward it for acceptance.

The apparent maturity of a promissory note, payable at sight or on demand, is:

1. If it bears interest, one year after its date ; or,

2. If it does not bear interest, six months after its date.

When a promissory note is payable at a certain time after sight or demand, such time is to be added to the period above mentioned.

A negotiable instrument is dishonored when it is either not paid or not accepted, according to its tenor, on presentation for the purpose, or without presentation when that is excused.

Notice of the dishonor of a negotiable instrument may be given:

1. By a holder thereof; or,

2. By any party to the instrument who might be compelled to pay it to the holder, and who would, upon taking it up, have a right to reimbursement from the party to whom the notice is given.

A notice of dishonor may be given in any form which describes the instrument with reasonable certainty, and substantially informs the party receiving it that the instrument has been dishonored.

A notice of dishonor may be given :

1. By delivering it to the party to be charged, personally, at any place ; or,

2. By delivering it to some person of discretion at the place of residence or business of such party, apparently acting for him ; or,

3. By properly folding the notice, directing it to the party to be charged, at his place of residence, according to the best information that the person giving the notice can obtain, depositing it in the post office most conveniently accessible from the place where the presentment was made, and paying the postage thereon.

In case of the death of a party to whom notice of dishonor should otherwise be given, the notice must be given to one of his personal representatives; or if there are none, then to any member of his family who resided with him at his death; or if there is none, then it must be mailed to his last place of residence.

A notice of dishonor given otherwise than by mail must be given on the day of dishonor, or on the next business day. When given by mail, it must be deposited in the post office in time for the first mail which closes after noon of the first business day succeeding the dishonor, and which leaves the place where the instrument was dishonored for the place to which the notice should be sent.

Every party to a negotiable instrument, receiving notice of its dishonor, has the like time thereafter to give similar notice to prior parties as the original holder had after its dishonor. But this additional time is available only to the particular party entitled thereto.

A notice of the dishonor of a negotiable instrument, if valid in favor of the party giving it, inures to the benefit of all other parties thereto whose right to give the like notice has not then been lost.

Notice of dishonor is excused:

1. When the party by whom it should be given cannot, with reasonable diligence, ascertain either the place of residence or business of the party to be charged; or,

2. When there is no post office communication between the town of the party by whom the notice should be given, and the town in which the place of residence or business of the party to be charged is situated; or,

3. When the party to be charged is the same person who dishonors the instrument; or,

4. When the notice is waived by the party entitled thereto.

Presentment and notice are excused as to any party who informs the holder, within ten days before maturity, that the instrument will be dishonored.

If before or after the maturity of an instrument an indorser has received full security for the amount thereof, or the maker has assigned all his estate to him as such security, presentment and notice to him are excused.

Delay in presentment, or in giving notice of dishonor, is excused when caused by circumstances which the party delaying could not have avoided by the exercise of reasonable care and diligence.

A waiver of presentment waives notice of dishonor also ; but a waiver of notice does not waive presentment.

A waiver of protest on any negotiable instrument, other than a foreign bill of exchange, waives presentment and notice.

Chapter XL.

PRINCIPAL AND AGENT.

An agent is one who represents another, called the principal, in dealings with third persons.

Any person having capacity to contract may appoint an agent, and any person may be an agent.

An agent for a particular act or transaction is called a special agent. All others are general agents.

An agent, unless specially forbidden by his principal to do so, can delegate his powers to another person in any of the following cases, and in no others :

1. When the act to be done is purely mechanical.

2. When it is such as the agent cannot himself, and the sub-agent can, lawfully perform.

3. When it is the usage of the place to delegate such powers.

4. When such delegation is specially authorized by the principal.

If an agent employs a sub-agent without authority, the former is a principal and the latter his agent, and the principal of the former has no connection with the latter.

A sub-agent, lawfully appointed, represents the principal in like manner with the original agent; and the original agent is not responsible to third persons for the acts of the sub-agent.

9

An agent has authority to do everything necessary or proper, and usual, in the ordinary course of business, for effecting the purpose of his agency.

An authority to sell personal property includes authority to warrant the title of the principal, and the quality and quantity of the property.

A general agent to .sell, who is intrusted by the principal with the possession of the thing sold, has authority to receive the price.

A special agent to sell has authority to receive the price on delivery of the thing sold, but not afterwards.

PART IV.

STATE OF NEVADA.

PREPARED EXPRESSLY FOR THIS WORK BY BISHOP & SABIN, PIOCHE

CHAPTER I.

COURTS, JURISDICTION, AND TERMS OF COURTS.

UNITED STATES COURTS.

United States Circuit Court, Ninth Circuit; composed of the Districts of California, Nevada, and Oregon. Judges—Stephen J. Field, Associate Justice U. S. Supreme Court; Lorenzo Sawyer, Circuit Judge, of San Francisco, California; District Judge, E. W. Hillyer, of Carson City, Nevada. U. S. Attorney, C. S. Varian, of Carson City. Marshal, R. S. Clapp, Carson City. Clerk, R. M. Daggett, Virginia City.

Terms of U. S. Circuit Court—At Carson City, second Mondays in March, June and October.

Terms of U. S. District Court—At Carson City, first Mondays in February, May and October.

(For the jurisdiction of the United States Courts, see Part II.)

STATE COURTS.

One Supreme Court, and nine District Courts.

The Supreme Court consist of three judges. The oldest in commission acts as chief justice. Judge—Thomas P. Hawley, C. J.; Warner Earll and Wm. H. Beatty, Associate Justices. Clerk, Charles F. Bicknall. All reside at Carson City.

Regular Terms—First Mondays of January, April, July and October.

The Supreme Court shall have appellate jurisdiction in all cases in equity ; also in all cases at law in which is involved the title or right of possession to, or the possession of, real estate or mining claims, or the legality of any tax, impost, assessment, toll, or municipal fine, or in which the demand, (exclusive of interest) or the value of the property in controversy, exceeds three hundred dollars ; also in all other civil cases not included in the general subdivision of law and equity, and also on questions of law alone, in all criminal cases in which the offense charged amounts to felony. The Court shall also have power to issue writs of mandamus, certiorari, prohibition, quo warranto and habeas corpus, and also all writs necessary or proper to the complete exercise of its appellate jurisdiction. Each of the justices shall have power to issue writs of habeas corpus to any part of the State, upon petition by, or on behalf of, any person held in actual custody, and may make such writs returnable before himself or the Supreme Court, or before any District Court in the State, or before any judge of said Courts.

DISTRICT COURTS.

Jurisdiction.—The District Courts in the several judicial districts of this State shall have original jurisdiction in all cases in equity ; also in all cases at law which involve the title or the right of possession to, or the possession of, real property or mining claims, or the legality of any tax, impost, assessment, toll, or municipal fine, and in all other cases in which the demand, (exclusive of interest) or the value of the property in controversy, exceeds three hundred dollars ; also in all cases relating to the estates of deceased persons, and the persons and estates of minors and insane persons, and of the action of forcible entry and unlawful detainer; and also in all criminal cases not otherwise provided for by law. They shall also have final appellate jurisdiction in cases arising in Justices' Courts and such other inferior tribunals as may be established by law. The District Courts, and the judges thereof, shall have power to issue writs of mandamus, injunction, quo warranto, certiorari, and all other writs proper and necessary to the complete exercise of their jurisdiction; and also have power to issue writs of habeas corpus, on petition by, or on behalf of, any person held in custody in their respective districts.

TIMES FOR HOLDING DISTRICT COURTS FOR 1876.

COUNTY.	COUNTY SEAT.	DIST.	WHEN HELD.
Storey	Virginia City	1st	First Monday of January, March, June, and October.
Ormsby	Carson	2d	First Monday of February. June, and November.
Washoe	Reno	2d	First Monday of January, March. June, and October.
Douglas	Genoa	2d	First Monday of May and December.
Lyon	Dayton	3d	First Monday of February, May, August and November.
Humboldt	Winnemucca	4th	First Monday of January, April, July, and October.
Churchill	Stillwater	5th	First Monday of May and December.
Lander	Austin	5th	First Monday of January, June, and October.
Nye	Belmont	5th	First Monday of March, August, and November.
Eureka	Eureka	6th	First Monday of March, July, and November.
White Pine	Hamilton	6th	First Monday of January, May, and September.
Lincoln	Pioche	7th	First Monday of January, April, July, and October.
Esmeralda	Aurora	8th	First Monday of June and December.
Elko	Elko	9th	First Monday of February, June, and October.

JUSTICES' COURTS.

Justices of the peace have jurisdiction in all civil cases when the demand, (exclusive of interest) does not exceed three hundred dollars. Are always open.

CHAPTER II.

TIME ALLOWED TO ANSWER—SERVICE BY PUBLICATION—PLACE OF TRIAL.

Defendant has ten days to answer summons, exclusive of day of service, from date of service, when served within the county, twenty days when served in the district but in another county than the one where the action was commenced, and in all other cases forty days, when personal service is had.

Service by publication may be had on defendant, upon filing of proper affidavit therefor. Summons to be published once a week for at least one month, against defendants residing in the States of California or Oregon, and the Territories of Utah and Washington; in all other cases the publication of summons to be for not less than three months.

PLACE OF TRIAL.

All actions pertaining to real estate, or to the recovery thereof, or any interest therein, must be commenced in the county wherein the real estate is situated. Transitory actions follow the person.

PROVISIONS IN JUSTICES' COURTS.

Defendant must be sued in the township in which he lives, unless he is served with summons in the county-seat, or has contracted to perform an obligation at a particular place; in which case he may be sued in the township, city, or precinct where such obligation is to be performed, or in the township in which he resides. Service must be made from one to ten days before return day of summons.

CHAPTER III.

LIMITATION OF ACTIONS.

Civil actions, except for recovery of real property, can only be commenced as follows :

Within Five Years.—Upon a judgment or decree of any Court of the United States, or of any State or Territory within the United States.

Within Four Years.—Upon any contract, obligation, or liability founded upon an instrument in writing.

Within Three Years.—Upon a liability created by statute, other than a penalty or forfeiture ; for trespass upon real property ; for taking, detaining, or injuring any goods or chattels ; including actions for the specific recovery of personal property ; for relief on the ground of fraud ; the cause of action not deemed to have accrued until discovery by party aggrieved of facts constituting a fraud.

Within Two Years.—Upon a contract, obligation, or liability not founded upon a written instrument.

Against a sheriff, coroner, or constable, upon the liability incured by the doing of an act in his official capacity and in virtue of his office, or an omission of an official duty, including non-payment of money collected upon execution. · Upon statute for a penalty or forfeiture where the action is given to an individual, or to · an individual and the State, except when the statute imposing it fixes a different limitation. For libel, slander, assault, battery, or false imprisonment. Upon statute for forfeiture or penalty to the State. Against a sheriff or other officer, for escape of a prisoner arrested or imprisoned on civil process. On open account for goods, wares or merchandise sold and delivered. For any article charged in a store acconnt. In case of mutual accounts, the statute begins to run from date of last entry in account of either party.

In all other cases, within four years after cause of action accrued.

General Provisions.

Limitation does not run against a party during absence from State, and if when a cause of action shall accrue against a party, he be out of the State, the action may be commenced within the time limited after his return to the State.

The statute does not run against a married woman, or a person under the age of twenty-one years; one insane, or imprisoned on criminal charge, where term of imprisonment does not extend to life.

An action upon a judgment, contract, obligation, or liability, for the payment of money or damages obtained, made, executed, or issued *out of the State*, can only be commenced as follows:

1. Within one year, when prior to passage of the act, (March 5, 1867) more than two and less than five years have elapsed since the cause of action accrued.

2. Within six months, when prior to the passage of the act, more than five years have elapsed since the cause of action accrued.

3. Within two years, in all other cases, after the cause of action accrued; a right of action shall be deemed to have accrued on a judgment at the time of its rendition.

When the cause of action has arisen in any other State or Territory of the United States, or in a foreign country, and by the laws thereof an action cannot be maintained against a person by reason of the lapse of time, no action thereon shall be maintained against him in this State.

No acknowledgment or new promise shall take the case out of the statute, except it be in *writing*, *signed* by the party to be charged.

Actions for recovery of possession of real estate must be commenced within five years, *except* actions for the recovery of mining ground, which must be commenced within two years, from time cause of action accrued.

CHAPTER IV.

ATTACHMENTS.

Writ of attachment may be issued with summons, or at any time afterwards :

1. In an action upon a contract for the direct payment of money, made, or by the terms thereof, payable in *this State*, which is not secured by mortgage, lien, or pledge upon real or personal property, situated or being in the State ; if so secured, when such security has been rendered nugatory by the act of the defendant.

2. In an action upon a contract against a defendant not residing in this State.

Writ to be issued upon filing of an affidavit to be made by plaintiff, or some one on his behalf, setting forth the statutory grounds for issuance of the writ.

Plaintiff must give bond to secure defendant against damage arising from the issuance of the writ, in case the attachment is dismissed, or the defendant recover in the action.

Real and personal property, debts and credits, stocks or shares in any corporation, may be attached in the manner pointed out by the statute.

CHAPTER V.

ARREST IN CIVIL ACTIONS.

The defendant may be arrested in the following cases :

1. In an action for the recovery of money or damages, on a cause of action arising upon contract, express or implied, when the

defendant is about to depart from the State with intent to defraud his creditors, or when the action is for libel or slander.

2. In an action for a fine or penalty, or for money or property embezzled, or fraudulently misapplied or converted to his own use by a public officer, or an officer of a corporation, or an attorney, factor, broker, agent, or clerk, in the course of his employment as such, or by any other person in a fiduciary capacity, or for misconduct or neglect in office, or in professional employment, or for willful violation of duty.

3. In an action to recover the possession of personal property unjustly detained, when the property or any part thereof has been concealed, removed, or disposed of, so that it cannot be found or taken by the sheriff.

4. When the defendant has been guilty of a fraud in contracting the debt or incurring the obligation for which the action is brought, or in concealing or disposing of the property, for the taking, detention, or conversion of which the action is brought.

.5. When the defendant has removed or disposed of his property, or is about to do so, with intent to defraud his creditors.

The order of arrest is only issued upon filing an affidavit and bond as required by statute—bond to be for a sum not less than four hundred dollars.

CHAPTER VI.

JUDGMENTS AND JUDGMENT LIENS.

From time judgment is docketed it becomes a lien upon all real property of the judgment debtor, not exempted from execution in the county, owned by him at the time, or which he may afterwards acquire, until the lien expires. Lien of judgment continues for two years, unless the judgment be previously satisfied. Personal property, not exempt from execution, is only held for satisfaction of judgment after the levy of execution thereon.

CHAPTER VII.

EXECUTIONS, EXEMPTIONS, SALE, AND REDEMPTION.

Execution may issue for the enforcement of a judgment at any time within five years after the entry thereof, and may be issued to the sheriff of any county in the State in proper cases.

EXEMPTIONS.

The following property of the judgment debtor is exempt from execution :

1. Chairs, tables, desks, and books to the value of $100.

2. Necessary household furniture, wearing apparel, beds, bedding, provisions, and firewood sufficient for one month.

3. Farming utensils ; also two oxen or two horses, or two mules and their harnesses; two cows, one cart or wagon ; and food for such oxen, horses, cows or mules, for one month ; also all seed grain or vegetables actually provided, reserved, or on hand for the purpose of planting or sowing, at any time within the ensuing six months, not exceeding in value $400.

4. The tools and implements of a mechanic or artisan necessary to carry on his trade ; the instruments and chests of a surgeon, physician, surveyor, and dentist, necessary to the exercise of their profession, with their scientific and professional libraries, and the libraries of an attorney or counsellor, and the libraries of ministers of the gospel.

5. The cabin or dwelling of a miner, not exceeding in value $500 ; also all tools and implements necessary for carrying on any mining operation not exceeding in value $500 ; and two horses, mules, or oxen, with their harnesses, and food for the same for one month, when necessary to be used in such mining operations.

6. Two oxen, two horses, or two mules, and their harness, and one cart or wagon, by the use of which a cartman, huckster, peddler, teamster, or other laborer, habitually earns his living ; and one horse, with vehicle and harness, or other equipments used by a physician or surgeon or minister of the gospel in making his professional visits, and food for such oxen, mules, or horses, for one month.

7. One sewing machine, not exceeding in value $150, in actual use by the debtor or his family.

8. All fire engines, hooks and ladders, and all apparatus and furniture belonging to any fire company or department.

9. All arms, uniforms, and accoutrements required by law to be kept by any person.

10. All court houses, jails, public offices and buildings, lots, grounds, and personal property ; the fixtures, furniture, books, papers, and appurtenances belonging and pertaining to the court house, jail, and public offices belonging to any county in this State ; and all cemeteries, public squares, parks and places, public buildings, town halls, public markets, buildings for the use of the fire departments and military organizations, and the lots and grounds thereto belonging and appertaining, owned or held by any town or incorporated city, or dedicated by such town or city to health, ornament, or public use, or for the use of any fire or military company organized under the laws of this State.

11. None of the above articles or species of property are exempt from execution issued upon a judgment recovered for its price, or upon a mortgage thereon.

12. The earnings of a judgment debtor arising from his personal services for the thirty days preceding the making of the order, (in supplemental proceedings) to the extent of fifty dollars, are exempt, when it shall be made to appear by the debtor's affidavit, or other-

wise, that such earnings are necessary for the use of a family supported wholly or partially by his labor.

For homestead exemption, see " Homesteads."

Sale.

Real property may be sold upon twenty days' notice, given as required by law ; and personal property after five days' notice of the time and place of sale, as required by law.

Redemption.

Real estate sold upon execution or order of sale, upon mortgage or otherwise, may be redeemed by the judgment debtor, or his successors in interest in the whole or any part of the property ; or by a creditor having a lien by judgment or mortgage upon the property sold, or some share or part thereof subsequent to that upon which the property was sold, within six months from the date of sale. Real property sold for taxes is not subject to redemption. Personal property, sold upon execution, is not subject to redemption.

Chapter VIII.

PROCEEDINGS SUPPLEMENTARY TO EXECUTION.

Upon return of execution unsatisfied, in whole or in part, issued upon any judgment, the defendant may be required to appear before the Court, and answer under oath concerning his property.

CHAPTER IX.

SECURITY FOR COSTS.

When plaintiff is a non-resident, or is a foreign corporation, security for costs may be required.

CHAPTER X.

APPEALS.

An appeal from a judgment rendered in a Justice's Court may be taken to the district court within thirty days after entry of judgment, upon filing a bond with two sufficient sureties for double the amount of judgment and costs, in case stay of execution is demanded.

An appeal may be taken from the District to the Supreme Court:

1. From a final judgment in action or special proceeding commenced in the Court in which the judgment is rendered, within one year after the rendition of judgment.

2. From an order granting or refusing a new trial, from an order granting or dissolving an injunction, and from an order refusing to grant or dissolve an injunction, and from any special order made after the final judgment, within sixty days after the order is made and entered in the minutes of the Court.

3. From an interlocutory judgment or order in cases of partition which determines the rights of the several parties, and directs partition, sale, or division to be made, within sixty days after the rendition of the same.

In all cases of appeal to the Supreme Court, a bond must be filed in the sum of $300 for payment of costs of appeal; and in case a stay of execution is demanded, then an additional bond must be filed in a sum for double the amount of the judgment and costs. Bonds to be given by appellant, and to be executed by two or more sureties.

CHAPTER XI.

ESTATES OF DECEASED PERSONS.

Claims against estates of deceased persons must be presented, proved, and allowed within *ten months* after the first publication of administrator's or executor's *notice* to *creditors*, *excepting* claims of persons who are *non-residents* of the State, who have not had *actual notice;* they may present their claims at any time before distribution of estate. Claims may be verified by residents before any officer authorized to administer oaths within the State. An affidavit taken before a justice of the peace of any other county in the State except the one where the administrator or executor resides, must, to entitle it to be used or filed, contain a certificate of the clerk of the county where such justice resides, reciting the facts that said justice is duly commissioned and acting as such justice of the peace; that the signature of such justice is genuine, and that full faith and credit are due to all his official acts.

Affidavits to correctness of accounts and claims, when made out of the State of Nevada, must, to insure their reception, be verified before some judge of a Court having a seal, under the seal thereof, or a commissioner of deeds duly commissioned and qualified, of the State of Nevada, or before a notary public whose official character is duly certified to by the secretary of State or Territory in which he and the party making proof reside.

Time in which the estate must be settled not limited by statute ; it is subject to the order of the Court.

District Courts have sole jurisdiction of all original proceedings in probate matters.

Chapter XII.

HOMESTEADS.

The homestead of a judgment debtor, consisting of a quantity of land, together with the dwelling house thereon and its appurtenances, not exceeding in value five thousand dollars, to be selected by husband and wife, or either of them, or other head of the family, is exempt from forced sale on execution or other process from any Court.

Homesteads are declared as follows :

The selection to be made by either the husband or wife, or both of them, or other head of a family, declaring their intention in writing to claim the same as a homestead. The same to be duly acknowledged and recorded as conveyances affecting real estate.

Declaration of intention to claim and hold a homestead may be made at any time prior to sale on execution or other process, excepting on sale of premises, on foreclosure of mortgage upon the premises executed by husband and wife ; or where the judgment is for the purchase price of the property claimed as a homestead. This exemption does not extend to any mechanic's, laborer's or vendor's lien upon the premises.

The homestead may be abandoned by a declaration in writing, signed and acknowledged by husband and wife, and recorded in

the office of the county recorder, in the same manner as the declaration to claim the same is required to be acknowledged and recorded.   On the death of husband or wife, the homestead and other
property exempt from sale on execution is required to be set apart
by the Court for the benefit of the surviving husband or wife, and
his or her legitimate children.

In cases where homestead property is appraised at a sum exceeding five thousand dollars, the same may be sold, and the sum
realized on sale in excess of five thousand dollars and costs will
pass to judgment creditor.

CHAPTER XIII.

OF WITNESSES AND DEPOSITIONS.

Parties to the action are not excluded from being witnesses upon
the ground of interest, except—

1. That no party to an action or proceeding is allowed to testify
therein, when the opposite party is the representative of a deceased
person, when the facts to be proved transpired before the death of
such deceased person.

2. Persons convicted of felony, unless pardoned, or the judgment is reversed on appeal, cannot be witnesses.

3. Attorneys or counsellors cannot, except by consent of their
client, be examined as to any confidential communications made to
them in the course of their professional employment, and the like
rule applies to physicians, surgeons, clergymen or priests, with
respect to confidential communications made to them in their professional capacity.

4. Husband or wife cannot be witnesses for or against each
other, except in actions brought by one against the other.

10

5. Public officers cannot be examined as witnesses in reference to communications made to them in official confidence, when the public interest would, by such disclosures, be injured.

6. Laws relative to the attestation of instruments required to be attested are reserved from the operation of the statute allowing parties in interest to testify.

Negroes can testify in all cases where whites are permitted to · act as witnesses.

The testimony of a witness in this State may be taken in an action at any time after the service of the summons, or the appearance of the defendant; and in a special proceeding, after a question of fact has arisen therein, in the following cases:

1. When the witness is a party to the action or proceeding, or a person for whose immediate benefit the action or proceeding is prosecuted or defended.

2. When the witness resides out of the county in which his testimony is to be used.

3. When the witness is about to leave the county where the action is to be tried, and will probably continue absent when the testimony is required.

4. When the witness, otherwise liable to attend the trial, is nevertheless too infirm to attend; or resides within the county, but more than fifty miles from the place of trial.

The deposition may be taken before any judge, or clerk of a Court, or any justice of the peace or notary public in this State, on serving upon the adverse party previous notice of the time and place of the examination, together with a copy of an affidavit showing that the case is one mentioned as above stated. Such notice shall be at least five days, and in addition one day for every twenty-five miles of the distance of the place of examination from the residence of the person upon whom notice is served, unless, for cause shown, a judge, by order, prescribe a shorter time. Either party may attend such examination, and put such questions, direct and cross, as may be proper.

The deposition, when completed and corrected, shall be signed by the witness and sealed and directed to the clerk of the Court in which the action is pending, or to such person as the parties, in writing, may agree upon, and either delivered by the officer taking the same to the clerk or such person, or transmitted through the mail, or by some safe private opportunity ; and such deposition may be used by either party upon the trial against any party giving or receiving such notice, subject to all legal objections. If the parties attend at the examination, no objection to the form of an interrogatory shall be made at the trial, unless the same was stated at the time of the examination.

If the deposition to be taken be by the reason of the absence or intended absence from the county of the witness, or because he is too infirm to attend, proof, by affidavit or oral testimony, shall be made at the trial that the witness continues absent or infirm, to the best of deponent's knowledge or belief.

Depositions thus taken may be also read, in case of the death of the witness.

When a deposition has been once taken, it may be read in any stage of the same action or proceeding by either party, and shall then be deemed the evidence of the party reading it.

DEPOSITIONS TAKEN OUT OF THE STATE.

The testimony of a witness out of the State may be taken by deposition in an action at any time after the service of the summons, or the appearance of the defendant; and in a special proceeding, at any time after a question of fact has arisen therein.

The deposition of a witness out of the State shall be taken upon commission issued from the Court, under the seal of the Court, upon an order of the judge or Court, on the application of either party, upon five days' previous notice to the other. It shall be issued to a person agreed upon by the parties, or if they do not agree, to any judge or justice of the peace selected by the officer granting the commission, or to a commissioner appointed by the governor of this State to take affidavits and depositions in other States or Territories.

Such proper interrogatories, direct and cross, as the respective parties may prepare, to be settled, if the parties disagree as to their form, by the judge or officer granting the order for the commission, at a day fixed in the order, or at the time of granting the order for commission, may be annexed to the commission ; or, when the parties agree to that mode, the examination may be without written interrogatories.

The commission shall authorize the commissioner to administer an oath to the witness, and to take his deposition in answer to the interrogatories, or when the examination is to be without interrogatories in respect to the questions in dispute, and to certify the deposition to the Court, in a sealed envelope directed to the clerk or other person designed or agreed upon, and forward to him by mail, or other usual channel of conveyance.

Chapter XIV.

JUDICIAL RECORDS, HOW PROVED.

A judicial record of this State, or the United States, or any Territory, may be proved by the production of the original, or a copy thereof, certified by the clerk or other person having the legal custody thereof, under the seal of the Court, to be a true copy of such record.

The records and judicial proceedings of the Courts of any other State of the United States, or of any Territory, may be proved or admitted in the Courts of this State, by the attestation of the clerk and seal of the Court annexed, if there be a seal, together with a certificate of the judge, chief justice, or presiding magistrate, as the case may be, that the said attestation is in due form.

A judicial record of a foreign country may be proved by the production of a copy thereof, certified by the clerk, with the seal of the Court annexed, if there be a seal, or by the legal keeper of the record, with the seal of his office annexed, if there be a seal, to be a true copy of such record, together with a certificate of a judge of the Court that the person making the certificate is the clerk of the Court, or the legal keeper of the record, and in either case that the signature is genuine, and the certificate in due form; and, also, together with the certificate of the minister or embassador of the United States, or of a consul of the United States, in such foreign country, that there is such a Court, specifying generally the nature of its jurisdiction, and verifying the signature of the clerk and judge, or other legal keeper of the record.

Second. A copy of the judicial record of a foreign country shall also be admissible in evidence upon proof:

1. That the copy offered has been compared by the witness with the original, and is an exact transcript of the whole of it.

2. That such original was in the custody of the clerk of the Court or other legal keeper of the same; and,

3. That the copy is duly attested by a seal, which is proved to be the seal of the Court where the record remains, if it be the record of a Court; or if there be no such seal, or if it be not the record of a Court, by the signature of the legal keeper of the original.

CHAPTER XV.

ACKNOWLEDGMENTS.

The proof or acknowledgment of every conveyance affecting any real estate shall be taken by some one of the following officers:

1. If acknowledged or proved within this State, by some judge or clerk of a Court having a seal, or some notary public, or justice of the peace: *Provided*, when the acknowledgment is taken before a justice of the peace in any other county than that in which

the real estate is situated, the same shall be accompanied with the certificate of the clerk of the District Court of such county, as to the official character of the justice taking the proof or acknowledgment, and the authenticity of his signature.

2. If acknowledged or proved without this State, but within the United States, shall be taken by some one of the following officers:

A judge or clerk of a Court having a seal, or some notary public or justice of the peace, or by any commissioner appointed by the Governor of this State for that purpose: *Provided*, that when the acknowledgment is taken by a justice of the peace, the same shall be accompanied by the certificate of the clerk of a Court of record of the county, having a seal, as to the official character of the justice and the authenticity of his signature.

3. If acknowledged or proved without the United States, by some judge or clerk of any Court of any State, Kingdom or Empire having a seal, or by any notary public therein, or by any minister, commissioner, or consul of the United States, appointed to reside therein.

CHAPTER XVI.

AFFIDAVITS, BEFORE WHOM TO BE TAKEN.

An affidavit to be used before any Court, judge, or officer of this State may be taken before any judge or clerk of any Court, or any justice of the peace, or notary public in this State.

An affidavit taken in another State, or in a Territory of the United States, to be used in this State, shall be taken before a commissioner appointed by the Governor of this State to take affidavits and depositions in such other State or Territory, or before any judge of a Court of record having a seal.

An affidavit taken in a foreign country, to be used in this State, shall be taken before an embassador, minister, or consul of the United States, or before any judge of a Court of record having a seal, in such foreign country.

When an affidavit is taken before a judge of a Court in another State, or in a Territory of the United States, or in a foreign country, the genuineness of the signature of the judge, the existence of Court, and the fact that such judge is a member thereof, shall be certified by the clerk of the Court, under the seal thereof.

Chapter XVII.

LIMITED PARTNERSHIPS

May be formed for the transaction of mercantile, mechanical, mining, or manufacturing business by two or more persons, as provided for by special statute. But nothing contained in the act shall authorize such partnerships for the purpose of banking or insurance.

In partnerships of this character there shall be one or more members of the firm to be known as general partners, and they are individually liable for the debts of the firm. The special partners are liable for the firm debts to the extent of their interest in the firm property or assets; also to the extent of any sums of money by them received, withdrawn, or divided, with interest thereon from the time they were so withdrawn from the firm.

The business of the partnership shall be conducted under a firm name, in which the names of the general partners only shall be inserted, and the general partners only shall transact the business. If the name of any special partner shall be used in said firm with his consent or privity, or if he shall personally make any contract respecting the concerns of the partnership with any person except the general partners, he shall be deemed and treated as a general partner.

Chapter XVIII.

MARRIED WOMEN

May become sole traders upon petition, and by order of District Court.

When they are sole traders, they become liable for debts incurred in the conduct of the business authorized to be carried on by them as such.

Chapter XIX.

CORPORATIONS

May be formed for all purposes under general statute.

Stockholders are not individually liable for any debt of the corporation.

Chapter XX.

CHATTEL MORTGAGES.

No chattel mortgage upon any personal property shall be valid for any purpose, except possession of the property mortgaged be given to and continuously retained by the mortgagee, except that growing crops may be mortgaged by the execution, acknowledgment and record of a mortgage, with delivery of possession.

Chapter XXI.

INTEREST AND USURY.

Where there is no express contract in writing, fixing a different rate of interest, interest shall be allowed at the rate of ten per cent. per annum for all moneys after they become due upon any bond, bill, or promissory note, or other instrument in writing, on any judgment recovered before any Court in this State, for money lent, money due on settlement of accounts from the day on which the balance is ascertained, and for money received for the use of another.

Parties may agree in writing for the payment of any rate of interest whatever upon money due, or to become due on any contract. Judgments rendered upon contracts shall conform thereto, and bear the interest agreed upon by the parties, which shall be specified in the judgment: *Provided*, only the amount of the original claim or demand shall draw interest after judgment.

Chapter XXII.

PROMISSORY NOTES AND BILLS OF EXCHANGE.

All notes in writing made and signed by any person, whereby he shall promise to pay to any other person, or to his order, or to the order of any other person, or to the bearer, any sum of money therein mentioned, shall be due and payable as therein expressed, and shall have the same effect, and be negotiable in like manner, as inland bills of exchange, according to the custom of merchants.

Days of grace are allowed upon bills and promissory notes, where not otherwise expressed.

Damages for non-acceptance of bills of exchange upon the usual protest are as follows, when drawn or negotiated in this State:

If such bills shall have been drawn upon any person or persons in any of the United States east of the Rocky Mountains, fifteen dollars upon the hundred upon the principal sum specified in such bill.

If such bill shall have been drawn upon any person or persons in any part or place in Europe, or in any foreign country, twenty dollars upon the hundred upon the principal sum specified in such bill.

Chapter XXIII.

MORTGAGES.

A mortgage of real property, whatever its terms, shall not be deemed a conveyance, so as to enable the owner of the mortgage to recover possession of the real property without a foreclosure and sale.

PART V.

STATE OF OREGON.

PREPARED EXPRESSLY FOR THIS WORK BY DOLPH, BRONOUGH, DOLPH & SIMON, PORTLAND, OREGON.

CHAPTER I.

COURTS AND THEIR JURISDICTION.

The judicial power of the State is vested in a Supreme Court, Circuit Courts, and County Courts, which are Courts of record.

Justices of the peace are invested with limited judicial powers, and Municipal Courts may be created to administer the regulations of incorporated towns and cities.

The Supreme Court consists of five justices, who are elected by the electors in each district, and who hold their offices for six years.

The Supreme Court has jurisdiction only to revise the final decisions of the Circuit Courts.

The Circuit Courts are held at least twice in each year, in each county organized for judicial purposes, by one of the justices of the Supreme Court. All judicial power, authority, and jurisdiction not vested exclusively in some other Court belongs to the Circuit Courts, and they have appellate jurisdiction and supervisory control over the County Courts, and all other inferior Courts, officers and tribunals.

County Courts have jurisdiction, but not exclusive, of actions at law, and all proceedings therein and connected therewith, when the claim or subject of the controversy does not exceed the value of five hundred dollars.

Justices' Courts have jurisdiction, but not exclusive, of the following actions:

1. For the recovery of money or damages only, where the amount claimed does not exceed $250.

2. For the recovery of specific personal property, when the value of the property claimed and the damages for the detention do not exceed $250.

3. For the recovery of a penalty or forfeiture, not exceeding $250.

4. To give judgment without action upon the confession of the defendant.

The jurisdiction does not, however, extend to an action in which the title to real property shall come in question, or to an action for false imprisonment, libel, slander, malicious prosecution, criminal conversation, seduction, or upon a promise to marry.

CHAPTER II.

TERMS OF COURT, WHEN AND WHERE HELD.

The following are the times and places of holding Courts, both Federal and State, in the several counties and districts of the State:

UNITED STATES CIRCUIT COURT, DISTRICT OF OREGON.

Regular terms held at Portland, on the second Monday of April, August and November.

Judges, Hon. Stephen J. Field, Associate Justice of the Supreme Court, and Hon. Lorenzo Sawyer, Circuit Judge. Clerk, Ralph Wilcox. Marshal, D. J. Malarkey.

UNITED STATES DISTRICT COURT, DISTRICT OF OREGON.

Regular terms held at Portland, on the first Monday of March, July and November.

Judge, Hon. Matthew P. Deady. Clerk, Ralph Wilcox. Marshal, D. J. Malarkey. U. S. District Attorney, Rufus Mallory. Register in Bankruptcy, H. H. Northup.

SUPREME COURT OF OREGON.

Regular terms held at Salem, on the second Monday in December of each year, and special terms held at such other times as the Court appoints.

CIRCUIT COURTS OF THE STATE OF OREGON.

COUNTIES.	TIMES OF HOLDING.
Baker	First Monday of October and third Monday of May.
Benton	Third Monday of November and second Monday of April.
Clackamas	Fourth Monday of April and fourth Monday of September.
Clatsop	Second Tuesday of August and fourth Tuesday of January.
Columbia	Second Monday of April.
Coos	Fourth Monday of May and second Monday of September.
Curry	First Monday of June.
Douglas	Third Monday of October and second Monday of May.
Grant	Third Monday of September and first Monday of June.
Jackson	Second Monday of February, June and November.
Josephine	Fourth Monday of April and fourth Monday of October.
Lake	Fourth Monday of June and November.
Lane	Third Monday of April and first Monday in November.
Linn	Second Monday in March and fourth Monday in October.
Marion	Fourth Monday of Feb., second Monday of June, and third Monday of Oct.
Multnomah	Second Monday of February, June, and October.
Polk	Second Monday of May and first Monday of December.
Umatilla	Fourth Monday of October and last Monday of April.
Union	Third Monday of October and first Monday of May.
Wasco	Second Monday of November and third Monday of June.
Washington	Fourth Monday of May and first Monday of October.
Yamhill	Fourth Monday of March and first Monday of October.

TERMS OF THE COUNTY COURTS.

In the counties of Josephine, Curry, Coos, Columbia, Clatsop,

Tillamook and Umatilla—on the first Monday of January, April, July and September.

In the counties of Grant, Baker, Lane and Wasco—on the first Monday of January, March, May, July, September and November.

In the county of Lake—on the first Monday of every alternate month.

In the county of Union—on the second Monday of May and the first Monday of January, March, July, September and November.

In the counties of Jackson, Douglas, Linn, Benton, Polk, Marion, Yamhill, Clackamas, Washington and Multnomah—on the first Monday of each month.

Chapter III.

COMMENCEMENT OF SUITS.

Actions at law are commenced by filing a complaint with the clerk of the Court.

At any time after the action is commenced, the plaintiff may cause a summons to be served on the defendant.

The summons must contain the name of the Court in which the complaint is filed, the names of the parties to the action, and the title thereof; it must be subscribed by the plaintiff or his attorney, and directed to the defendant, and require him to appear and answer the complaint, or the plaintiff will take judgment for a sum specified therein.

If the defendant be served within the county in which the action is commenced, he must appear and answer the complaint within ten days from the date of the service; but if served in any other county in the State, he must appear and answer the complaint within twenty days from the date of service.

Chapter IV.

PLACE OF TRIAL OF CIVIL ACTIONS.

Actions for the recovery of real property, or an estate, or interest therein, or for injury thereto, and for the recovery of any personal property distrained for any cause, shall be commenced and tried in the county in which the subject of the action, or some part thereof, is situated.

In all other cases the action shall be commenced and tried in the county in which the defendants or either of them reside, or may be found at the commencement of the action. If none of the parties reside in this State, the same may be tried in any county which the plaintiff may designate in his complaint.

Chapter V.

LIMITATION OF ACTIONS.

The periods prescribed for the commencement of actions are as follows :

Within Twenty Years :

Actions for the recovery of real property, or for the recovery of the possession thereof.

Within Ten Years:

Actions upon a judgment or decree of any Court of the United States, or of any State or Territory within the United States.

Actions upon sealed instruments.

Within Six Years:

An action upon a contract or liability express or implied, excepting those already mentioned.

An action upon a liability created by statute, other than a penalty or forfeiture.

An action for waste or trespass upon real property.

An action for taking, detaining or injuring personal property, including an action for the specific recovery thereof.

Within Three Years:

An action against a sheriff, constable or coroner, upon a liability incurred by the doing of an act in his official capacity, or by the omission of an official duty; but this does not apply to an action for an escape.

An action upon a statute for a penalty or forfeiture.

Within Two Years:

An action for libel, slander, assault, battery, or false imprisonment; for criminal conversation, or for an injury to the person or rights of another not arising on contract.

An action upon a statute for a forfeiture or penalty to the State.

Within One Year:

An action against a sheriff or other officer for the escape of a prisoner arrested or imprisoned on civil process.

An action for any cause not hereinbefore provided for shall be commenced within ten years after the cause of action accrued.

CHAPTER VI.

ATTACHMENTS.

In an action for the recovery of money or damages, the plaintiff, at any time after the commencement of the action, and before judgment, may have the property of the defendant attached, by filing with the clerk of the Court an undertaking with one or more sureties equal to the amount for which the plaintiff demands judgment, and not less than $100 ; and the plaintiff, or some one in his behalf, making and filing an affidavit that the defendant is either a foreign corporation or a non-resident of the State, or has departed therefrom with intent to delay or defraud his creditors, or to avoid the service of a summons, or keeps himself concealed therein with like intent, or has removed or is about to remove his property from the State with intent to delay or defraud his creditors, or has assigned, secreted, or disposed of any of his property, or is about to do so, with intent to delay or defraud his creditors, or that the debt was fraudulently contracted.

CHAPTER VII.

ARRESTS IN CIVIL ACTIONS.

The defendant may be arrested in the following cases :

In an action for the recovery of money or damages on a cause of action arising out of contract, when the defendant is not a resident of the State, or is about to remove therefrom ; or when the action is for an injury to person or character, or for injuring or

11

wrongfully taking, detaining, or converting property. In an action for a fine or penalty, or on a promise to marry, or for money received, or property embezzled or fraudulently misapplied or converted to his own use by a public officer, or an attorney, officer, or agent of a corporation, factor, agent or broker, or other person in a fiduciary capacity. In an action to recover the possession of any personal property unjustly detained, when the property or any portion thereof has been concealed, removed, or disposed of.

When the defendant has been guilty of a fraud in contracting the debt or incurring the obligation for which the action is brought.

When the defendant has removed or disposed of his property, or is about to do so, with intent to defraud his creditors.

No female can be arrested in any action, except for an injury to person, character, or property.

Chapter VIII.

JUDGMENTS AND JUDGMENT LIENS.

A judgment, when entered, becomes a lien upon the real estate owned by the defendant in the county at the time of the entry, and such as he may subsequently acquire. The lien continues for ten years.

CHAPTER IX.

EXECUTIONS, EXEMPTIONS, SALE, AND REDEMP-
TION.

The party in whose favor a judgment is given which requires the payment of money, the delivery of real or personal property, or either of them, may, at any time after the entry thereof, have a writ of execution issued for its enforcement.

There are three kinds of execution: one against the property of the judgment debtor, another against his person, and the third for the delivery of real or personal property.

In the Circuit and County Courts executions are returnable in sixty days, and in Justices' Courts in thirty days.

In the Circuit and County Courts there is no stay of execution, except pending an appeal; in Justices' Courts execution may be stayed for thirty days upon filing bond.

The following personal property is exempt from sale under an execution:

Books, pictures, and musical instruments, to the value of $75; wearing apparel to the value of $100, and if a householder, to the value of $50 for each member of the family; tools, implements, apparatus, team, vehicle, harness, or library, when necessary in the occupation or profession of a judgment debtor, to the amount of $400; if the judgment debtor be a householder, ten sheep with one year's fleece, two cows, five swine, household goods, furniture, and utensils, to the value of $300. No article of property is exempt from execution issued upon a judgment for the purchase price.

Upon a sale of real property, when the estate is less than a leasehold of two years' unexpired term, the sale is absolute. In all other cases such property is subject to redemption.

The judgment debtor, or his successor in interest, may redeem such property within sixty days from the date of the order confirming the sale, by paying the amount of the purchase money, with interest at the rate of two per cent. per month from the time of sale, together with the amount of taxes the purchaser may have paid thereon.

A creditor having a lien by judgment, decree or mortgage, on any portion of the property subsequent in time to that on which the property was sold, may also redeem. .

Chapter X.

PROCEEDINGS SUPPLEMENTARY TO EXECUTION.

After the issuing of an execution against property, and upon proof by the affidavit of the plaintiff, in the writ or otherwise, to the satisfaction of the Court or judge thereof, that the judgment debtor has property liable to execution which he refuses to apply towards the satisfaction of the judgment, such Court or judge may by an order require the judgment debtor to appear and answer under oath concerning the same. If it appear from such examination that the judgment debtor has property liable to execution, the Court or judge shall make an order requiring the judgment debtor to apply the same in satisfaction of the judgment. Disobedience to any such order may be punished as for a contempt.

Chapter XI.

SECURITY FOR COSTS.

Security for costs can only be required in Justices' Courts. If the plaintiff is a non-resident of the county, the justice may require him to give an undertaking with one or more sureties for the costs and disbursements of the action before issuing the summons, and if at any time before the commencement of the trial the defendant apply therefor, the justice must require such plaintiff to give such undertaking. Upon application of defendant, and in the discretion of the justice, the plaintiff, if a resident of the county, may be required to give an undertaking for costs. The undertaking may be in the following form : " I, A B, or We, A B and C D, undertake to pay E F, the defendant in this action, all costs and disbursements that may be adjudged to him in this action."

The sureties must possess the qualifications of bail upon arrest, and if required by the defendant, must justify in a sum not less than $50.

CHAPTER XII

APPEALS.

Any party to a judgment or decree, other than a decree or judgment for want of an answer, or by confession, may appeal therefrom.

An appeal to the Supreme Court shall be taken by serving and filing a notice of appeal within six months from the entry of the judgment or decree appealed from, or to the Circuit Court within thirty days after such entry, and not otherwise.

Appeals from the Circuit Courts are taken to the Supreme Court, and from County Courts and Justices' Courts to the Circuit Court of the county.

Upon an appeal from the Circuit or County Court, the appellant must file an undertaking, with one or more sureties, to the effect that the appellant will pay all damages, costs and disbursements which may be awarded against him on the appeal; and if the judgment or decree appealed from be for the recovery of money or personal property, or the value thereof, to obtain a stay of proceedings the undertaking must further provide, that if the judgment or decree appealed from be affirmed, the appellant will satisfy it so far as affirmed.

Upon an appeal from Justice's Court, the undertaking is to the effect that the appellant will pay all costs and disbursements that may be awarded against him on the appeal, and that he will satisfy any judgment that may be given against him in the appellate court on the appeal.

Chapter XIII.

ESTATES OF DECEASED 'PERSONS.

Every executor or administrator must, immediately after his appointment, publish a notice thereof in some newspaper published in the county, for four successive weeks. Such notice must require all persons having claims against the estate to present them to the administrator or executor, within six months from the date of such notice, with the proper vouchers. A claim not presented within six months is not barred, but it cannot be paid until the claims presented within that period have been satisfied. A claim not due or contingent must, nevertheless, be presented as any other claim. Until administration has been completed, a claim against the estate may be presented, allowed and paid out of any assets not otherwise appropriated or liable.

Every claim must be verified by the affidavit of the claimant, or some one on his behalf, who has personal knowledge of the facts, to the effect that the amount claimed is justly due, that no payments have been made thereon except as stated, and that there is no just counter-claim to the same.

There is no specified time in which estates are required to be settled.

CHAPTER XIV.

DESCENT OF REAL PROPERTY.

When any person dies, seized of any real property, or any right thereto, or any interest therein, not having lawfully devised the same, such real property descends, subject to his debts, as follows :

1. In equal shares to his children and to the issue of any deceased child by right of representation ; and if there be no child of the intestate living at the time of his death, such real property descends to all his other lineal descendants ; and if all such descendants are in the same degree of kindred to the intestate, they take such real property equally ; or otherwise, they take according to the right of representation.

2. If the intestate leaves no lineal descendants, such property descends to his wife ; and if he leaves no wife, it descends to his father.

3. If the intestate leaves no lineal descendants, wife nor father, such real property descends in equal shares to his brothers and sisters, and to the issue of any deceased brother or sister by right of representation ; but if the intestate leaves a mother also, she takes an equal share with such brothers and sisters.

4. If the intestate leaves no lineal descendants, wife, father, brother nor sister living, at his death, such real property descends to his mother, to the exclusion of the issue of his deceased brothers or sisters.

5. If the intestate leaves no lineal descendants, wife, father, mother, brother nor sister, such real property descends to his next of kin in equal degree, excepting that when there are two or more collateral kindred in equal degree, but claiming through different ancestors, those who claim through the nearest ancestor are preferred to those claiming through a more remote ancestor.

6. If the intestate leaves one or more children, and the issue of one or more deceased children, and any of such surviving children shall die under age, without having been married, all such real

property that came to such deceased child by inheritance from such intestate, descends in equal shares to the other children of the intestate, and to the issue of any other children of such intestate who shall have died, by right of representation; but if all the other children of such intestate are also dead, and any of them shall have left issue, such real property so inherited by such deceased child descends to all the issue of such other children of the intestate in equal shares, if they are in the same degree of kindred to such deceased child; otherwise, they take by right of representation.

7. If the intestate leaves no lineal descendants or kindred, such real property escheats to the State of Oregon.

CHAPTER XV.

DESCENT OF PERSONAL PROPERTY.

When any person dies possessed of any personal property, not having lawfully bequeathed the same, such personal property is applied and distributed as follows:

1. If the intestate leaves a widow, she is allowed all her articles of apparel and ornaments, according to the degree and estate of the intestate, and such property and provisions for the use and support of herself and minor children as shall be allowed and ordered.

2. The personal property of the intestate remaining after such allowance is applied to the payment of the debts of the intestate, and the charges and expenses of administration.

3. The residue, if any, of the personal property is distributed among the persons who would be entitled to the real property, except as otherwise provided.

4. If the intestate leaves a husband, such husband is entitled to the whole of the personal property.

5. If the intestate leaves a widow and issue, such widow is entitled to receive one-half of such personal property ; but if there be a widow and no issue, she is entitled to the whole of such personal property.

6. If there be no husband, widow or kindred, the whole escheats to the State.

CHAPTER XVI.

HOMESTEADS AND DOWER.

HOMESTEADS.

There is no homestead law in this State.

DOWER.

The widow of every deceased person is entitled to dower, or the use during her natural life of one-third part of all the lands of which her husband was seized of an estate of inheritance at any time during the marriage, unless she is lawfully barred thereof.

CHAPTER XVII.

DEPOSITIONS.

The deposition of a witness out of the State may be taken upon commission issued from the Court, or without commission before a commissioner appointed by the governor of this State to take depositions in other States or countries. The commission may be issued by the clerk of the Court, or the justice in a cause pending in Justice's Court, on the application of either party upon five days' previous notice to the other. It is issued to a person agreed upon by the parties, or if they do not agree, to a judge, justice of the peace, notary public, or clerk of a Court selected by the officer issuing it. Such interrogatories, direct and cross, as the parties may prepare may be annexed to the commission.

The following form may be used:

In the———Court of the State of Oregon for———County.

A B, Plaintiff, }
    vs. }
C D, Defendant. }

Deposition of E F, a witness on behalf of the———————.
in the above entitled action, taken before me, a commissioner named in the attached commission, and a (notary public) in and for —————————county, State of——————— on the—————— day of——————187——— at my office at the city of——— ———in said·county and State, who being first duly sworn in answer to the direct and cross interrogatories attached to said commission in their order, testified as follows:

1. To the first direct interrogatory he answers, etc.

When completed, the deposition should be read to the witness, and then subscribed by him.

The following form of certificate should be added to the deposition:

STATE OF———
    COUNTY OF——— } ss.

I,—————a (notary public) in and for said county and State, and commissioner, before whom the foregoing deposition was taken, do hereby certify that the deposition of said witness, E F, was taken before me, at my office in the city of—————————in said county and State, on the———day of—————————18—— between the hours of———o'clock A.M., and———o'clock—M. of said day, and the same was endorsed by me; that before proceeding to the examination, the witness was duly sworn to tell the truth, the whole truth, and nothing but the truth; that when completed, the deposition was carefully read over by me to said witness, and then by him subscribed.

In witness whereof, I have hereunto set my hand and official seal, this————day of—————————187——

[SEAL.]

Notary Public, etc.
and Commissioner.

Endorse upon the envelope the title of the Court and cause, and the words " deposition of—————————" and forward by mail to the officer issuing the commission.

CHAPTER XVIII.

JUDICIAL RECORD.

The judicial record of a sister State is proved by the production of a copy thereof, certified by the clerk or other person having the legal custody of the record, with the seal of the Court affixed thereto, if there be a seal, together with the certificate of the chief judge, or presiding magistrate, that the certificate is in due form, and made by the clerk or other person having the legal custody of the original.

CHAPTER XIX.

ACKNOWLEDGMENTS.

Deeds may be acknowledged within this State before any judge of the Supreme Court, county judge, justice of the peace, notary public, or clerk of a Court. No acknowledgment of any conveyance having been executed shall be taken by any officer, unless he shall know or have satisfactory evidence that the person making such acknowledgment is the individual described in and who executed such conveyance.

When a married woman, residing in this State, shall join with her husband in a deed of conveyance of real estate situated within this State, the acknowledgment of the wife shall be taken separately and apart from her husband, and she 'shall acknowledge that she executed such deed freely and without fear or compulsion from any one. If any deed shall be executed in any other State, Territory or District of the United States, such deed may be executed and acknowledged according to the laws of such State, Territory or District, or before any commissioner appointed by the governor of this State for such purpose ; and unless the acknowledgment be taken before such commissioner, it must be certified by the clerk or other proper certifying officer of a Court of record of the county or district within which such acknowledgment was taken, under the seal of his office, that the person whose name is subscribed to the certificate of acknowledgment was, at the date thereof, such officer as he is therein represented to be, and that he believes the signature of such person subscribed thereto to be genuine, and that the deed is executed and acknowledged according to the laws of such State, Territory or District.

CHAPTER XX.

LIMITED PARTNERSHIPS.

. Limited partnerships for the transaction of mercantile, mechanical and manufacturing business may be formed in this State. The persons forming such partnership make and severally subscribe and acknowledge a certificate in duplicate, which contains the name assumed by the partnership, the names and respective places of residence of all the general and special partners, the amount of capital which each special partner contributes, the general nature of the business to be transacted, and the time when the partnership is to commence and terminate; one copy of such certificate is filed with the clerk of the county in which the principal place of business of the partnership is to be. A copy of the same is required to be published for four weeks in some weekly newspaper published in the county. The business must be conducted under a name in which the names of the general partners only shall be inserted, without the addition of the word company, or any other general term.

Special partners are not personally liable for any debts of the partnership.

During the continuance of any such partnership no part of the capital stock can be withdrawn, nor any division of interests or profits made, so as to reduce such capital stock below the sum stated in the certificate.

CHAPTER XXI.

MARRIED WOMEN.

The constitution of the State provides that the property and pecuniary rights of every married woman at the time of marriage, or afterwards acquired by gift, devise or inheritance, shall not be subject to the debts or contracts of the husband, and laws shall be passed providing for the registration of personal property: which has been done. The property, both real and personal, acquired by any married woman during coverture, is free from and not liable for the debts, liabilities or contracts of her husband.

CHAPTER XXII.

CORPORATIONS.

Corporations are only formed under general laws, and cannot be created by special laws.

The stockholders of all corporations and joint stock companies are liable for the indebtedness of such corporations to the amount of their stock subscribed and unpaid, and no more.

No bank, banking company or moneyed institution can be created under the laws of this State ; nor can any bank, company or institution exist in the State with the privilege of making, issuing, or putting in circulation any bill, check, certificate, promissory note or other paper, or the paper of any bank, company or person, to circulate as money.

CHAPTER XXIII.

CHATTEL MORTGAGES.

Chattel mortgages are valid against third parties when the property is retained in the possession of the mortgagor, provided the mortgage or a copy thereof is filed in the office of the county clerk. Such mortgage, however, ceases to be valid as against creditors and subsequent purchasers, or mortgagors in good faith, after the expiration of one year from the filing of the same, unless within thirty days preceding the expiration of the year an affidavit, setting forth the interest which the mortgagee has in the property by virtue of such mortgage, is made and annexed to the instrument or copy on file. The effect of such affidavit does not continue beyond one year, when a similar affidavit must be made.

CHAPTER XXIV.

INTEREST AND USURY.

Ten per cent. per annum is the legal rate of interest; but on contracts, interest at the rate of one per cent. per month may be charged by express agreement of the parties.

Usury entails the forfeiture of the principal sum, without interest, to the school fund of the county in which the suit is brought.

PART VI.

UTAH TERRITORY.

PREPARED EXPRESSLY FOR THIS WORK BY LEWIS BURNES, SALT LAKE CITY.

CHAPTER I.

THE COURTS AND THEIR JURISDICTION.

The Supreme Court of the Territory has general appellate jurisdiction only.

There are three United States District Courts in the Territory, with unlimited jurisdiction in all chancery and law actions.

THE PROBATE COURTS,

One in each county: Their jurisdiction is limited to strictly probate business, except that they may try divorce cases where both parties agree upon that forum ; removable, however, at the pleasure of either party, to the District Court. The judges have the right to enter town sites, and preside over the board of selectmen; in other words, the County Court.

12

JUSTICES' COURTS

Have jurisdiction in all actions where the amount involved is less than three hundred dollars, except in cases involving titles to real estate.

CHAPTER II.

THE TERMS OF COURTS AND PLACES OF HOLDING SAME.

The Supreme Court sits the first Monday of January, and the second Monday of June, of each year, at Salt Lake City.

The District Courts sit at Salt Lake City, third district; Provo, second district; Beaver City, first district. The times are fixed by the Governor at pleasure, and often change to suit convenience or absence of the judges, and now the assignment is only temporary.

The Probate Courts and Justices' Courts are always open for the transaction of business; the former at their respective county court houses, and the latter in their respective precincts.

CHAPTER III.

COMMENCEMENTS OF SUITS AND TIME ALLOWED DEFENDANTS TO PLEAD.

Suits may be commenced at any time. Ten days after service are allowed the defendants to plead, answer, demur, or file motions in cases in the District Courts and Supreme Court.

In Justices' Courts, defendants may be required to answer within two days after service, and not longer than ten days after service.

.

Chapter IV.

LIMITATIONS OF ACTIONS.

Actions for the recovery of real estate can only be brought within seven years after the plaintiff's having been lawfully seized and possessed of the premises by himself, grantor, ancestor, or predecessor.

Actions for the recovery of money on notes, bonds, or judgments recovered in a foreign State must be brought within four years after the cause of action accrued; and on accounts, within two years.

Chapter V.

ATTACHMENTS

Can only issue upon the filing of an affidavit on behalf of the plaintiff, showing the existence of a debt upon contract, specifying the nature and amount thereof, as near as may be, over and above all legal set-offs or counter-claims; that the same has not been secured by any mortgage, lien, or pledge upon real or personal estate within the Territory, or if so secured, that such security has

been rendered nugatory by the act of the defendant ; that the
defendant is not residing in this Territory, or that the defendant has
departed the Territory or county where the action is brought, or
that the defendant stands in defiance of an officer, or conceals himself so that process cannot be served upon him, or that he is disposing of his property with the intent to defraud his creditors ; that
the debt is an actual bona fide existing demand due and owing from
the defendant to the plaintiff, and that the action is not sought or
prosecuted to hinder, delay, or defraud any creditor of the defendant.

There must also be executed and filed an undertaking, with two
sufficient sureties, in a sum not less than $200, nor exceeding the
amount claimed by the plaintiff, conditioned, that if the defendant
recover judgment in the action, the plaintiff will pay all costs that
may be awarded to the defendant, not exceeding the amount specified in the undertaking.

CHAPTER VI.

ARRESTS IN CIVIL ACTIONS

Are issued upon filing an undertaking and affidavit, the same in
effect as those required in attachment cases, except that in addition to the liability of sureties in attachment cases for costs, in
cases of arrest they are liable for any damage which the defendant
may sustain by reason of the arrest, not exceeding the sum
specified in the undertaking, and the undertaking must be in a
sum not less than $500. In either case, the sureties must an-
nex an affidavit to the undertaking ; that he is a resident and
householder, or freeholder within the Territory, and worth double
the sum specified in the undertaking, over and above all his debts
and liabilities, exclusive of property exempt from execution.

The affidavit in cases of arrest differs from attachment affidavits only in this, that the arrest may be made in any action for a fine, or for money or property embezzled, or fraudulently misapplied, or converted to his own use by a public officer, or an officer of a corporation, or an attorney, factor, or broker, agent or clerk, in the course of his employment, or by any person in a fiduciary capacity for misconduct or neglect in office, or in a professional employment, or for a willful violation of duty or in an action to recover the possession of personal property, unjustly detained; when the property, or any part thereof, has been concealed, removed or disposed of, so that it cannot be found or taken by the Territorial marshal, his deputy, or the sheriff or his deputy; or where the defendant has been guilty of fraud in contracting the debt or incurring the obligation for which the action is brought, or is concealing or disposing of the property for the taking, detention or conversion of which the action is brought; or when the defendant has removed or disposed of his property or is about to do so, with the intent to defraud his creditors.

CHAPTER VII.

JUDGMENTS AND JUDGMENT LIENS.

A judgment is collectable by execution, which may be issued any time after judgment, within three years after its rendition, and is a lien upon the real estate of the defendant within the county where it is rendered, from its rendition; executions may be issued to other counties, but the judgment constitutes a lien there, only from the time of filing a transcript of the judgment for record in the office of the county recorder of the county to which it is sent.

CHAPTER VIII.

EXECUTIONS, EXEMPTIONS, SALES, AND REDEMPTION.

Property, real or personal, may be sold on twenty days' notice, under execution, but the execution may issue returnable in not less. then ten days nor more than ninety days, and the execution may require the officer to satisfy the judgment in the particular kind of money ordered in the judgment.

The following property is exempt from execution:

1. Chairs, tables, desks and books, to the value of one hundred dollars belonging to the judgment debtor.

2. Necessary household, table and kitchen furniture belonging to the judgment debtor, including stoves, not to exceed one stove for every five persons of the family. Stove pipe and stove furniture, wearing apparel, one bedstead, one bed, and the necessary bedding for every two persons in the family, and provisions and fuel for the family sufficient for sixty days.

3. The farming utensils or implements of husbandry of the judgment debtor. Also, two oxen or two horses, or two mules and their harness; one cow and calf for every five persons in the family; one cart or wagon, and food for such oxen, horses, cows, or mules, for sixty days; also all seed grain, or vegetables, actually provided, reserved, or on hand, for the purpose of planting or sowing at any time within the ensuing six months, not exceeding in value one hundred dollars.

4. The tools, tool chest, and implements of a mechanic or artisan, necessary to carry on his trade. The instruments and chests of a surgeon, physician, surveyor, or dentist, necessary to the exercise of their professions, with their scientific and professional libraries, and the law library of an attorney or counsellor, and the libraries of ministers of the gospel.

5. The tent or cabin of a miner, including a table, camp stools, a bed and bedding, and necessary tools used in mining, not exceed-

ing the value of four hundred dollars, with provisions necessary to his support for thirty days.

6. Two oxen or two horses or two mules, and their harness, and one cart and wagon, by the use of which a cartman, teamster, or other laborer habitually earns his living, and food for such oxen, horses, or mules for sixty days; and a horse, harness, and vehicle used by a physician, surgeon, or minister of the gospel, in making his professional visits.

7. One sewing machine not to exceed in value $100.00, in actual use by the debtor or his family. If the debtor be head of a family, then there shall be a further exemption of five head of sheep and the wool therefrom for every person in his family, two hogs and three pigs under three months old, and the necessary food for all such animals for sixty days. All flax raised by the debtor and the manufactures therefrom, and all cloth manufactured in the family of the debtor for their own use; all spinning wheels and looms and other instruments of domestic labor kept for family use. The earnings of such debtor for his personal service, or those of his family, at any time within sixty days next preceding the levy.

8. All fire engines, hooks and ladders, with the carts, trucks and carriages, hose, buckets, implements and apparatus. All furniture and uniforms of any fire company or department now existing, or which may be under the laws of this territory hereafter organized.

9. All arms, ammunitions, uniforms, and accoutrements, required by law to be kept by a person.

10. All court-houses, jails, public offices and buildings, school houses, and houses of public worship, lots, grounds and personal property appertaining thereto. The fixtures, furniture, books, papers, and appurtenances belonging and appertaining to the court-house, jail, and public offices belonging to any county, or for the use of schools or houses of public worship; and all cemeteries, public squares, parks and places, town halls, markets for the use of fire departments and military organizations, and the lots and grounds thereto belonging, or held by any town or incorporated city, or dedicated to such town or city to health, ornament, or public use, to the use of any fire or military company now existing or hereafter organized.

11. For homestead exemption, see " Homestead."

REDEMPTION

Of real property may be made by the defendant, or any creditor subsequent to plaintiff's lien, any time within six months from the day of sale.

Chapter IX.

PROCEEDINGS IN AID OF EXECUTIONS.

On the return by a sheriff or marshal of an execution " unsatisfied," the judgment creditor upon affidavit or otherwise showing to the satisfaction of the Court, or of the judge thereof, that the judgment debtor has property which he unjustly refuses to apply towards the satisfaction of the judgment, may apply, and the Court or judge may, by an order, require the judgment debtor to appear at a specified time and place before such judge, or a referee appointed by him, to answer under oath concerning the same ; and such proceedings may thereupon be had for the application of the property of the judgment debtor towards the satisfaction of the judgment, as are provided upon the return of an execution ; that is, to require the appearance of witnesses, and hear the same, and make orders in relation thereto.   And on proof by .affidavit, or otherwise, that any person or corporation has property of such judgment debtor, or is indebted to him in an amount exceeding $50, the judge may by order require such person, or corporation, or any officer or member thereof, to appear at a specified time and place before him, or a referee appointed by him, and answer concerning the same.

The judge or referee may order any property of the judgment

debtor not exempt from execution in the hands of such debtor, or any other person, or due to the judgment debtor, to be applied towards the satisfaction of the judgment.

If it appear that a person or corporation, alleged to have property of the judgment debtor or indebted to him, claims an interest in the property adverse to him, or denies the debt, the Court or judge may authorize, by an order made to that effect, the judgment creditor to institute an action against such person or corporation for the recovery of such interest or debt; and the Court or judge may, by order, forbid a transfer or other disposition of such interest or debt, until an action can be commenced and prosecuted to judgment. Such order may be modified or vacated by the judge granting the same, or the Court in which the action is brought, at any time, on such terms as may be just.

CHAPTER X.

SECURITY FOR COSTS.

It is made the duty of the clerk of the District Court, in all civil actions, to require the party commencing the suit to pay in advance or secure by bond with security the payment of the probable amount of the costs of the action, provided that the said costs shall at the conclusion of the trial be paid by the party against whom said costs are adjudged by the Court.

Chapter XI.

APPEALS

From Justices' Courts to the proper District Court may be taken any time within thirty days after rendition of judgment, except where the judgment is for an amount less than $20, by filing a notice of such appeal, and serving a copy on the opposite party; and by filing with the justice, within five days after filing the notice of appeal, an undertaking with two good sureties, who shall justify under oath.

Appeals from the District Court

May be taken to the Supreme Court from any *final* judgment or order in a civil action, except when expressly made final by the act, any time within one year after the rendition of judgment. From any order granting or refusing a new trial, or from an order granting or dissolving an injunction, or from an order refusing to grant or dissolve an injunction, and from any special order made after the final judgment, within sixty days after the order is made and entered upon the minutes of the Court; or from any interlocutory judgment or order in cases of partition, sale or division, to be taken within sixty days after the rendition of the same.

The appeal is taken by filing with the clerk of the Court with whom the judgment or order appealed from is entered, a notice stating the appeal from the same, or some specific part thereof, and serving a copy of the notice on the adverse party or his attorney. To render the appeal effectual for any purpose, in any case, a written undertaking shall be executed on the part of the appellant, by at least two sureties, to the effect that the appellant will pay all damages and costs which may be awarded against him on the appeal; or a sum not exceeding $100 shall be deposited with the clerk with whom the judgment or order was entered, to abide the event of the appeal; such undertaking shall be filed, or such de-

posit made with the clerk, within at least five days after the notice
of appeal is filed.

An appeal from a judgment or order for the payment of money
shall not stay the execution of the judgment or order, unless a
written undertaking is executed on the part of the appellant, by
two or more sureties, stating their places of residence and occupation, to the effect that they are bound in double the amount named
in the judgment or order appealed from; and should the judgment
or order appealed from, or any part thereof, be affirmed, the
appellant shall pay the amount directed to be paid by the
judgment or order, or the part thereof which shall be affirmed,
and all damages and costs which may be awarded against the appellant, and in the kind of money in which the Court to which it is
appealed shall order the payment thereof.

The sureties shall file affidavit as to their worth, over all just
debts and liabilities, exclusive of property exempt from execution.

When the appeal shall be thus perfected, it shall stay all proceedings upon the judgment, until the action of the appellate Court
shall be had.   The appellee may object to the sureties, as to their
sufficiency, and if the objection be well taken, and the appellant,
upon five days' notice, fail to give additional security, the appeal
shall be regarded as if not taken.

Upon trial in the appellate Court, the successful party is entitled
to have the judgment remitted to the Court from which the appeal
was taken, for execution.

CHAPTER XII.

ESTATES OF DECEASED PERSONS.

Claims against deceased estates must be made within two years
after administration begins.

Satisfactory proof of the amount due must be made to the Probate Court ; this may be made after expiration of two years, provided notice of the claim be given within the two years.

The executor or administrator of the estate has as long to make final settlement in, as the Probate Court will permit, which is usually, as long as he can show any unsettled business of the estate.

The widow or other members of the family are entitled to the homestead, and such further allowance as the Probate Court may deem proper for the maintenance of the widow.

The largest discretion is given the Court in making orders respecting the estate.

Chapter XIII.

HOMESTEADS.

There shall be allowed homestead exemption, to be selected by the debtor, consisting of lands and appurtenances thereon not exceeding in value one thousand dollars for the judgment debtor, and the further sum of two hundred and fifty dollars for each member of the family, (which, in some instances, amount to thirty or forty, including wives and children). If the premises amount in value to more than the homestead exemption, it may be ordered sold or partitioned, and in case of sale, the excess over the exemption valuation is subject to execution ; and in case of partition, the part divided off from the homestead is subject to sale on execution, the valuation to be made by persons chosen by the debtor and the officers having the execution.

CHAPTER XIV.

DEPOSITIONS

May be taken in any action at any time after service of summons, or the appearance of the defendant, and in a special proceeding after a question of fact has arisen therein, in the following cases:

1. When the witness is a party to the action or proceeding, or a person for whose immediate benefit the action or proceeding is prosecuted or defended.

2. When the witness resides out of the county in which his testimony is to be used.

3. When the witness is about to leave the county where the action is to be tried, and will probably continue absent when his testimony is required.

4. When the witness, otherwise liable to attend the trial, is too infirm to attend, or resides within the county but more than fifty miles from the place of trial.

Either party may have a deposition of a witness taken before a notary public, justice of the peace, judge, or clerk of a court, by serving notice on the adverse party of the time and place of examination, together with a copy of the affidavit showing the case to be one of the kind above mentioned. The notice must be served at least five days, and one additional day for every twenty-five miles of distance of the place of examination from the residence of the person served, unless for cause the Court prescribes a shorter time.

The witness may be cross-examined, and after having his testimony carefully examined and read to him, he shall sign it; and the officer taking the deposition shall certify it up to the proper Court, enclosed in an envelope, and addressed to the clerk of the Court in which the action is pending, or to such person as the parties may agree upon, or transmit through the mail; and such deposition may be used by either party on the trial. No objections to the form of an interrogatory at the trial will be heard, unless made at the time of taking, if the party making the objection is in attendance at the taking.

If a deposition be taken on account of the absence from the county, or intended absence, or because the witness is too infirm to attend, before being used proof must be made by affidavit or oral testimony that the witness' disability continues, to the best of affiant's knowledge. The deposition may be read in case of his death.

Depositions once taken may be read in any stage of the cause by either party, and shall be deemed evidence of the party reading them.

If a deposition be taken out of the Territory, it must be upon a commission issued by the Court, under its seal, upon five days' notice to the adverse party of the application for a commission, and shall be issued to a person to be agreed upon between the parties; and, in case of disagreement, then to such person as the Court may appoint, or to a commissioner appointed by the Governor of this Territory to take affidavits and depositions in the States or Territories.

Such interrogatories, direct and cross, as the parties prepare, or, in case of disagreement, such as the Court shall settle, shall be annexed to the commission. The cause shall not be continued on account of the non-return of the commission and deposition, unless upon evidence satisfactory to the Court, that the testimony of the witness is necessary, and that proper diligence has been used to obtain it.

The statute also provides for the taking of testimony, and for its perpetuation, upon application to the Court, showing that the applicant expects to be a party to an action in this Territory, and giving the names of persons whom he expects will be adverse parties; that the proof of some facts is necessary to perfect the title to property in which he is interested, or to establish a marriage, descent, heirship, or any other matter which it may hereafter become material to establish; though no suit may at the time be anticipated. The names of the witnesses and the general outline of the facts expected to be proven, to be stated. Affidavits or other proofs filed with the testimony shall be *prima facie* evidence of the facts stated therein. No particular form of the certificate of the officer taking the deposition is prescribed by the statute.

Chapter XV.

JUDICIAL RECORDS, HOW PROVEN.

A judicial record of this Territory, or of the United States, or of any State or Territory of the United States, may be admitted in the Courts of this Territory by the attestation of the clerk, with the seal of the Court annexed, together with the certificate of the judge, chief justice, or presiding magistrate, as the case may be, that said attestation is in due form.

A judicial record of a foreign country may be proved by the production of a copy thereof, certified by the clerk, with the seal of the Court annexed, if there be a clerk and seal, to be a true copy of such record, together with a certificate of the judge of the Court that the person making the certificate is the clerk of the Court, or the legal keeper of the records; and in either case, that the signature is genuine, and the certificate in due form; together with the certificate of the minister or embassador of the United States, or of a consul of the United States, in such foreign country, that there is such a Court, specifying generally its jurisdiction, and verifying the signature of the judge and clerk, or other legal keeper of the record.

A copy of the judicial record of a foreign country shall also be admissible in evidence, upon proof, first, that the copy offered has been compared by the witness with the original, and is an exact transcript of the whole of it; and that such original was in the custody of the clerk of the Court, or other legal keeper of the same; and that the copy is duly attested by the seal which is proved to be the seal of the Court where the record remains, if it be the record of a Court; or if there be no such seal, or if it be not a record of a Court, by the signature of the legal keeper of the original.

Chapter XVI.

ACKNOWLEDGMENTS.

Deeds, mortgages, powers of attorney, or other instruments affecting the title to real estate, must be acknowledged or proved before they can legally be placed upon record.

The following is the form of the acknowledgment certificate:

STATE OR TERRITORY OF———-⎫
———————————County, ⎬ ss.

On this———day of———A. D. 187 , personally appeared before me ———, a notary public in and for said county, ———, who is personally known to me to be the person described in and who executed the foregoing instrument, who acknowledged to me that he executed the same freely and voluntarily, and for the uses and purposes therein mentioned. In witness whereof, I have hereunto set my hand and official seal, on the day and year last above written.   ———————————,

[SEAL.]   Notary Public.

The following officers are authorized to take acknowledgments, and certify to them:

If acknowledged or proven within this Territory, by some judge or clerk of a Court having a seal, or some notary public, or county recorder, or by a justice of the peace of the county where the conveyance is executed, and to be recorded.

If acknowledged or proved out of this Territory, and within any State or Territory in the United States, by some judge or clerk of any Court of the United States, or of any State or Territory having a seal, or by a notary public, or by a commissioner appointed by the Governor of this Territory for that purpose.

If acknowledged or proved without the United States, by some judge or clerk of any Court of any State, Kingdom, or Empire having a seal, any notary public therein, or any minister, commissioner, or consul of the United States appointed to reside therein. Such officers may take and certify such proofs or acknowledgments by their respective deputies, in the names of their principals.

When granted by a judge or clerk, the certificate shall be under the seal of his Court.

When granted by an officer who has an official seal, it shall be under such seal.

By a justice of the peace, under his hand.

Chapter XVII.

PARTNERSHIPS.

The statute provides how partners may be summoned, and how judgments against partners may be rendered, but is thus brief and pointed.

When two or more persons, associated in any business, transact such business in a common name, whether it comprises the names of such persons or not, the associates may be sued by such common name, the summons in such cases being served on one or more of the associates, but the judgment in such cases shall bind only the joint property of the associates. The private property of persons engaged in copartnership shall be held liable for the debts of the firm, only when the partnership property shall prove insufficient to pay them. The assignment of a partner in trade to satisfy a creditor of the firm shall be deemed valid in law, but is not to be construed to authorize the assignment of partnership effects to satisfy individual claims of any of the parties.

13

CHAPTER XVIII.

MARRIED WOMEN.

All property owned by either spouse before marriage, and that acquired after marriage by gift, bequest, devise, or descent, is the separate property of that spouse by whom the same is owned or acquired ; and as such, may be held, owned and controlled, and transfered and disposed of by the spouse so owning or acquiring it, without any limitation or restriction by reason of marriage.

Either spouse may sue and be sued in law. No right of dower shall be allowed.

CHAPTER XIX.

CORPORATIONS.

Any number of persons, not less than six, one-third of whom being residents of the Territory, may incorporate for purposes of manufacturing, mining, or conducting any commercial or other industrial pursuit, or for constructing roads, ditches, colonization and improvements for lands, colleges, seminaries, churches, libraries, or any benevolent, charitable, christian or scientific associations, or for any rightful subject consistent with the Constitution of the United States, and the laws of the Territory.

Stock may be subscribed and paid up in property. No individual liability upon stockholders. The probate judge is the officiating officer in effecting an incorporation.

CHAPTER XX.

CHATTEL MORTGAGES.

We have no statute defining what property is the subject of chattel mortgage, but an action for the recovery of debts secured by a mortgage on either real or personal property, or both, is provided for by statute, giving power to the Courts to render judgment, and make decree of foreclosure, and order of sale of the mortgaged property, in satisfaction of the debt, and providing for an ordinary judgment lien and execution for unpaid balance, after sale of the mortgaged property.

CHAPTER XXI.

INTEREST AND USURY.

Ten per cent. per annum interest is allowed on debts due, where no contract as to interest exists. There is no usury statute, and parties are at liberty to contract for rates of interest without limit, and any agreed rate is collectable.

PART VII.

IDAHO TERRITORY.

PREPARED EXPRESSLY FOR THIS WORK BY JONAS W. BROWN,
IDAHO CITY.

CHAPTER I.

COURTS, THEIR JURISDICTION AND TERMS.

The judicial power of the Territory is vested in a Supreme Court, three District Courts, Probate Courts for each county, and Justices of the Peace.

THE SUPREME COURT

Has appellate jurisdiction in all civil cases where the amount in dispute exceeds in value one hundred dollars, and in all criminal cases tried in District Courts. Meets at Boise City annually, on the first Monday of January.

DISTRICT COURTS

Have original jurisdiction in all civil cases where the amount in dispute exceeds one hundred dollars, and in all criminal cases prosecuted by indictment. Their appellate jurisdiction extends to hearing all cases on appeal from Probate Courts and Justices' Courts. They have exclusive jurisdiction in all equity cases, and in all cases involving the title to real estate.

The terms of the District Courts are fixed annually for the several counties by the Supreme Court.

THE PROBATE COURTS

Have jurisdiction of all probate matters, same as in California. They have also concurrent jurisdiction (by special act of Congress) with the District Courts in all civil actions, when the amount in controversy shall not exceed five hundred dollars, exclusive of interest; and the same rules of practice govern in Probate Courts in civil cases as in the District Courts, except in the matter of appeals to the District Court. The terms of the Probate Courts commence on the fourth Monday in each month.

JUSTICES' COURTS

Have jurisdiction in all civil actions where the sum or damages claimed do not exceed one hundred dollars, excepting matters where the boundaries of land are in dispute. These Courts are always open for business.

CHAPTER II.

COMMENCEMENT OF ACTIONS.

Civil actions in the District Courts and the Probate Courts shall be commenced by the filing of a complaint with the clerk of the Court in which the action is brought: *Provided*, that after the filing of the complaint, a defendant in the action may appear, answer, or demur, whether the summons has been issued or not, and such appearance, answer, or demurrer be deemed a waiver of summons.

The clerk shall indorse on the complaint the day, month, and year the same is filed ; and at any time within one year after the filing of the same, the plaintiff may have a summons issued. The act defining jurisdiction of Probate Courts provides that the summons may be issued at any time within six months from the filing of the complaint.

In the District Court the defendant must answer in ten days, if served within the county in which the action is brought ; in twenty days, if served without the county, but within the judicial district in which the action is brought. In all other cases, thirty days. In the Probate Court, answer must be filed in ten days.

CHAPTER III.

PLACE OF TRIAL OF CIVIL ACTIONS.

Actions for the following causes shall be tried in the county in which the subject of the action, or some part thereof, is situated, subject to the power of the Court to change the place of trial:

1. For the recovery of real property, or of an estate or interest therein, or for the determination, in any form, of such right or interest, or for injuries to real property.

2. For the partition of real property.

3. For the foreclosure of a mortgage of real property ; provided, when such real property is situate partly in one county and partly in another, the plaintiff may select either of said counties, and the county so selected shall be the proper county for the trial of such action.

Actions for the following causes shall be tried in the county where the cause, or some part thereof, arose ; subject to the like power of the Court to change the place of trial :

1. For the recovery of a penalty or forfeiture imposed by a statute, except that when it is imposed for an offense committed on a lake, river, or other stream of water situated in two or more counties, the action may be brought in any county bordering on such lake, river, or other stream, and opposite the place where the offense was committed.

2. Against a public officer, or person especially appointed to execute his duties, for an act done by him in virtue of his office, or against a person who, by his command, or in his aid, does anything touching the duties of such officer.

In all other cases, the action shall be tried in the county in which the defendants, or any of them, may reside at the commencement of the action ; or if none of the defendants reside in this Territory, or, if residing in this Territory, the county in which they so reside be unknown to the plaintiff, the same may be tried in any county which the plaintiff may designate in his complaint ; and if any defendant or defendants may be about to depart from the Territory, such action may be tried in any county where either of the parties reside or may be found, or service be had ; subject, however, to the power of the Court to change the place of trial, as provided in the act.

CHAPTER IV.

LIMITATIONS OF CIVIL ACTIONS.

Five Years :

Real estate, including quartz mines or lodes, judgments or decrees of any Court of the United States, or of any State or Territory of the United States.

Four Years:

Any contract, obligation, or liability founded upon an instrument of writing.

Three Years:

Trespass upon real property, taking, detaining or injuring goods or chattels or for the specific recovery of personal property. Relief on ground of fraud.

Two Years:

Contract or liability not founded on an instrument of writing, including accounts.   An action for libel or slander.

One Year:

Placer mining claims.

General Provisions:

An action upon any contract, obligation or liability for the payment of money, founded upon an instrument of writing executed out of this Territory, or any other Territory from which this Territory is in part formed, can only be commenced as follows:

1. Within one year, when more than two and less than five years have elapsed since the cause of action accrued.

An action upon any judgment, contract, obligation or liability for the payment of money or damages, obtained, executed, or made out of this Territory, or any other Territory from which this Territory is in part formed, shall only be commenced within three years after the party making such liabilities shall be a resident of this Territory.

No acknowledgment of promise shall be sufficient evidence of a new continuing contract, whereby to take the case out of the operation of the statute, unless the same be contained in some writing signed by the party to be charged thereby.

Chapter V.

ATTACHMENTS.

The plaintiff, at the time of issuing the summons, or at any time afterward, may have the property of the defendant attached as security for the satisfaction of any judgment that may be recovered, unless the defendant give security to pay such judgment, in the following cases:

1. In an action upon a contract, express or implied, for the direct payment of money, which contract is not secured by a mortgage, lien, or pledge upon real or personal property; or if so secured, that such security has, without any act of the plaintiff, or the person to whom the security was given, become valueless.

2. In an action upon a contract, express or implied, against a defendant not residing in this Territory.

The clerk of the Court shall issue the writ of attachment upon receiving an affidavit by or on behalf of the plaintiff, which shall be filed, setting forth—

1. That the defendant is indebted to the plaintiff, specifying the amount of such indebtedness over and above all legal set-offs and counter-claims, upon a contract, express or implied, for the direct payment of money; and that the payment of the same has not been secured by any mortgage, lien, or pledge upon real or personal property; or, if so secured, that such security has, without any act of the plaintiff, or the person to whom the security was given, become valueless; or,

2. That the defendant is indebted to the plaintiff, specifying the amount of the indebtedness as near as may be, over and above all legal set-offs and counter-claims, and that the defendant is a non-resident of the Territory; and,

3. That the attachment is not sought, and the action is not prosecuted, to hinder, delay, or defraud any creditor or creditors of the defendant.

Before issuing the writ, the clerk must require a written undertaking on the part of the plaintiff, in a sum not less than two hundred dollars, and not exceeding the amount claimed by the plaintiff, with sufficient sureties, to the effect that if the defendant recover judgment, the plaintiff will pay all costs that he may sustain by reason of the attachment, not exceeding the sum specified in the undertaking, if the attachment be wrongfully issued.

Chapter VI.

ARREST IN CIVIL ACTION.

The defendant may be arrested, as hereinafter provided, in the following cases:

1. In an action for the recovery of money or damages on a cause of action arising upon contract, express or implied, when the defendant is about to depart from the Territory, with intent to defraud his creditors; or when the action is for willful injury to person, to character, or to property, knowing the property to belong to another.

2. In an action for a fine or penalty, or on a promise to marry, or for money or property embezzled, or fraudulently applied, or converted to his own use by a public officer, or an officer of a corporation, or an attorney, factor, broker, agent, or clerk, in the course of his employment as such, or by any other person in a fiduciary capacity, or for misconduct or neglect in office, or in a professional employment, or for a willful violation of duty.

3. In an action to recover the possession of personal property unjustly detained, when the property, or any part thereof, has been concealed, removed, or disposed of, to prevent its being found or taken by the sheriff.

4. When the defendant has been guilty of fraud in contracting the debt or incurring the obligation for which the action is brought, or in concealing or disposing of the property, for the taking, detention, or conversion of which the action is brought.

5. When the defendant has removed or disposed of his property, or is about to do so, with intent to defraud his creditors.

To obtain an order of arrest, it must appear to the judge, by the affidavit of the plaintiff or some other person, that a sufficient cause of action exists, and that the case is one of those above mentioned. The affidavit must be positive, or upon information and belief. Before making an order, the judge must require a written undertaking on the part of plaintiff, with sureties in an amount to be fixed by the judge, which must be at least five hundred dollars.

CHAPTER VII.

JUDGMENTS AND JUDGMENT LIENS.

In an action on a contract or obligation, in writing, for the direct payment of money, made payable in a specified kind of money or currency, judgment for the plaintiff may follow the contract or obligation, and be made payable in the kind of money or currency specified therein.

From the time the judgment is docketed it becomes a lien upon all the real property of the judgment debtor, not exempt from execution in the county, owned by him at the time, or which he may afterwards acquire, until the lien expires. The lien continues for two years.

A transcript of the original docket, certified by the clerk, and filed with the recorder of any other county, becomes a lien on the property of the judgment debtor in such county, and continues for two years.

A transcript of a judgment of a Probate Court, filed and docketed in the office of the district clerk, becomes a lien upon the real estate of the judgment debtor for two years from date of filing and docketing.

A transcript of a judgment of a justice of the peace becomes a lien upon real estate by being filed and recorded in the county recorder's office. By filing and docketing same in district clerk's office, the clerk may issue execution to any other county in the Territory.

CHAPTER VIII.

EXECUTIONS, EXEMPTIONS, SALE AND REDEMPTION.

A writ of execution to enforce the judgment may be issued at any time within five years after the entry thereof. In all cases other than for the recovery of money, the judgment may be enforced or carried into execution after the lapse of five years from the date of its entry, by leave of the Court, upon motion or by judgment for that purpose, founded upon supplemental pleadings.

EXEMPTIONS FROM EXECUTION.

1. Chairs, tables, desks and books, to the value of one hundred dollars, belonging to the judgment debtor.

2. Necessary household, table and kitchen furniture belonging to the judgment debtor, including stove, stovepipe, and stove furniture of whatever kind, wearing apparel, beds, bedding and bedsteads, and provisions actually provided for individual or family use sufficient for three months.

3. The farming utensils or implements of husbandry of the

judgment debtor; also, two oxen, or two horses, or two mules, and their harness; two cows, one cart or wagon, and food for such oxen, horses, cows or mules for three months; also, all seed grain or vegetables actually provided, reserved, or on hand for the purpose of planting or sowing at any time within the ensuing six months, not exceeding in value the sum of two hundred dollars; the tools and implements of a mechanic necessary to carry on his trade; the instruments and chests of a surgeon, physician, surveyor, and dentist necessary to the exercise of their profession, with the professional library, and the law libraries of an attorney and counsellor; also, the wardrobe and books of an actor.

4. The tents and furniture, including a table, camp stools, bed and bedding of a miner; also his rocker, shovels, spades, wheelbarrows, pumps, and other instruments used in mining, with provisions necessary for his support for three months.

5. Two oxen, two horses, or two mules, and their harness, and one cart or wagon, by the use of which a cartman, teamster, or other laborer habitually earns his living, and the food for such oxen, horses, or mules, for three months; and a horse used by a physician in making his professional visits.

6. All fire engines, with carts, buckets, hose, and apparatus thereto appertaining, of any fire company or department organized under any law of this Territory.

7. All arms and accoutrements required by law to be kept by any person.

8. All court-houses, jails, public offices and buildings, lots, ground and personal property, the fixtures, furniture, books, papers, and appurtenances belonging to any county in this Territory; and all cemeteries, public squares, parks and public buildings, town halls, markets, buildings appertaining to the fire departments, and the lots and grounds thereto belonging and appertaining, owned or held by any town or incorporated city, or dedicated by such town or city to health, ornament, or public use.

No article above mentioned shall be exempt from execution issued upon a judgment recovered for its price, or upon a mortgage thereon.

SALE OF PROPERTY UNDER EXECUTION.

In case of perishable property, by posting written notices of the time and place of sale in three public places of the precinct, for a reasonable time, considering the condition of property.   In case of other personal property, by posting similar notices in three public places of the precinct, township or city where the sale is to take place, not less than five, nor more than ten days successively.   In case of real property, by posting similar notices, particularly describing the property, for twenty days successively, in three public places of the precinct, township, or city where the property is situated, and also where the property is to be sold, and publishing a copy thereof once a week for the same period in some newspaper published in the county, if there be one.   All sales of property under execution shall be made at auction to the highest bidder, and shall be made between the hours of nine in the morning and five in the afternoon.

REDEMPTION.

Real estate sold on execution under a judgment may be redeemed within six months from the date of the sale, either by the judgment debtor or his successor in interest in the whole or any part of the property, or by a creditor having a lien by judgment or mortgage on the property sold, by paying to the purchaser the amount of his purchase with eighteen per cent. thereon in addition.   The purchaser is entitled to the rents, issues, and profits.

Sale upon foreclosure of mortgage held to be final.   No redemption.

Chapter IX.

PROCEEDINGS SUPPLEMENTARY TO EXECUTION.

After return of execution unsatisfied, the judgment debtor may be required to answer concerning his property.

A judgment debtor unjustly refusing to apply property which he has to the satisfaction of a judgment against him, may be required to appear and answer concerning the same.

After the issuing or return of execution, or upon proof by affidavit or otherwise, to the satisfaction of the judge, that any person or corporation has property of judgment debtor, or is indebted to him in an amount exceeding fifty dollars, such person or corporation may be required to appear and answer concerning same.

Chapter X.

SECURITY FOR COSTS.

When the plaintiff in an action resides out of the Territory, or is a foreign corporation, security for costs and charges that may be awarded against such plaintiff may be required by the defendant. When required, all proceedings shall be stayed until an undertaking, as required, be filed to pay all costs, not exceeding the sum of three hundred dollars, with two sureties. If such security be not given within thirty days from the service of notice that security is required, the Court may order the action dismissed.

CHAPTER XI.

APPEALS IN GENERAL.

An appeal may be taken: 1. From a final judgment in an action or special proceeding, commenced in the Court in which the judgment is rendered, within one year after the entry of judgment. But an exception to the decision or verdict, on the ground that it is not supported by the evidence, cannot be reviewed on appeal from the judgment, unless the appeal is taken within sixty days. after the rendition of the judgment.

2. From a judgment rendered by a Probate or Justice's Court,. within twenty-one days from the entry of judgment.

3. From an order granting or refusing a new trial; from an order granting or dissolving an injunction ; from an order refusing to grant or dissolve an injunction; from an order dissolving or refusing to dissolve an attachment; from an order granting or refusing to grant a change of the place of trial ; from any special order made after final judgment, and from an interlocutory judgment in actions for partition of real property, within thirty days after the order or interlocutory judgment is made and entered in the minutes of the Court, or filed with the clerk.

In the District Court, an undertaking must be filed on the part of the appellant by at least two sureties, to the effect that the appellant will pay all the damages and costs, not exceeding three hundred dollars : or that sum must be deposited with the clerk.

If a stay of proceedings is desired, an undertaking in double the amount of the judgment and costs must be filed.

In the Probate and Justices' Courts, appeals are allowed in all cases where the demand, exclusive of interest, or the value of the property in controversy, amounts to twenty-five dollars.

Appeals in Probate and Justices' Courts must be taken in twenty days from the rendition of the judgment.

14

CHAPTER XII.

HOMESTEADS.

The homestead consisting of a quantity of land, together with the dwelling house thereon and its appurtenances, not exceeding in value the sum of five thousand dollars, to be selected by the husband and wife, or either of them, or other head of a family, shall not be subject to forced sale in execution, or any final process from any Court.

The person or persons claiming a homestead shall do so by written declaration, setting forth that they, or either of them, are married, or if not married, that he or she is the head of a family ; that they or either of them, as the case may be, are, at the time of making such declaration, residing with their family, or with the person under their care and maintenance, on the premises, particularly describing said premises, and it is their intention to use and claim the same as a homestead, which declaration shall be signed by the party making the same, and acknowledged and recorded in the office of the county recorder. Such exemption shall not extend to any mechanic's, laborer's or vendor's lien, lawfully obtained, nor to a mortgage or alienation to secure the purchase money or pay the purchase money, if the signature of the wife be obtained to the same, and acknowledged by her separate and apart from her husband.

CHAPTER XIII.

ESTATES OF DECEASED PERSONS.

Every executor or administrator shall, immediately after his appointment, cause to be published in some newspaper published in the county—if there be one ; if not, then in such newspaper as may be designated by the Court—a notice to the creditors of the deceased requiring all persons having claims against the deceased to exhibit them, with the necessary vouchers, within ten months after the first publication of the notice to such executor or administrator, at the place of his residence or transaction of business, to be specified in the notice.

If a claim be not presented within ten months—unless the value of the estate does not exceed fifteen hundred dollars ; in which case notice to creditors shall be given to present their claims within four months—after the first publication of the notice, it shall be barred forever : *provided*, if it be not then due, or if it be contingent, it may be presented within ten months after it shall become due or absolute : and *provided* further, that when it shall be made to appear by the affidavit of the claimant, to the satisfaction of the executor or administrator and the probate judge, that the claimant had no notice, as provided in this act, by reason of absence from this Territory, it may be presented at any time before a decree of distribution is entered.

Every claim presented to the administrator shall be supported by the affidavit of the claimant that the amount is justly due, that no payments have been made thereon, and that there are no off-sets to the same to the knowledge of the claimant or affiant : *provided,* that when the affidavit is made by any other person than the claimant, he shall set forth in the affidavit the reason it is not made by the claimant. The oath may be taken before any officer authorized to administer oaths. (If the claimant is a non-resident, the affidavit must be made before a judge or clerk of a Court having a seal, or a commissioner for Idaho Territory.) The executor or administrator shall also require satisfactory vouchers or proofs to be produced in support of the claim.

The amount of interest shall be computed and included in the statement of the claim, and the rate of interest determined ; *provided*, that no claim which shall have been due and payable thirty days prior to the death of the deceased shall bear greater interest than ten per cent. per annum from and after the time of issuing letters.

When a claim, accompanied by the affidavit required, has been presented to the executor or administrator he shall endorse thereon his allowance or rejection, with the day and date thereof. If he allow the claim, it shall be presented to the judge for his approval, who shall in the same manner endorse upon it his allowance or rejection.

If the executor or administrator, or the judge, refuse or neglect to endorse such allowance or rejection for ten days after the claim shall have been presented to him, such refusal or neglect shall be deemed a rejection: if allowed and approved, it must be filed in the Probate Court within thirty days.

If the claim be founded on a bond, bill, note, or other instrument, the original instrument shall be presented, and the allowance and approval, or rejection, shall be endorsed thereon or attached thereto.

If the claim, or any part thereof, be secured by a mortgage or other lien, such mortgage or evidence of lien shall be attached to the claim and filed therewith, unless the same be recorded in the office of the recorder of the county in which the land lies; in which case it shall be sufficient to describe the mortgage or lien, and refer to the date, volume and page of its record.

In all cases the claimant may withdraw his claim from file on leaving a certified copy, with a receipt endorsed thereon, by himself or his agent. If the original instrument be lost or destroyed, then, in lieu thereof, the claimant shall be required to file his affidavit particularly describing such instrument, and stating the loss or destruction thereof.

When a claim is rejected, either by the executor or administrator or probate judge, the holder shall bring suit in the proper Court against the executor or administrator, within three months after the date of its rejection, if it be then due, or within three months after it becomes due, otherwise the claim shall be forever barred.

No claim shall be allowed which is barred by the statute of limitations.

The executor, administrator or probate judge may allow a claim in part, and if the claimant fail to recover a greater sum he is allowed no costs.

The debts of the estate are paid in the following order:

1. Funeral expenses.

2. The expenses of the last sickness.

3. Debts having preference by the laws of the United States.

4. Judgments rendered against the deceased in his lifetime, and mortgages in the order of their date.

5. All other demands against the estate.

The mortgages in preference extend only to the proceeds of the property mortgaged; any deficiency must be classified and paid under the fifth head.

Executors and administrators should make a settlement of the estate at the expiration of one year; except where the value of the estate does not exceed fifteen hundred dollars, the Court may order the estate settled in six months.

CHAPTER XIV.

DEPOSITIONS.

The deposition of a witness in this Territory, who is a party to the action or proceeding; or who resides out of the county, or is about to leave the county where the action is to be tried; or is too infirm to attend the trial; or when the testimony is required upon a motion, or in any other case where the oral examination of the witness is not required, may be taken by either party, before any judge or clerk, or any justice of the peace, or notary public in this Territory, on serving upon the adverse party previous notice of the time and place of the examination, together with a copy of an affidavit, showing that the case is one of the above mentioned. Such notice shall be at least five days, and in addition one day for every twenty-five miles of the distance of the place of examination from the residence of the person to whom the notice is given, unless a shorter time is prescribed by the judge.

The deposition of a witness out of this Territory may be taken upon commission issued from the Court, under the seal of the Court, upon an order of the judge or Court, or probate judge, on the application of either party, upon five days' notice to the other. If issued to any place within the United States, it may be directed to a person agreed upon by the parties, or if they do not agree, to any judge or justice of the peace, or commissioner selected by the officer issuing it.

If issued to any country out of the United States, it may be directed to a minister, ambassador, consul, vice consul, or consular agent of the United States in such country, or to any person agreed on by the parties.

The commission shall authorize the commissioner to administer an oath to witness, and to take his deposition in answer to the interrogatories; or when the examination is to be made without interrogatories, in respect to the matter in dispute; and to certify the deposition to the Court, in a sealed envelope, directed to the clerk or other person designated or agreed upon, and forward to him by mail or other usual channel of conveyance.

CHAPTER XV.

JUDICIAL RECORDS.

A judicial record of this Territory or of the United States may be proved by the production of the original or copy thereof, certified by the clerk, or other person having the legal custody thereof, under the seal of the Court, to be a true copy of such record.

The records or judicial proceedings of the Courts of any State of the United States may be proved or admitted in the Courts of this Territory, by the attestation of the clerk and the seal of the

Court annexed, (if there be a seal) together with the certificate of the judge, chief justice or presiding magistrate, as the case may be, that the attestation is in due form.

A seal of a Court or public officer, when required, may be impressed with wax, wafer or any other substance, and then attached to the instrument or document; or it may be impressed on the paper alone.

Chapter XVI.

ACKNOWLEDGMENTS.

Acknowledgments are required in all conveyances affecting real estate. The same certificate required as in California.

May be taken by :

1. If acknowledged or proved within this Territory, by some judge or clerk of a Court having a seal, or some notary public, recorder or justice of the peace of the proper county.

2. If acknowledged or proved without this Territory, and within the United States, by some judge or clerk of any Court of the United States, or of any State or Territory having a seal, or by any commissioner appointed by the Governor of this Territory.

3. If acknowledged or proved without the United States, by some judge or clerk of any Court, (having a seal) of any State, Kingdom or Empire, or by a notary public therein, or by any minister, commissioner, or consul of the United States appointed to reside therein.

The act concerning conveyances of real estate, or any interest therein, and mortgages, is the same as in California.

Chapter XVII.

LIMITED PARTNERSHIPS.

Limited partnerships for the transaction of mercantile, mechanical, mining or manufacturing business may be formed, but not for the purpose of banking or insurance.

No such partnership shall be deemed to have been formed until a certificate which shall contain the name or firm under which said partnership is to be conducted, the names and respective places of residence of all the general and special partners, distinguishing who are general, and who are special partners, the amount of capital which each special partner has contributed to the capital stock, the general nature of the business to be transacted, the time when the partnership is to commence and terminate, shall be made and severally signed and acknowledged by all the partners, before an officer authorized to take acknowledgment of deeds, and recorded in the office of the recorder of the county in which the principal place of business of the partnership is located. If there shall be a place of business in different counties, said certificate shall be recorded in each of such counties; a copy of such certificate shall be published three successive weeks in the county where the principal place of business is located.

Any false statement in the certificate makes all the partners liable as general partners.

The special partners shall not be personally liable for any debts of the partnership, except their names be used in said firm with their consent or privity, or shall personally make any contract respecting the concerns of the partnership with any person except the general partner.

Chapter XVIII.

MARRIED WOMEN.

All property both real and personal, of the wife before marriage, and that acquired afterwards, by gift, bequest, devise or descent, is her separate property, and all the husband's is his separate property. All other property acquired after marriage is common property.

The wife is required to make, sign, acknowledge, and have recorded a complete inventory of her separate property, in the office of the recorder of the county where the property is situated. The husband has the management and control of the wife's separate property during marriage, but cannot alienate or create a lien or incumbrance on the same, except by instrument signed and acknowledged by both husband and wife.

The District Court may, on application of the wife, appoint a trustee to take charge of and manage her separate property, if the husband mismanages it or commits waste.

The husband has entire control of common property and his own separate property, and the rents and profits of all the separate property of both husband and wife are deemed common property, unless expressly provided in the instrument or devise to the contrary. Upon dissolution of the community by death, half of the common property goes to the survivor and half to the descendants, if there are any; if not, all to the survivor. Upon dissolution by decree of Court, the common property must be equally divided, unless the decree is granted on the ground of adultery or extreme cruelty, when the division of the same is left to the discretion of the Court granting the decree.

The separate property of the husband is not liable for the debts of the wife contracted before marriage, but the separate property of the wife is liable for all such debts.

Chapter XIX.

CORPORATIONS.

There is a general law for the formation of corporations, by which three or more persons may form a corporation by filing a certificate in writing with the clerk of the District Court of the district in which the principal place of business of the corporation is intended to be located, and a certified copy of the same, under the hand of the clerk and the seal of the Court, in the office of the secretary of the Territory. Said certificate must state the corporate name of the company, the object for which it is formed, amount of capital stock, term of existence, (not to exceed fifty years) number of shares, number of trustees and their names who shall manage the concerns of the corporation for the first three months, and principal place of business.

The total amount of the debts of the corporation shall not, at any time, exceed the amount of the capital stock actually paid in; and in case of any excess, the trustees under whose administration the same may have happened, except those who have caused their dissent therefrom to be entered at large on the minutes of the board of trustees at the time, and except those not present at the time when the same did happen, shall, in their individual and private capacities, be liable jointly and severally to the said corporation, and in the event of its dissolution, to any of the creditors thereof, for the full amount of such excess.

Each stockholder shall be individually and personally liable for his proportion of all the debts and liabilities of the corporation, contracted or incurred during the time that he was a stockholder, for the recovery of which joint or several actions may be instituted; and when a judgment in such action shall be recovered against joint stockholders, the Court on the trial thereof shall apportion the amount of the liability of each, and in the execution thereof no stockholder shall be liable beyond his proportion so ascertained.

CHAPTER XX.

CHATTEL MORTGAGES

May be given upon all kinds of personal property. To be valid against subsequent incumbrancers, or purchasers in good faith, for a valuable consideration, the mortgage must show the residence, and the profession, trade or occupation of both the mortgagor and mortgagee, and each of the parties must make affidavit thereto, that the mortgage is made in good faith, and without any design to hinder, delay or defraud creditors. When so made and recorded in the office of the recorder of deeds, such mortgage is good against all persons.

CHAPTER XXI.

INTEREST AND USURY.

Ten per cent. per annum is the legal rate of interest. Parties may agree in writing for any rate of interest not exceeding two per cent. per month, but any judgment rendered upon such contract bears only ten per cent. per annum. The penalty for a greater rate than above specified is three times the amount so paid, and the person receiving a greater rate than two per cent. per month is liable to a fine of three hundred dollars, or six months' imprisonment, or both. Interest does not commence to run on open accounts until a balance is struck and agreed to, or a settlement is had.

Chapter XXII.

AFFIDAVITS.

An affidavit to be used before any Court, judge or officer of this Territory may be taken before any judge or clerk of any Court, or any justice of the peace or notary public in this Territory.

An affidavit taken in another State or Territory of the United States, to be used in this Territory, shall be taken before a commissioner appointed by the Governor of this Territory to take affidavits and depositions in such other State or Territory, or before the judge of a Court of record having a seal. An affidavit taken in a foreign country, to be used in this Territory, shall be taken before an ambassador, minister, or consul of the United States, or before any judge of a Court of record having a seal in such foreign country, or before a commsssioner of deeds appointed by the governor.

When an affidavit is taken before a judge of a Court in another State or Territory, or a foreign country, the genuineness of the signature of the judge, the existence of the Court, and the fact that such judge is a member thereof, shall be certified by the clerk of the Court under the seal thereof.

Chapter XXIII.

SOLE TRADERS.

A married woman may become a sole trader by the judgment of the Probate Court of the county in which she has resided for six months next preceding the application.

A person intending to make application to become a sole trader must publish notice of such intention in a newspaper published in the county, or if there be none, then in a newspaper published in an adjoining county, for four successive weeks.

The notice must specify the term and the day upon which application will be made, the nature and place of the business proposed to be conducted by her, and the name of her husband.

Ten days prior to the day named in the notice, the applicant must file a verified petition, setting forth :

1. That the application is made in good faith, to enable the applicant to support herself, and others dependent upon her, giving their names and relation.

2. The fact of insufficient support from her husband, and the causes thereof, if known.

3. Any other grounds for application, which are good causes for a divorce, with the reason why a divorce is not sought ; and,

4. The nature of the business proposed to be conducted, and the capital to be invested therein, if any, and the sources from which it is derived.

The applicant may invest in the business proposed to be conducted a sum derived from the community property or of the separate property of the husband, not exceeding five hundred dollars.

Any creditor of the husband may oppose the application by filing in the Court (prior to the day named in the notice) a written opposition, verified, containing either :

1. A specific denial of the truth of any material allegation of the petition, or setting forth—

2. That the application is made for the purpose of defrauding the opponent ; or,

3. That the application is made to prevent, or will prevent him from collecting his debt.

Issues of fact must be tried as in other cases.   If the facts found sustain the petition, the Court must render judgment, authorizing the applicant to carry on in her own name and on her own account, the business specified in the notice and petition.

The sole trader must make and file with the clerk of the Court an affidavit, in the following form :

" I, A B, do, in presence of Almighty God, solemnly swear
that this application was made in good faith, for the purpose of
enabling me to support myself, (and any dependent, such as husband, parent, sister, child, or the like, naming them, if any) and
not with any view to defraud, delay or hinder any creditor or creditors of my husband ; and that, of the moneys so to be used by me
in business, not over five hundred dollars have come, either directly or indirectly, from my husband ; so help me God."

A certified copy of the decree, with this oath endorsed thereon,
must be recorded in the office of the recorder of the county where
the business is to be carried on.

A married woman who is adjudged a sole trader is responsible
and liable for the maintenance of her minor children.

The husband of a sole trader is not liable for any debt contracted by her in the course of her sole trader's business, unless contracted upon his written consent.

PART VIII.

WYOMING TERRITORY.

PREPARED EXPRESSLY FOR THIS WORK BY E. P. JOHNSON, CHEYENNE.

CHAPTER I.

COURTS AND THEIR JURISDICTION.

The Courts provided for this Territory are a Supreme Court, District Courts, Probate Courts, and Justices of the Peace.

The Supreme Court has no original jurisdiction, except in habeas corpus cases. It exercises an appellate jurisdiction, principally in cases coming up from the District Courts.

The District Courts have chancery and common law jurisdiction, and jurisdiction in appeals from the Justice and Probate Courts.

The Probate Court has no jurisdiction, except over probate business proper.

The Justices of the Peace have no jurisdiction of any matter in controversy where the title or boundaries of land may be in dispute, or where the debt or sum claimed shall exceed one hundred dollars.

CHAPTER II.

TERMS OF COURTS, WHEN AND WHERE HELD.

The Territory is divided into three judicial districts. Laramie county composes the first ; Albany and Carbon the second; Sweetwater and Uinta the third. Terms of Court are held in each, as follows :

At Cheyenne, commencing on the fourth Monday of May and first Monday of November of each year.

At Laramie, commencing on the first Monday of February and August of each year.

At Rawlins, commencing on the first Monday of April and second Monday of September of each year.

At Areen River, on the first Monday of May and October of each year.

At Evanston, commencing on the first Monday of January and July of each year.

CHAPTER III.

COMMENCEMENT OF ACTIONS, TIME TO ANSWER, PLACE OF TRIAL.

Actions are commenced by filing in the office of the clerk of the proper Court a petition, and causing a summons thereon to be issued. The summons is returnable on the second Monday after the day of its date, and the answer or demurrer of the defendant shall be filed on or before the third Saturday after the return day of the summons.

Civil actions must be tried in the county in which they are commenced, unless upon application for a change of venue based upon sufficient reasons the Court orders the place of trial to be changed; and in such case, the Court must send the cause to the most convenient county.

Chapter IV.

LIMITATION OF ACTIONS.

Actions for the recovery of real property can only be brought within twenty-one years after the cause of action shall have accrued, except actions of forcible entry and detainer, or forcible and unlawful detention, only of real property, which must be commenced within two years after the cause of action shall have accrued.

An action upon a specialty, or any agreement, contract or promise in writing, or on a foreign judgment, must be brought within fifteen years. And actions upon contract not in writing, express or implied, or upon a liability created by statute, must be brought within six years after the cause of action shall have accrued.

This Territory makes no discrimination against causes of action arising outside of its borders. With respect to limitation, all causes of action stand on the same footing, without reference to the place of contract or rendition of judgment.

15

CHAPTER V.

ATTACHMENTS.

The creditor in a civil action for the recovery of money may, at or after the commencement thereof, by filing the necessary affidavit, have an attachment against the property of the debtor, and upon the grounds herein stated:

1. When the debtor, or one of several debtors, is a foreign corporation, or a non-resident of this Territory.

2. Has absconded with the intent to defraud his creditors.

3. Has left the county of his residence to avoid the service of a summons.

4. So conceals himself that a summons cannot be served upon him.

5. Is about to remove his property, or a part thereof, out of the jurisdiction of the Court, with the intent to defraud his creditors.

6. Is about to convert his property, or a part thereof, into money, for the purpose of placing it beyond the reach of his creditors.

7. Has property or rights in action which he conceals.

8. Has assigned, removed, or disposed of, or is about to dispose of his property, or a part thereof, with the intent to defraud his creditors.

9. Fraudulently contracted the debt or incurred the obligation for which suit is about to be or has been brought.

But an attachment shall not be granted on the ground that the debtor is a foreign corporation, or a non-resident of this Territory, for any other claim than a debt or demand arising upon contract, judgment, or decree.

When a foreign corporation or non-resident is defendant, the writ may issue without an undertaking. In all other cases the writ will not be issued by the clerk of the Court until there has been executed and filed in his office an undertaking, with sureties

approved by him, in double the amount of plaintiff's claim, to the
effect that plaintiff shall pay all damages which defendant may sustain by reason of the attachment, if the writ be wrongfully obtained.

CHAPTER VI.

ARREST IN CIVIL ACTIONS.

No person can be imprisoned for debt in any civil action on mesne
or final process, unless in case of fraud.   An order for the arrest
of the debtor shall be made by the clerk of the Court in which the
action is brought, when there is filed in his office an affidavit of the
creditor, or his authorized agent or attorney, made before any judge
of any Court of the Territory, or clerk thereof, or justice of the
peace, stating the nature of the creditor's claim, that it is just, and
the amount thereof as nearly as may be, and establishing one or
more of the following particulars :

1. That the debtor has removed, or begun to remove, any of his
property out of the jurisdiction of the Court, with intent to defraud
his creditors.

2. That he has begun to convert his property, or a part thereof,
into money, for the purpose of placing it beyond the reach of his
creditors.

3. That he has property or rights of action which he fraudulently
conceals.

4. That he has assigned, removed, or disposed of, or has begun
to dispose of his property, or a part thereof, with intent to defraud
his creditors.

5. That he fraudulently contracted the debt or incurred the obligation for which suit is about to be or has been brought.

The affidavit must also contain a statement of the facts claimed to justify the belief in the existence of one or more of the above particulars. The creditor, before the issuing of the order of arrest, must give bond in double the amount of the claim stated in the affidavit. The death of a person under arrest does not satisfy the judgment.

Chapter VII.

JUDGMENT LIENS.

A judgment is a lien on the lands and tenements of a judgment debtor from the first day of the term at which it is rendered; but judgments by confession and judgments rendered at the same term at which the action is commenced bind such lands only from the date of their rendition.

If execution is not sued out within five years from the date of the rendition of judgment, such judgment becomes dormant, and ceases to operate as a lien. The judgment may subsequently be revived, but the lien is not restored, except from the date of revivor.

Chapter VIII.

EXECUTIONS, SALE, REDEMPTION AND EXEMPTIONS.

Executions are of three kinds:
1. Against the property of the judgment debtor.
2. Against his person.

3. For the delivery of the possession of real property, with damages for witholding the same and costs.

The officer having the writ must levy first on the goods and chattels of the debtor, but if no goods be found, he shall endorse on the writ " no goods," and forthwith levy the writ of execution upon the lands and tenements of the debtor liable to satisfy the judgment.

The officer may sell goods and chattels seized, by first publishing notice of the time and place of sale, for a period of ten days. Notice of the sale of lands and tenements must be published thirty days prior to the sale.

There is now in this Territory no statute providing for the redemption of property, either real or personal, sold on execution.

The exemptions from levy, or seizure, are a homestead not exceeding in value $1500, so long as it is actually occupied as such by the debtor and his family, the value to be ascertained by appraisers.

So, too, the following personal property, when owned by the head of a family who is residing with the same: Furniture, bedding, and provisions, and such other articles as the debtor may select, not exceeding in value $500.

There is also exempt the necessary wearing apparel of every person, not exceeding in value $50.

The tools, team, and implements, or stock in trade of any mechanic, miner or other person, used and kept for the purpose of carrying on his trade or business, not exceeding in value $300. Also the library, instruments and implements of any professional man, not exceeding in value $300.

There is no exemption in favor of a person not an actual resident of the Territory, nor one about to remove or abscond therefrom. And no article of property is exempt from attachment or sale, upon execution for the purchase money of said article of property.

CHAPTER IX.

PROCEEDINGS IN AID OF EXECUTIONS.

Proceedings in aid of executions may be had, in which the debtor may be examined and compelled to disclose and appropriate to the payment of the judgment any property which he may have unjustly refused to apply to that purpose.

A receiver may be appointed to take and dispose of such property of the judgment debtor that may be unearthed on examination, either legal or equitable, and appropriate the proceeds to the payment of the judgment.

CHAPTER X.

SECURITY FOR COSTS.

In all cases in which the plaintiff is a resident of the county in which the action is brought, he must furnish security for costs before commencing such action.

CHAPTER XI.

APPEALS.

In actions at law, final judgments and orders may be reviewed on writ of error, or petition in error sued out any time within three years after rendition.

In chancery cases, review may be had by appeal, if the appeal is perfected within thirty days after the decree complained of.

Where the judgment or decree sought to be reviewed is for the payment of money, security must be given in double the amount of the decree or judgment. In other cases the amount of security is fixed by the Court.

CHAPTER XII.

ESTATES OF DECEASED PERSONS.

Estates of deceased persons are settled in the Probate Courts through the usual means of executors and administrators.

Claims against the estate must be presented within one year after the granting of letters testamentary or of administration, and if not so presented, are forever barred.

Every executor and administrator must exhibit a statement of the accounts of his administration for settlement, with proper vouchers, to the Probate Court, at its first term after the end of six months from the date of his letters, and at the corresponding term of Court every six months until administration be completed.

Chapter XIII.

DESCENTS AND DISTRIBUTION OF PROPERTY.

1. Whenever any person having title to any real estate, or property having the nature or legal character of real estate, or personal estate undisposed or otherwise limited by marriage settlement, shall die intestate as to such estate, it shall descend and be distributed in parcenary to his kindred, male and female, subject to the payment of his debts, in the following course and manner, namely : If such intestate leave a husband or wife and children, or the descendants of any children, him or her surviving, one-half of such estate shall descend to such surviving husband or wife, and the residue thereof to such surviving children and descendants of children as hereinafter limited ; if such intestate leave a husband or wife and no child nor descendants of any child, then the real and personal estate of such intestate shall descend as follows, to wit : Three-fourths thereof to such surviving husband or wife, and one-fourth thereof to the father and mother of the intestate, or the survivor of them. *Provided,* That if the estate of such intestate, real and personal, does not exceed in value the sum of ten thousand dollars, then the whole thereof shall descend to and vest in the surviving husband or wife as his or her absolute estate, subject to the payment of debts as aforesaid. Dower and the tenancy by the courtesy are abolished, and neither husband nor wife shall have any share in the estate of the other save as herein provided. Except in cases above enumerated, the estate of any intestate shall descend and be distributed as follows:

First.—To his children surviving, and the descendants of his children who are dead, (the descendants collectively taking the share their parent would have taken if living).

Second.—If there be no children nor their descendants, then to his father, mother, brothers and sisters, and to the descendants of brothers and sisters who are dead, (the descendants collectively taking the share their parent would have taken if living) in equal parts.

Third.—If there be no children nor their descendants, nor father, mother, brothers, sisters, nor descendants of deceased brothers or sisters, nor husband nor wife living, then to the grandfather, grandmother, uncles, aunts and their descendants, (the descendants taking collectively the share of their immediate ancestors) in equal parts.

2. All posthumous children or descendants of the intestate shall inherit in like manner as if born in the lifetime of the intestate ; but no right of inheritance shall accrue to any person other than the children or descendants of the intestate, unless they are in being, and capable in law of taking as heirs at the time of the intestate's death.

3. Children, and descendants of children of the half-blood, shall inherit the same as children and descendants of the whole blood, but collateral relations of the half-blood shall inherit only half the measure of collateral relatives of the whole blood, if there be any of the last named class living.

4. Where any of the children of the intestate shall have received in his lifetime any real or personal estate, by way of advancement, and the other heirs desire it to be charged to him, the probate judge shall cite the parties to appear before him, shall hear proof upon the subject, and shall determine the amount of such advancement or advancements to be thus charged.

5. The maintenance, education or supply of money to a child under the age of majority, without any view to apportion or settlement in life, shall not be deemed an advancement under section four.

6. The alienage of the descendants shall not invalidate any title to real estate which shall descend from him or her.

7. Illegitimate children shall inherit the same as those born in wedlock, if the parents subsequently intermarry, and such children be recognized after such intermarriage by the father to be his. Illegitimate children inherit from the mother, and the mother from the children.

8. Divorces of husband and wife shall not affect the right of children personally together, to inherit their property.

9. Probate judges and administrators of the estates of persons dying intestate within this Territory, shall apportion and distribute estates of intestates according to this Act.

10. The rule of descent of all property of whatsoever kind or nature, real or personal, of any bastard or illegitimate person, dying intestate in this Territory, and leaving property and effects therein, shall be as follows, to wit : On the death of any such person intestate, his or her property, estate and effects shall descend to and vest in the widow, or the surviving husband and children, as the property and effects of other persons in like cases. In case of the death of any such illegitimate person leaving no children, or descendants of a child or children, then the whole property and estate, rights, credits and effects shall descend to and vest in the widow or surviving husband. In case of any such illegitimate person leaving no widow, surviving husband, or descendants, then the property and estate of such person shall descend to and vest in the mother and her children, and their descendants ; to the mother one-half, and the other half to be equally divided between her children and their descendants, the descendants of a child taking the share of their deceased parent or ancestors. In case of the death of any such illegitimate person leaving no heirs as above provided, then the property and effects, of whatsoever kind or nature, shall pass to and vest in the next of kin to the mother of such illegitimate person, in the same manner as the estate of a legitimate person would, by law, pass to the next of kin.

11. If any decedent leaves a widow residing in this Territory, in all cases she shall be allowed to have and retain as her sole and separate property one bed and bedding, wearing apparel for herself and family, two cows, her saddle and bridle, one horse, household furniture for herself and family, and also the same amount and species of property, real and personal, as is or may be by law exempt from execution. Said property shall be retained by the widow, and set apart to her by the executor or administrator, and shall in no case be subject to the payment of debts of the deceased.

12. When an inventory shall have been made of the personal estate of any testator or intestate, the widow may relinquish her right to all of the specified articles of property allowed to her by

the preceding section ; or in case the intestate shall not leave any
or all of the articles specified, in either case she shall be entitled to
other property, or the value of the same in money ; and it shall be
the duty of the administrator or Court of probate to allow the value
of the articles specified by law to be set apart to the widow of any
intestate, to be allowed her in money, or other personal property, at
her election.

13.   The right of a widow to her separate property shall in no
case be affected by her renouncing, or failing to renounce, the benefit of the provisions made for her in the will of her husband, or otherwise.

CHAPTER XIV.

DEPOSITIONS.

No person is disqualified as a witness by reason of his interest
in the event of suit.

Depositions may be taken as soon as a case is commenced, and
may be used when the witness does not reside in the county where
the action is pending, or is absent therefrom ; or when from age or
infirmity or imprisonment of the witness he is unable to attend
Court, or is dead ; or when in any case oral examination is not
required ; or in cases of appeal from Justices' Courts.

They may be taken in or out of the Territory, before a justice
of the peace, chancellor, or judge of any Court of record, notary
public, mayor, or chief magistrate of any city or town corporate,
a commissioner appointed by the Governor of the Territory, or any
person authorized by special commission from the Territory.

They may be taken in narrative form or by questions and
answers, except in chancery cases, in which they must be taken on
interrogatories and cross-interrogatories, settled before issuing the

commission. In law cases they may be taken on notice or commission issued by the clerk of the Court.

Chapter XV.

JUDICIAL RECORDS.

The judicial records of another State must be proven in accordance with the provisions of the Act of Congress, except judgments of justices of the peace, whose proceedings may be authenticated by his own certificate, supported by the official certificate of the clerk of any Court of record in the county in which such justice resides, that his signature is genuine, and that he is an acting justice of the peace of that county.

Chapter XVI.

ACKNOWLEDGMENTS.

Deeds or mortgages, executed within this Territory, of lands or any interest in lands, shall be executed in the presence of two witnesses, who shall subscribe their names to the same as such; and the person executing such deeds or mortgages may acknowledge the execution thereof before any judge or commissioner of a Court of record, or before any notary public or justice of the peace within the Territory; and the officer taking such acknowledgment shall indorse thereon a certificate of the acknowledgment thereof, and the true date of making the same, under his hand, and seal of office if there be one.

If any such deed or mortgage shall be executed in any other State, Territory or District of the United States, such deed or mortgage may be executed according to the laws of such State, Territory or District, by any officer authorized by the laws of such State, Territory or District to take the acknowledgment of deeds or mortgages therein, or before any commissioner appointed by the Governor of this Territory for such purposes.

In the cases provided for in the last preceding section, unless the acknowledgment be taken before a commissioner appointed by the Governor of this Territory for that purpose, such deed or mortgage shall have attached thereto a certificate of the clerk or other proper certifying officer of the Court of record of the county or district within which such acknowledgment was taken under the seal of his office, that the person whose name is subscribed to the certificate of acknowledgment was, at the date thereof, such officer as he is therein represented to be, that he knows the signature of such person subscribed thereto to be genuine, and that the deed or mortgage is executed and acknowledged according to the laws of such State, Territory, or District.

CHAPTER XVII.

LIMITED PARTNERSHIPS.

There is no statute concerning limited partnerships in the Territory.

Chapter XVIII.

MARRIED WOMEN.

Married women retain their property, real and personal, which they had at marriage, or which they acquire thereafter from any person other than their husband, in good faith, as their own, free from the husband's control, and free from liability for his debts. They may bargain, sell and convey personal property as if they were sole ; may make a will, be sued and sue as if they were sole ; may carry on any trade or business on their own account. The husband is not liable for the debts of the wife contracted before marriage. When judgment is rendered against both for the tort of the wife the judgment must be satisfied first out of the property of the wife, if she have any.

Chapter XIX.

CHATTEL MORTGAGES.

Chattel mortgages must be executed in the presence of two witnesses, and acknowledged before some one authorized to take acknowledgment of deeds, and filed in the office of the county recorder of the county where the property is ; and it then becomes a lien on the property described therein for one year ; and if it so provide, the property mortgaged may be left in possession of the mortgagor. All goods and chattels may be mortgaged.

CHAPTER XX.

INTEREST AND USURY.

The legal rate of interest is twelve per cent. per annum ; but any rate that may be agreed on is legal.   Judgments draw twelve per cent. from the date of their rendition.

PART IX.

MONTANA TERRITORY.

PREPARED EXPRESSLY FOR THIS WORK BY W. E. CULLEN, HELENA.

CHAPTER I.

COURTS, THEIR JURISDICTION AND TERMS:

The Courts of the Territory are a Supreme Court, District Courts, Probate Court, and Justices of the Peace.

The Supreme Court has appellate jurisdiction only.

The District Courts have original jurisdiction of all civil cases where the amount in controversy exceeds fifty dollars, and of all felonies; also appellate jurisdiction from the Probate and Justices' Courts.

The Probate Court, in addition to probate matters, has jurisdiction in civil actions to the amount of five hundred dollars, except where the title or right to the possession of land is in question, and in chancery and divorce cases. The Probate Court also has jurisdiction of such criminal cases arising under the laws of the Territory as do not require the intervention of a grand jury.

Justices of the Peace have jurisdiction where the title of land is not in dispute, and where the debt or sum claimed does not exceed one hundred dollars.

The District Court, when sitting at Helena, Deer Lodge, and

16

Bozeman, has the same jurisdiction as the Circuit and District Courts of the United States, and the first six days of each term at said places are appropriated to the trial of causes arising under the constitution and laws of the United States.

TERMS OF DISTRICT COURTS, 1876.

COUNTY.	COUNTY SEAT.	DIST.	WHEN HELD.
Beaverhead...	Bannack.......	2d....	First Monday in June, second Monday in October.
Deer Lodge...	Deer Lodge.....	2d....	Second Monday in April, first Monday in September.
Gallatin......	Bozeman.......	1st ...	First Monday in May, second Monday in October.
Jefferson......	Radersburg.....	3d....	First Monday in April, first Monday in October.
Madison	Virginia City...	1st ...	Third Monday in March, third Monday in September.
Meagher......	Diamond City...	3d....	Fourth Monday in May, fourth Monday in October.
Meissoula	Meissoula	2d....	Fourth Monday in June, Second Monday in November.
Lewis & Clark.	Helena.........	3d....	First Monday in March, second Monday in September, and first Monday in November.

Terms of the Supreme Court are held at the capital, Helena,. on first Monday in January and second Monday in August.

CHAPTER II.

TIME ALLOWED DEFENDANT TO ANSWER—PLACE OF TRIAL OF CIVIL ACTIONS.

TIME ALLOWED DEFENDANT TO ANSWER.

Ten days if served in the county, twenty days if served outside the county but in the district; forty days in all other cases.

PLACE OF TRIAL OF CIVIL ACTIONS.

Actions for the recovery of real estate, or for injuries thereto,

for partition thereof, or for foreclosure of mortgage thereon, must
be tried in the county where the same is situated.

Actions for the recovery of a penalty or forfeiture imposed by
statute, or against a public officer, must be tried in the county
where the cause arose.

In all other cases the action is to be tried in the county in
which the defendant may reside, or in the county where the plaintiff resides and the defendant may be found.

CHAPTER III.

LIMITATION OF ACTIONS.

Upon a judgment or decree of a United States Court, or of any
State or Territory, ten years.

Upon any contract, obligation or liability, founded upon an instrument of writing, ten years.

Actions for waste or trespass upon real property ; for a liability
created by statute, other than a penalty or forfeiture ; for taking,
detaining or injuring goods or chattels, and for relief on the ground
of fraud, must be commenced within three years.

Actions against a sheriff, coroner or constable, for any act in his
official capacity, must be commenced within two years.

Actions upon an account, contract, obligation or liability not
grounded upon an instrument of writing, must be commenced within five years.

An action for a penalty or forfeiture given by statute, or for
libel, slander, assault, battery or false imprisonment, must be commenced within two years.

Actions for relief not provided for, as above, must be commenced within three years after the cause of action accrued.

If the party against whom the action accrues is out of the
Territory at the time, the statute does not run until his return, and
if, after the action has accrued, he depart from the Territory, the
time of his absence is not a part of the time limited for the commencement of an action.   A part payment revives a debt which
has been barred.   No acknowledgment or promise is sufficient to
take a case out of the statute, unless it be in writing and signed by
the party to be charged.   A cause of action arising in any other
State or Territory, and barred by the laws of such State or Territory, cannot be maintained here.

Chapter IV.

ATTACHMENTS—ARRESTS IN CIVIL CASES.

Attachments.

An attachment will issue in all cases where an affidavit is made
by or on behalf of the plaintiff, that the defendant is indebted to
the plaintiff upon a contract for the payment of money, gold dust
or other property then due, which is not secured by a mortgage,
lien or pledge upon either real or personal property; and upon
giving an undertaking in double the amount of the debt sought to
be recovered, if the same does not exceed in amount $1000, and
in the amount sought to be recovered if over $1000, conditioned
that the plaintiff will pay all costs that may be awarded to the defendant, and all damages which he may sustain by reason of such attachment, if the defendant recovers judgment, or the Court finally
decides that the plaintiff was not entitled to an attachment.

ARRESTS IN CIVIL CASES.

Arrest may be had in all cases of fraud, or when the action is for willful injury to person or character, or to property, knowing the property to belong to another.

CHAPTER V.

JUDGMENT LIENS, EXECUTIONS, EXEMPTIONS, SALE AND REDEMPTION.

A judgment rendered by the District Court is a lien upon all the real estate of defendant in the county wherein it is docketed, and is such lien for the period of two years.

Execution may be issued at any time within five years after the entry of the judgment. Executions may be issued to several counties at the same time.

The following articles are exempt from execution: wearing apparel of judgment debtor and family, also all chairs, tables, desks, to the value of $100; all necessary household and kitchen furniture, including stoves, stovepipes and stove furniture, beds, bedding and provisions, and fuel actually provided for use sufficient for one month; and also one horse, two cows with their calves, two swine and fifty domestic fowls; one sewing machine not exceeding the value of $100, in actual use by the debtor or his family; also to a farmer, farming utensils, also two oxen or horses, or two mules and their harness, two cows, one cart or wagon, and food for such animals for one month; also all seed grain or vegetables actually reserved for planting.

To a mechanic or artisan, tools or implements necessary to carry on his trade.

To a physician, the instruments and chest necessary to the exercise of his profession, together with his library and one horse and vehicle.

To an attorney at law, or a minister of the Gospel, their libraries.

To a miner, his cabin, sluices, mining tools and appliances not to exceed in value $500; also two horses, mules or oxen, and food for the same for one month, and their harness, when necessary to be used for any windlass, derrick or pump.

To a cartman, truckster, peddler, teamster or laborer, two horses, two mules, or two oxen and their harness, and one cart or wagon, by the use of which such person habitually earns his living.

Also the earnings of the judgment debtor for thirty days' next preceding the levy of execution, when such earnings are necessary for the support of the debtor's family.

A homestead not exceeding in value $2500; if agricultural land, not more than eighty acres; if within the limit of a town or city or village, not more than one-fourth of an acre.

The sheriff is required to give notice of sale as follows: by posting notice of the time and place of such sale in three public places of the township or city where the sale is to take place, for such time as may be reasonable in case of perishable property; in case of other personal property, not less than five nor more than ten days.

In case of real property, by posting a similar notice for twenty days, and publishing a copy thereof once a week for the same period in some newspaper published in the county, if there be one. In all sales of real property, where the estate is greater than the unexpired term of a two years' lease, the same may be redeemed within six months from such sale, by—first, the judgment debtor, second, a creditor having a lien by judgment or mortgage on the property sold, or some part thereof.

CHAPTER VI.

PROCEEDINGS SUPPLEMENTARY TO EXECUTIONS.

When an execution is returned unsatisfied, the judgment credit-or may compel the debtor to appear before a judge and answer concerning his property, and upon such hearing witnesses may be examined. If any property is found, the judge may order the same applied on execution.

CHAPTER VII.

SECURITY FOR COSTS—APPEALS.

SECURITY FOR COSTS.

Security may be required in all cases where suit is brought by a non-resident ; and where such security is required, all proceedings are stayed, and the action will be dismissed unless an undertaking is filed in such amount as may be fixed by the Court within thirty days. Security may also be required of the plaintiff, where the defendant makes oath that the plaintiff is insolvent.

APPEALS.

Same as in California.

CHAPTER VIII.

ESTATES OF DECEASED PERSONS—HOMESTEADS.

ESTATES OF DECEASED PERSONS.

Demands against the estate of a deceased person must be exhibited for allowance within two years after granting letters, or they will be barred.   Any officer authorized to administer an oath may take proof of claims.   There is no time limited for the settlement of an estate.

HOMESTEADS.

Not exceeding in value $2500, to consist of not more than eighty acres of land ; or if within the limits of a town site, not to exceed one-fourth of an acre is exempt.

CHAPTER IX.

DEPOSITIONS—JUDICIAL RECORDS—ACKNOWLEDG-MENTS.

DEPOSITIONS.

Same law as in California, from which our code was taken.

JUDICIAL RECORDS

Of another State or Territory are proved by the production of exemplified copies.

ACKNOWLEDGMENTS.

Every conveyance affecting real estate must be in writing and acknowledged, or proved and certified. The following is a general form of acknowledgment, viz:

TERRITORY OF MONTANA, } ss.
     COUNTY OF————— }

Be it remembered, that on this——day of———, 187—, personally appeared before the undersigned, a [title of office] within and for the county aforesaid, personally appearing, came——— —— to me, personally known to me to be the same person mentioned in and who executed the foregoing instrument, and he acknowledged to me that he had so executed the same freely and voluntarily, and for the uses and purposes therein expressed.

Witness my hand, etc.

If a married woman is a party, the certificate must state that the officer examined her apart from and without the hearing of her husband, and that she then acknowledged that she executed the same freely and voluntarily, without fear of or under compulsion of her said husband, and that she did not wish to retract the execution of the same.

CHAPTER X.

LIMITED PARTNERSHIPS

May be created by two or more persons who shall be responsible as general partners, and two or more persons who shall contribute to the common stock a specific sum in actual cash payments.

The special partners not to be liable for any debt of the partnership. In order to create such partnership it is necessary that a certificate, stating the name of the partnership firm, the place of residence of each of the general and special partners, the amount of the capital which each special partner has contributed, the general nature of the business, the time when the partnership is to commence and when it is to terminate, shall be made, acknowledged and recorded in the office of the county recorder of the county in which the principal place of business of the partnership is located. Any false statement in such certificate subjects all parties to liability as general partners.

CHAPTER XI.

MARRIED WOMEN

Are liable on their contracts made for benefit of or with reference to their separate property. They may become sole traders by filing a certificate in the county recorder's office, and conduct business as a *femme sole*.

CHAPTER XII.

CORPORATIONS—CHATTEL MORTGAGES—INTEREST.

CORPORATIONS.

There is no individual liability of stockholders for indebtedness of a corporation, beyond the amount of the unpaid stock which they hold.

CHATTEL MORTGAGES.

All personal property may be pledged or mortgaged, and such mortgages must be foreclosed promptly when due. No chattel mortgage can be made for a longer period than twelve months.

INTEREST AND USURY.

The legal rate of interest is ten per cent., but any rate for which parties may contract is collectable. There is no usury law.

PART X.

WASHINGTON TERRITORY.

PREPARED EXPRESSLY FOR THIS WORK BY JAMES K. KENNEDY, WALLA WALLA.

CHAPTER I.

COURTS AND THEIR JURISDICTION.

The Territory is divided into three judicial districts, each having a judge, who together compose the Supreme Court.

The Supreme Court has appellate jurisdiction only, and causes are removed to it from the District Courts by writs of error or appeals.

The several District Courts have general common law and chancery jurisdiction, in all matters where the amount in controversy exceeds one hundred dollars. They have also general jurisdiction in causes arising under the laws of the United States, and in admiralty and bankruptcy.

There is a Probate Court in each county, holding four terms each per annum, having statutory jurisdiction in all matters pertaining to decedents' estates, and the guardianship and estates of minors and insane persons. They have no common law jurisdiction except such as is strictly necessary to carry out and enforce that defined by statute.

Justices of the Peace have jurisdiction coëxtensive with the limits of their respective counties, over all causes arising on contract for the recovery of money only, when the sum claimed does not exceed one hundred dollars, and in actions for damages for injury to person or property, or for taking or detaining personal property, if the damages claimed do not exceed one hundred dollars; also in actions on undertakings or bonds, when the penalty or amount claimed does not exceed one hundred dollars; also in actions for the foreclosure of mortgages, or the enforcement of liens on personal property, when the debt secured does not exceed one hundred dollars; also in actions for damages for fraud and deceit in the sale, purchase, or exchange of personal property, when the damages claimed do not exceed one hundred dollars; also in actions of forcible entry and detainer; also in actions to try the right of possession to mining claims. They may also take and enter judgment on the confession of a defendant, or upon default for a failure to appear or answer.

CHAPTER II.

TERMS OF COURTS—WHEN AND WHERE HELD.

The Supreme Court holds one term in each year, at Olympia, commencing on the second Monday of July.

The District Court of the first judicial district, Hon. S. C. Wingard, judge, is held for the counties of Walla Walla and Columbia, at Walla Walla City, on the first Monday of May and third Monday of October; for the county of Yakima, at Yakima City, on the first Monday of October of each year; for the counties of Stevens and Whitman, at Colfax, on the first Monday of June of each year.

The District Court of the second judicial district, Hon. R. S. Green, judge, is held for the counties of Klickitat, Skamania and Clark, at Vancouver, on the third Monday of March and third Monday of November of each year ; for the counties of Cowlitz, Wahkiakum and Pacific, at Kalama, on the first Monday in January and the fourth Monday in June ; for the counties of Thurston, Lewis, Mason and Chehalis, at Olympia, on the first Monday in April and first Monday in December.

The District Court of the third judicial district, Hon. J. R. Lewis, C. J., judge, is held for the county of Pierce, at Steilacoom, on the first Monday of January and first Monday of August ; for the counties of King, Kitsap and Snohomish, at Seattle, on the fourth Monday of January and third Monday of August ; for the counties of Jefferson, Island, Whatcom, San Juan and Clallam, at Port Townsend, on the fourth Monday of February and fourth Monday of September.

In addition to the above terms of Court, prescribed by Act of the Legislative Assembly, power is given to the judges of each district to appoint, by rule from time to time, two special terms in each year, at which to transact all business, except trials by jury, and the hearing causes on their merits.

Terms of the Probate Courts are held at the county seat of each county on the fourth Mondays of January, April, July and October, of each year.

Justices' Courts are always open for the transaction of business.

CHAPTER III.

COMMENCEMENT OF SUITS—TIME ALLOWED TO ANSWER.

Actions in the District Courts are commenced by filing the complaint with the clerk, and the issuing a summons thereon at any time within one year of such filing. The defendant is required to answer the complaint as follows: if served within the county where the action is brought, twenty days; if served out of the county but in the district in which the action is brought, thirty days; in all other cases, sixty days. If the defendant fails to appear and answer according to the requirements of the summons, the plaintiff is entitled to have the default entered, and judgment for the amount specified in the summons, or for the relief prayed for in the complaint. The complaint and all subsequent proceedings in an action, except a demurrer, must be verified by the party, (his agent or attorney, in the county where the action is brought) to the effect that he believes it to be true. All common law forms of pleadings, and all distinctions between law and equity as to form, are abolished, and the code system adopted.

In Probate Court, most of the business can be commenced, preliminary orders granted, and writs issued by the judge in vacation. Orders or decrees for the sale of real estate, the settlement of estates, and discharge of executors, administrators, or guardians, and final orders and decrees generally, must be heard and decided in term time.

Actions are commenced in Justices' Courts by filing with the justice a complaint or account, verified by the party, his agent or attorney, to the effect that he believes it to be true, and the issuance of a summons or notice thereon. The summons or notice is returnable in not less than six, nor more than twenty days, from the filing the complaint.

CHAPTER IV.

PLACE OF TRIAL OF CIVIL ACTIONS.

Actions for the recovery of the possession of, or for the foreclosure of a mortgage on, or in any wise affecting the title to real property, and all questions involving the right or title to personal property, or for the detention or injury to such property, shall be brought in the county in which the subject of the action or some part thereof is situated.

Actions for a penalty or forfeiture imposed by statute, or against public officers, shall be tried in the county or district where the cause of action or some part thereof arose.

Actions against corporations may be brought in any county where the corporation has an office for the transaction of business, or any person resides upon whom process against such corporation may be served. In all other cases the action shall be commenced and tried in the district embracing the county in which the defendants, or either of them reside, or may be served with process; or if none of them reside in the Territory, the same may be tried in any district or county which the plaintiff may designate in his complaint.

CHAPTER V.

LIMITATION OF ACTIONS.

The period prescribed for the limitation of actions, from the time the cause of action accrues, is as follows:

For the recovery of real property, or the possession thereof, twenty years; upon a judgment or decree of any Court of the United States, or of any State or Territory within the United States, or upon a contract in writing or liability, express or implied, arising out of a written agreement, or for the rents and profits, or use and occupation of real estate, six years; for waste or trespass upon real property, or for taking, detaining, or injuring personal property, including an action for the recovery thereof, or for any other injury to the person or rights of another not hereinafter

17

enumerated ; upon a contract or liability, express or implied, which is not in writing, and does not arise out of any written instrument; for relief upon the ground of fraud, (the cause of action in such case not to be deemed to have accrued until the discovery by the aggrieved party of the facts constituting the fraud) against a ministerial officer upon a liability incurred by the doing an act in his official capacity, or by the omission of an official duty, including the non-payment of money collected upon execution ; upon a statute for a penalty or forfeiture, and for seduction aud breach of marriage contract, three years ; for libel, slander, assault, assault and battery and false imprisonment, actions upon a statute for a forfeiture or penalty to the Territory, two years ; against a sheriff or other officer, for the escape of a prisoner arrested or imprisoned on civil process, one year.

When the cause of action arises in another State or Territory, between a resident of that State or Territory and of this Territory, the foregoing limitations apply.   When the cause of action arises in another State or Territory between non-residents of this Territory, and the same would be barred there by the lapse of time, it will be barred here.   An action shall be deemed commenced as to each defendant when the complaint is filed.

Chapter VI.

ATTACHMENTS.

The plaintiff, at the time of issuing the summons, or at any time thereafter, and before judgment, may have the property of the defendant attached as security for the satisfaction of such judgment as he may recover, whenever he or any one on his behalf shall make and file an affidavit that a cause of action exists against the de-

fendant, and the grounds thereof, and that the defendant is either—
first, a foreign corporation ; or second, that he is not a resident of
this Territory, or has departed therefrom with intent to delay or defraud his creditors, or to avoid the service of process, or keeps
himself concealed therein with like intent ; or third, that he has
removed or is about to remove any of his property from the Territory with intent to delay or defraud his creditors ; or fourth, that
he has assigned, secreted or disposed of any of his property, or is
about to assign, secrete or dispose of it with intent to delay or defraud his creditors ; or fifth, that the defendant has been guilty of a
fraud in contracting the debt or incurring the obligation for which
the action is brought.

Before the writ issues the plaintiff must file with the clerk a
bond, with one or more sureties, in a sum not less than one hundred dollars and equal to the amount for which the plaintiff demands
judgment, to the effect that the plaintiff will pay all costs that may
be adjudged to the defendant, and all damages which he may sustain by reason of the attachment, if the same be wrongful, oppres-
sive, or without sufficient cause.   All property may be attached
not by law exempt from execution, including debts owing to defendant. The defendant may have the property attached delivered
to him by executing to the sheriff a bond, with surety approved by
him, to the effect that such property shall be properly kept and delivered upon demand, to be held on execution ; or that he will pay
the appraised value thereof; or the defendant may, before the time
for answering expires, apply to the Court or judge for the discharge
of the attachment, on the grounds that it was improperly or improvi-
dently issued.

Writs of attachment may be issued by justices of the peace,
upon any of the foregoing grounds, except that the debt was contracted in fraud, and on the additional grounds that the defendant
is a non-resident of the county, or is secretly leaving or has left the
county, with the intent to hinder, delay, or defraud his creditors.

Chapter VII.

ARREST IN CIVIL ACTIONS.

The defendant, upon an order of the Court or judge of the Supreme Court, may be arrested in the following cases, and no other:

1. In an action for the recovery of damages on a cause of action not arising out of contract, where the defendant is a non-resident of the Territory, or is about to remove therefrom, or where the action is for an injury to person or character, or for injuring or wrongfully taking, detaining, or converting property.

2. In an action for a fine or penalty, or on a promise to marry, or for money received, or property embezzled or fraudulently misapplied, or converted to his own use by a public officer, or by an attorney, or by an officer or agent of a corporation in the course of his employment as such, or by any factor, agent, broker, or other person in a fiduciary capacity, or for any misconduct or neglect in office, or in a professional employment.

3. In an action to recover the possession of personal property unjustly detained, when the property, or any part thereof, has been concealed, removed, or disposed of, so that it cannot be found or taken by the sheriff, with the intent that it should not be so found or taken, or with the intent to deprive the plaintiff of the benefit thereof.

4. When the defendant has been guilty of fraud in contracting the debt or incurring the obligation for which the action is brought, or in concealing or disposing of the property for the taking, detention, or conversion of which the action is brought.

5. When the defendant has removed or disposed of his property, or is about to do so, with intent to defraud his creditors.

6. When the action is to prevent threatened injury to, or destruction of, property, and the danger is imminent that such property will be destroyed, or its value impaired, to the injury of plaintiff.

7. On the final judgment or order of any Court in the Territory,

when the defendant having no property subject to execution, or not
sufficient to satisfy the judgment, has money which he ought to apply in payment upon such judgment, which he refuses to apply,
with intent to defraud plaintiff; or when he refuses to comply with
the legal order of the Court, with intent to defraud the plaintiff.

The Court or judge making the order shall first be satisfied by
affidavit of the party, his agent or attorney, *and other proof in
writing*, that one or more of the above causes exist. Before the
order of arrest issues, the plaintiff, or some one in his behalf, shall
file a bond with the clerk in such amount as the Court or judge
may have fixed in the order, with sureties to the satisfaction of the
clerk, conditioned to pay to the defendant all damages he shall
suffer and all expenses he shall incur by reason of such arrest and
imprisonment, if the order be vacated, or if the plaintiff fail to recover in his action. The defendant may, on motion, apply to the
Court to vacate the order of arrest on the ground of insufficiency
of the proof, or he may show that the facts alleged are untrue, or
he may give bail.

The grounds for issuing a warrant of arrest by a justice of the
peace are the same as above.

CHAPTER VIII.

JUDGMENTS AND JUDGMENT LIENS.

In addition to judgments of non-suit and judgments upon the
merits, either on trial by jury or by the Court, the plaintiff may
have judgment by failure of the defendant to appear and answer,
or upon the confession of judgment by defendant. A judgment in
the District Court is a direct lien on the real estate of the defendant in the county where the judgment is rendered for twenty days

after the expiration of the term. The plaintiff, to continue the lien, must, at the expiration of said·twenty days, file a transcript of the judgment in the office of the county auditor of any county where the real estate is situated, which lien shall continue for five years from the date of the judgment.

To make a judgment in Justices' Courts a lien on real estate, the plaintiff must file a transcript of such judgment in the office of the clerk of the District Court, and file such transcript, certified by the clerk, in the office of the county auditor of the county where the real estate is situated.

Chapter IX.

EXECUTIONS, EXEMPTIONS, SALES, AND REDEMPTIONS.

The plaintiff may have execution on a judgment at any time within five years after its rendition; if the period of five years shall have elapsed without an execution having been issued, none shall issue unless the creditor or his assignee shall file a motion with the clerk of the Court to issue an execution, verified in like manner as a complaint, and shall cause notice of such motion to be served on the judgment debtor in like manner and with like effect as a summons. The motion shall be tried as any other action. Upon hearing the motion, the Court may order that judgment be entered and docketed as other judgments. Executions require the sheriff to exhaust the personal property of the defendant, not exempt from execution, before levying on real estate. They can be issued to any sheriff in the Territory, when the defendant has property, by plaintiff, his agent or attorney, making an affidavit that the defendant has not sufficient property in the county where the execution issued, to satisfy the judgment, but that he has property subject to execution in such other county. Execution may be stayed by defendant on giving a bond to the opposite party in double the amount of the judgment and costs, with surety to the satisfaction of the clerk, conditioned to pay said judgment, interest, costs, and increased costs, at the expiration of the period of the stay, which is as follows : In the Supreme Court, on all sums under $500, thirty days ; on all sums over $500 and under $1500, sixty days ; on all sums over $1500, ninety days.   In the District Court, on all sums under $300, two months ; on all sums over $300 and under $1000, five months ; on all sums over $1000, six months.   In Justices' Courts, on any sum not exceeding twenty-five dollars, one month ; more than twenty-five dollars, two months.

EXEMPTIONS.

All property, real and personal, belonging to a married woman at the time of her marriage, and all which she may subsequently acquire in her own right, and all the personal earnings, and all the issues, rents, and profits of such real estate, shall not be liable to attachment or execution upon any liability or judgment against the husband, so long as she or any minor heir of her body shall be living.   Every householder being the head of a family is entitled, as exempt from attachment and execution, to a homestead not exceeding in value the sum of one thousand dollars, while occupied as such by the owner thereof, or his or her family.   The following property shall also be exempt from execution : All wearing apparel, private libraries, family pictures, and keepsakes ; to each house-holder one bed and bedding, and one additional bed and bedding for every two members of the family, and other household goods, utensils, and furniture not exceeding $150, coin, in value ; two cows and calves, five swine, two stands of bees, twenty-five domestic fowls, and provisions and fuel for the comfortable main-tenance of such householder and family for six months.   To a farmer, one span of horses and harness, or two yoke of oxen, with yokes and chains, and one wagon ; also farming utensils, actually used about the farm, not exceeding in value $200 in coin.   To a mechanic, the tools of his trade, also material not exceeding in value $500 coin. To a physician, his library not exceeding in value $500 coin; also one horse and buggy, the instruments used in his practice, and medicines not exceeding in value $200 coin. To attorneys, clergymen, and other professional men, their libraries, not exceeding $500 coin value, and office furniture, fuel, and stationery, not exceeding $200 coin value. All firearms kept for the use of any person or family. To all persons, a canoe, skiff, or small boat, with its oars, sails and rigging, not exceeding $50 coin. To a person engaged in lightering for his support, one or more lighters, barges, or scows, and a small boat, with oars, sails and rigging, not exceeding in the aggregate $250 coin value. To a teamster or drayman, his team: the word team meaning a span of horses, harness, and one wagon or dray; a sufficient quantity of hay, grain or feed to keep the animals herein exempt for six months. No property shall be exempt from an execution issued on a judgment for the price or any part of the price thereof.

SALES.

Personal property is sold by the sheriff upon ten days' notice of the time and place of such sale, posted in three public places of the county: real estate, by posting similar notices, particularly describing the property, for four weeks in three public places of the county where the property is to be sold, and publishing a copy thereof once a week, for the same period, in a newspaper of the county. All sales of property upon execution shall be by auction. Sales of personal property shall be in view of the property, and of real estate, at the Court-house door.

REDEMPTION.

Sales of real estate are confirmed at the next term of the District Court, and the defendant, or his successor in interest, or any person having a lien thereon, may redeem such real estate within six months after confirmation, by paying the amount, with two per cent. interest per month.

CHAPTER X.

PROCEEDINGS SUPPLEMENTARY TO EXECUTION.

The plaintiff in proceedings supplementary to execution may upon a proper showing to the Court or judge, have an order requiring defendant to appear and answer as to any property which he may have subject to execution, and which ought to be applied on the judgment; or if it appears there is danger of the defendant absconding, the order may require his arrest, and upon being brought before the judge he may be ordered to enter into bond, with surety, that he will appear from time to time during such proceedings, and will not in the meantime dispose of any of his property subject to execution. Any person indebted to the defendant in a sum exceeding fifty dollars, may be required to appear and answer concerning the same.

CHAPTER XI.

SECURITY FOR COSTS.

When the plaintiff resides out of the district or county, or is a foreign corporation, security for costs may be required by the defendant; when required, all proceedings in the action shall be stayed until a bond, executed by two or more persons, be filed with the clerk, conditioned that they will pay such costs and charges as may be awarded against plaintiff, not exceeding the sum of $200.

Chapter XII.

APPEALS AND WRITS OF ERROR

May be taken from the District Courts to the Supreme Court of the Territory within six months from the date of the order, judgment or decree appealed from, and not afterwards. To stay proceedings in the Court below, the appellant or plaintiff in error must file a bond with sureties to the satisfaction of the clerk. Appeals from the Probate Court to the District Court must be taken within sixty days from the rendition of the decision or judgment, and from Justices of the Peace to the District Court, within twenty days from the date of the judgment. The party appealing shall execute and file with the justice a bond with one or more sureties in the sum of $100, to the effect that the appellant will pay all costs ; or if a stay of proceedings be claimed, a bond with two or more sureties in a sum equal to twice the amount of the judgment.

Chapter XIII.

ESTATES OF DECEASED PERSONS.

Claims against decedents' estates must be filed within one year from the publication of notice to creditors. The Court may, however, in its discretion, order a shorter time in any particular case, but not less than six months from the date of notice. To entitle a claim to be filed, it must be supported by the affidavit of the claimant that the amount is justly due, that no payments have been made thereon, and that there are no offsets to the same to the knowledge of the claimant. The oath may be taken before any officer authorized to administer oaths, and in a neighboring State or Territory, the oath, if not administered by a commissioner for the Territory, must be properly authenticated, the certificate stating that such person is authorized to administer oaths, and that his signature is genuine, with the seal of a Court of record to such certificate. The claim being thus proved, must be presented to the administrator for his allowance ; if he allow it, it is presented to the probate judge for his allowance, when, if allowed by him, the same is filed. If either the administrator or probate judge reject it, the party has three months within which to bring suit on it. Estates must be settled within one year, unless further time be granted by the Court.

CHAPTER XIV.

HOMESTEADS.

See Exemptions. A homestead may consist of a house and lot, or lots, in any city, or of a farm of any number of acres, so that their value does not exceed $1000.   To entitle a person to a homestead, he or she shall cause the word " homestead " to be entered of record in the margin of his or her recorded title to the same,

CHAPTER XV.

DEPOSITIONS

Of witnesses residing in the Territory may be taken, when the witness resides out of the district, and more than twenty miles from the place of trial; or when the witness is about to leave the district, and go more than twenty miles from the place of trial; or when he is sick, infirm, or aged, so as to make it probable he will not be able to attend the trial, before any judge of the District Court, justice of the peace, clerk of the Supreme or District Courts, mayor of a city or notary public, upon serving on the adverse party, or his attorney, three days' notice of the time and place of examination, and one day for every ten miles of the distance of the place of examination from the residence of the person to whom notice is given. The deposition must be read to the witness and signed by him, and certified by the officer taking the same. The deposition of a witness out of the Territory, but residing within a hundred miles of the place of holding Court, may be taken under a notice in the same manner, and before like character of officers as above. In all other cases, the deposition of a witness out of the Territory shall be taken upon a commission by the clerk, under the seal of the Court, upon the order of the Court or a judge thereof, upon giving to the opposite party or his attorney ten days' previous notice in writing, together with a copy of the interrogatories that may be put to the witness.

CHAPTER XVI.

JUDICIAL RECORDS OF OTHER STATES, HOW PROVED.

The records and proceedings of any Court of the United States, or any State or Territory, shall be admissible in evidence in all cases in Washington Territory, when authenticated by the attestation of the clerk, prothonotary, or other officer having charge of the records of such Court, with the seal of such Court annexed.

CHAPTER XVII.

ACKNOWLEDGMENTS.

All deeds affecting the title to real estate, or of any interest therein, and all contracts creating or evidencing any encumbrance on real estate, shall be by deed. All deeds must be acknowledged before one of the following officers, if made in the Territory: a judge of the Supreme Court, a judge of the Probate Court, a justice of the peace, a county auditor, a clerk or a regularly appointed deputy clerk of the District or Supreme Court, or a notary public, duly qualified. If made out of the Territory, but in the United States, they may be acknowledged before any person authorized to take acknowledgments of deeds by the laws of the State or Territory wherein the acknowledgment is taken, or before any commissioner appointed by the Governor of Washington Territory for such purpose. Unless such acknowledgment be taken before a commissioner,

such deed shall have attached thereto a certificate of the clerk or
other proper certifying officer of a Court of record of the county or
district within which the acknowledgment was taken, under the seal
of his office, that the person whose name is subscribed to the certificate of acknowledgment was, at the date thereof, such officer as
he is therein represented to be ; that he is authorized by law to take
acknowledgments of deeds ; and that he believes the signature of
the person subscribed thereto to be genuine.   If made in a foreign
country, out of the United States, they shall be acknowledged or
proved by two witnesses before any minister plenipotentiary, *charge
d'affaires*, consul, " general consul," vice-consul, or commercial
agent appointed by the government of the United States to any
foreign country, or the proper officer of any Court of such country,
or the mayor or other chief magistrate of any city, town, or corporation therein.   Such officer shall make and sign officially a certificate of acknowledgment, or of the proof by two witnesses, as the
case may be, which shall be annexed to the deed.

There are no particular requisites of an acknowledgment, except
in case of a married woman.   She shall not be bound by any deed
affecting her own real estate or any interest in real estate, unless
she shall be joined in the conveyance by her husband, and shall,
upon an examination by the officer taking the acknowledgment,
separate and apart from her husband, acknowledge that she did
voluntarily, of her own free will, and without the fear of or coercion
from her husband, execute the deed ; and the officer shall make
known to her the contents of the deed, and shall certify that he has
made known to her its contents, and examined her separate and
apart from her husband, as is above provided.   In case the husband and wife mortgage the homestead, the officer shall certify
that she did freely and voluntarily, separate and apart from her
husband, sign and acknowledge said mortgage, and the officer taking
the acknowledgment shall fully apprise her of her rights and the
effect of signing such mortgage.

Chapter XVIII.

LIMITED PARTNERSHIPS.

There is no law of limited partnerships in this Territory.   The liability of partners is unrestricted.

Chapter XIX.

MARRIED WOMEN

Cannot become sole traders in this Territory.   All property owned by the wife at the time of her marriage, and that acquired afterwards by gift, bequest, devise or descent, is her separate property, but is liable for her husband's debts, unless she has a recorded inventory of the same in the office of the county auditor of the county where the property is situated.   The wife can make no contract in her own right, except in particular cases affecting her separate property.

Chapter XX.

CORPORATIONS.

Each and every stockholder shall be personally liable to the creditors of the company *to the amount of what remains unpaid on his subscription to the capital stock, and not otherwise.*

CHAPTER XXI.

CHATTEL MORTGAGES

May be made upon locomotives, engines, and the other rolling stock of a railroad; steam machinery and machinery used by machinists, foundrymen, and mechanics; steamboat engines and boilers; mining machinery; printing presses and material; professional libraries; instruments of a physician, surgeon, or dentist; upholstery and furniture used in hotels or boarding-houses, when mortgaged to secure the purchase money of the articles mortgaged; growing crops; vessels of more than five tons burden. The mortgage must be accompanied by the affidavit of all the parties thereto that it is made in good faith, and without any design to hinder, delay, or defraud creditors. It must be acknowledged or proved, certified, and recorded in the same manner as deeds to real estate. It must be recorded in the office of the county auditor where the mortgagor resides, and also of the county in which the property mortgaged is situated, or to which it may be removed, and must be recorded in books kept for chattel mortgages exclusively.

CHAPTER XXII.

INTEREST.

The legal rate of interest is ten per cent. per annum, in the absence of any contract in writing, fixing a different rate. Parties may contract in writing for any rate of interest that they may agree upon.

PART XI.

ARIZONA TERRITORY.

CHAPTER I.

COURTS AND THEIR JURISDICTION.

The following are the Courts of justice for the Territory :

1. The Supreme Court. 2. The District Courts. 3. The Probate Courts. 4. The Justices' Courts.

The Supreme Court has appellate jurisdiction in all cases wherein the legality of any tax, toll, impost, or municipal fine is in question. It also has jurisdiction to review upon appeal—

First. A judgment in action or proceeding commenced in a District Court, or brought into that Court from another Court, where the matter in dispute exceeds one hundred dollars, or when the possession of, or title to lands or tenements is in controversy ; and to review upon the appeal from such judgment any intermediate or collateral order of the Court or judge at chambers, involving the merits and necessarily affecting the judgment.

Second. An order granting or refusing a new trial, sustaining or overruling a demurrer, or affecting a substantial right in an action or proceeding.

The District Courts have jurisdiction as follows :

Original jurisdiction in all civil cases where the amount exceeds

18

one hundred dollars, exclusive of interest, and in cases involving the title or possession of real property.

Appellate jurisdiction in Justice Court actions, and orders of judgments of the Probate Courts in certain cases.

The Probate Courts have jurisdiction of estates of deceased persons.

Justices' Courts have jurisdiction as follows:

1. Of an action arising on contract for the recovery of money only, if the sum claimed does not exceed three hundred dollars.

2. Of an action for damages for injury to the person, or for taking or detaining personal property, or for injuring real or personal property, if the damages claimed do not exceed three hundred dollars.

3. Of an action upon a bond conditioned for the payment of money not exceeding three hundred dollars, though the penalty exceed that sum, the judgment to be given for the sum actually due; when the payments are to be made by installments, an action may be brought for each installment as it becomes due.

4. Of an action for the foreclosure of any mortgage, or the enforcement of any lien on personal property, where the debt secured does not exceed three hundred dollars.

5. Of an action to recover personal property, when the value of such personal property does not exceed three hundred dollars.

Their jurisdiction does not extend to civil actions in which the title to real property is brought in question.

CHAPTER II.

TERMS OF COURTS, WHEN AND WHERE HELD.

The Supreme Court is held at Tucson, commencing on the first Monday in January of each year.

The District Courts in the several counties are held as follows:

Pima County, on the second Monday of February and first Monday in August, of each year.

Yuma County, on the third Monday of March and first Monday of December, in each year.

Yavapai County, on the first Monday of May and first Monday of October, in each year.

Maricopa County, on the first Monday of April and first Monday in September, of each year.

Mohave County, on the first Monday of June and the second Monday in November, of each year.

Pinal County, on the first Monday of June, in each year.

District Court is held at the county seat of each county.

Probate Court is held at the county seat of each county, on the first Monday of January, April, July and October, in each year, and the judge may hold such adjourned or special terms as he thinks proper.

Justices' Courts are always open for the transaction of business.

CHAPTER III.

COMMENCEMENT OF SUITS.

Civil actions are commenced by filing a complaint with the Court or justice, and issuing a summons thereon.

The defendant is required to answer the complaint in District Court actions as follows:

1. If the defendant is served within the county in which the action is brought—twenty days.

2. If the defendant is served out of the county, but in the district in which the action is brought—thirty days.

3. In all other cases—forty days.

Where personal service cannot be had, by reason of the defendant being out of the Territory, or where he conceals himself to avoid service of process, service is made by publication, upon an order made by the judge or justice of the peace.

In District Court actions the order shall direct the publication to be made in some newspaper to be designated as most likely to give notice to the defendant; the last of such insertions to be sixty days from the first; the order prescribes the time for publication. In Justice Court actions the publication shall be once a week for at least four weeks, and the justice shall issue a new summons returnable in not less than sixty, nor more than seventy days from its date.

In Justice Court actions the time mentioned in the summons for the appearance of the defendant and the time of service shall be as follows:

1. When the summons is accompanied by an order to arrest the defendant, it shall be returnable immediately.

2. When the defendant is not a resident of the county, it shall be returnable not more than two days from its date, and shall be served at least one day before the time for appearance.   ·

3. In all other cases it shall be returnable in not less than six nor more than ten days from its date, and shall be served at least four days before the time for appearance.

CHAPTER IV.

PLACE OF TRIAL OF CIVIL ACTIONS.

Actions for the following causes shall be tried in the county in which the subject of the action, or some part thereof, is situated:

1. For the recovery of real property, or of an estate or interest therein, or for the determination in any form of such right or interest, and for injuries to real property.

2. For the partition of real property.

3. For the foreclosure of a mortgage of real property.

Actions for the following causes shall be tried in the county where the cause, or some part thereof, arose :

1. For the recovery of a penalty or forfeiture imposed by statute.

2. Against a public officer.

In other cases the action shall be tried in the county in which the parties, or some of them, reside, at the commencement of the action, or the defendant may be found ; or if none of the parties reside in the Territory, the same may be tried in any county which the plaintiff may designate in his complaint.

The Court may, on motion, change the place of trial.

1. When the county designated in the complaint is not the proper county.

2. When there is reason to believe that an impartial trial cannot be had therein.

3. When the convenience of witnesses and the ends of justice would be promoted by the change.

4. When from any cause the judge is disqualified from acting in the action.

No person shall be held to answer to any summons issued against him from a Justice's Court in a civil action, in any precinct other than the one in which he or the plaintiff shall reside, except in the cases following :

1. Where there shall be no Justice's Court for the precinct or village in which the defendant or plaintiff may reside, or no justice competent to act in the case.

2. When two or more persons shall be jointly or jointly and severally bound in any debt or contract, or otherwise jointly liable in the same action, and reside in different precincts of the same county, or in different counties, the plaintiff may prosecute his action in a Justice's Court of the precinct or county in which any of the debtors or other persons liable may reside.

3. In case of injury to the person, or to real and personal property, the plaintiff may prosecute his action in the precinct where the injury was committed, or where the defendant may be found.

4. Where personal property, unjustly taken or detained, is

claimed, or damages therefor are claimed, the plaintiff may bring his action in any precinct or county in which the property may be found, or in which the property was taken.

5. When the defendant is a non-resident of the county, he may be sued in any precinct, village or city wherein he may be found.

6. When a person has contracted to perform any obligation at a particular place, and resides in another, he may be sued in the precinct in which such obligation is to be performed or in which he resides.

7. When the foreclosure of a mortgage, or the enforcement of a lien upon personal property, is sought by the action, the plaintiff may sue in the precinct, village or city where the property is situated.

CHAPTER V.

LIMITATION OF ACTIONS.

The periods prescribed for the commencement of actions are as follows:

Within five years—An action for the recovery of real property or the possession thereof; an action upon a judgment or decree of any Court of the United States, or of any State or Territory within the United States.

Within four years—An action upon any contract, obligation, or liability founded upon an instrument of writing.

Within three years—An action for trespass upon real property; an action for taking, detaining or injuring any goods or chattels, including actions for the specific recovery of personal property; an action for relief on the ground of fraud, the cause of action in such case not to be deemed to have accrued until the discovery by the aggrieved party of the facts constituting the fraud.

· Within two years—An action upon a contract, obligation or liability, not founded upon an instrument of writing; also, an action
against a sheriff, coroner, or constable, upon the liability incurred
by the doing of an act in his official capacity, and in virtue of his
office, or by the omission of an official duty, including the non-
payment of money collected upon an execution. The above does
not apply to open accounts for goods, wares and merchandise sold
and delivered, nor to an action for an escape.

Within one year—An action for libel, slander, assault, battery,
or false imprisonment; an action against a sheriff or other officer
for the escape of a prisoner arrested on civil process; an action on
an open account for goods, wares and merchandise sold and delivered.

The statute begins to run from the time the cause of action accrued.

Part payment does not prevent the statute running; but in
an action brought to recover a balance due upon a mutual, open account, where there have been reciprocal demands between the
parties, the cause of action shall be deemed to have accrued from
the time of the last item proved in the account on either side.

An action upon a contract, obligation or liability for the payment
of money, founded upon an instrument of writing, executed out of
this Territory, can only be commenced as follows:

First. Within one year, when more than two and less than five
years have elapsed since the cause of action accrued.

Second. Within six months, when more than five years have
elapsed since the cause of action accrued.

When the cause of action has arisen in another State, Territory,
or foreign country, and is there outlawed, no action will lie in this
Territory. If when the cause of action accrues against a person, he
is out of the Territory, the action may be commenced within the
term herein limited, after his return to the Territory; and if after
the cause of action accrues he departs from the Territory, the time
of his absence shall not be part of the time limited for the commencement of the action.

Chapter VI.

ATTACHMENTS.

Attachments in District Court actions can only be issued :

1. In an action upon a contract, express or implied, for the direct payment of money, and which is not secured by a mortgage upon real or personal property.

2. In an action upon a contract, express or implied, against a defendant not residing in this Territory.

Before issuing the writ of attachment, an affidavit on the part of the plaintiff must be filed, showing :

That the defendant is indebted to the plaintiff (specifying the amount of the indebtedness over and above all legal set-offs or counter claims) upon a contract, express or implied, for the direct payment of money, and that such contract was made or is payable in the Territory, and that the payment of the same has not been secured by any mortgage on real or personal property, and showing also the existence of either of the following causes :

1. That the defendant is not a resident of this Territory.

2. That he is about to remove his property and effects beyond the limits of this Territory.

3. That he has absconded from his usual place of abode in this Territory, so that the ordinary process of law cannot be served upon him.

4. That he is about fraudulently to conceal or make away with his property and effects, so as to defraud, hinder, or delay his creditors.

5. That he has fraudulently concealed or made away with his property and effects, so as to defraud, hinder, or delay his creditors.

6. That he is about fraudulently to convey, assign, or dispose of his property, so as to defraud, hinder, or delay his creditors.

7. That he has fraudulently conveyed, assigned, and disposed of his property, to defraud, hinder, or delay his creditors.

8. That the defendant is a non-resident corporate body.

9. That he is about to remove from this Territory to avoid the ordinary process of law.

A written undertaking is required on behalf of the plaintiff, in a sum not less than double the amount claimed, with sufficient sureties, to the effect that if the defendant recover judgment the plaintiff will pay all costs awarded the defendant, and all damages which he may sustain by reason of the attachment, not exceeding the amount specified in the undertaking.

In Justices' Courts, an attachment may be issued in an action upon a contract, express or implied, for the direct payment of money, which contract is made or is payable in this Territory, and is not secured by a mortgage upon real or personal property.

Upon filing with the justice an affidavit, on the part of the plaintiff, setting forth the above facts, and the amount of such indebtedness over and above all legal set-offs and counter claims; and upon the filing of an undertaking on the part of the plaintiff, with two or more sufficient sureties, to the effect that if the defendant recover judgment the plaintiff will pay all costs awarded the defendant, and all damages which he may sustain by reason of the attachment, the writ shall issue.

CHAPTER VII.

ARREST IN CIVIL ACTIONS.

The defendant may be arrested in the following cases :

1. In an action for the recovery of money or damages, in a cause of action arising upon contract, express or implied, when the defendant is about to depart from the Territory with intent to defraud his creditors ; or when the action is for willful injury to person, to character, or to property known to belong to another.

2. In an action for a fine or penalty, or for money or property embezzled, or fraudulently misapplied, or converted to his own use by a public officer, or an officer of a corporation, or an attorney, factor, broker, agent or clerk, in the course of his employment as such, or by any other person in a fiduciary capacity, or for misconduct or neglect in office, or in a professional employment, or for a willful violation of duty.

3. In an action to recover the possession of personal property unjustly detained, when the property, or any part thereof, has been concealed, removed, or disposed of, so that it cannot be found or taken by the officer.

4. When the defendant has been guilty of a fraud in contracting the debt or incurring the obligation for which the action is brought, or in concealing or disposing of the property, for the taking, detention, or conversion of which the action is brought.

5. When the defendant has removed or disposed of his property, or is about to do so, with intent to defraud his creditors.

An affidavit is required on behalf of the plaintiff, setting forth the grounds of arrest, and also an undertaking with sufficient sureties, in an amount of at least five hundred dollars.

CHAPTER VIII.

JUDGMENTS AND JUDGMENT LIENS.

A judgment is the final determination of the rights of the parties in an action or proceeding.

Immediately upon the docketing of a judgment it becomes a lien upon all the real estate of the judgment debtor not exempt from execution in the county, owned by him at the time, or which he may afterwards acquire, until the lien expires. The lien con-

tinues two years.   A transcript of the original docket, certified by
the clerk, may be filed with the recorder of any other county, and
thereby constitute a lien upon the lands of the judgment debtor in
such county.

CHAPTER IX.

EXECUTIONS, EXEMPTIONS, SALE, AND REDEMPTION.

Execution may be issued at any time within five years after the
entry of judgment.   Until a levy is made, property is not affected
by execution.

The following property is exempt from execution :

1. The homestead, consisting of a quantity of land, together
with the dwelling house thereon and its appurtenances, and the
water rights and privileges pertaining thereto sufficient to irrigate
the land, not exceeding in value the sum of five thousand dollars,
allowed to the head of a family.   The homestead may be set apart
after execution levied.

2. All spinning-wheels, weaving-looms with the apparatus, and
stoves put up and kept for use in any dwelling-house.

3. A seat, pew, or slip occupied by such person or family in any
house or place of public worship.

4. All cemeteries, tombs, and rights of burial, while in use as
repositories of the dead.

5. All arms and accoutrements kept for use ; all wearing apparel of every person or family.

6. The library and school books of every individual and family,
not exceeding one hundred and fifty dollars, and all family pictures.

7. To each householder ten goats or sheep, with their fleeces,
and the yarn or cloth manufactured from the same ; two cows, five

swine, and provisions and fuel for the comfortable subsistence such household and family for six months.

8. To each householder, all household goods, furniture and utensils, not exceeding in value six hundred dollars.

9. The tools, implements, materials, stock, apparatus, team, vehicle, horses, harness, or other things to enable any person to carry on the profession, trade, occupation or business in which he is wholly or principally engaged, not exceeding in value six hundred dollars.

10. One sewing machine and one musical instrument.

11. A sufficient quantity of hay, grain, feed, and roots for properly keeping the above named animals three months.

An execution may be made returnable in not less than ten nor more than sixty days after its receipt by the sheriff.

Notice of sale must be given as follows :

1. In case of perishable property, a reasonable time.

2. In case of personal property, not less than five nor more than ten days.

3. In case of real property, twenty days.

Upon the sale of real property, when the estate is less than a freehold of two years unexpired term, the sale shall be absolute. In all other cases, the real property is subject to redemption within six months after the sale, upon paying to the purchaser the amount of the purchase, with eighteen per cent. in addition, and all taxes or assessments paid by the purchaser.

CHAPTER X.

PROCEEDINGS SUPPLEMENTARY TO EXECUTION.

When an execution is returned unsatisfied in whole or in part, the judgment creditor, at any time after such return is made, is entitled to an order from the judge of the Court, requiring such judgment debtor to appear and answer concerning his property before such judge or a referee appointed.

Chapter XI.

ESTATES OF DECEASED PERSONS.

Immediately after the appointment of the executor or administrator, he shall give notice through a newspaper published in the county, if there be one, and if not, then in such newspaper designated by the Court, requiring all persons having claims against the deceased to present them, with the necessary vouchers, within ten months after publication of the notice. If a claim be not presented within the ten months, it shall be forever barred ; however, if it be not then due or is contingent, it may be presented within ten months after it shall become due or absolute ; and when it shall be made to appear by the affidavit of the claimant, to the satisfaction of the executor or administrator, and the probate judge, that the claimant had no notice by reason of being out of the Territory, it may be presented at any time before a decree of distribution is entered. Every claim presented to the executor or administrator shall be supported by the affidavit of the claimant, that the amount is justly due, that no payments have been made thereon, and that there are no offsets to the same to the knowledge of the claimant or other affiant ; *provided*, that when the affidavit is made by any other person than the claimant, he shall set forth in the affidavit the reason it is not made by the claimant.

The affidavit may be sworn to before any officer authorized to take oaths.

When a claim is presented and allowed by the executor or administrator, it shall then be presented to the probate judge for his approval, and within thirty days thereafter filed with the Probate Court.

If a claim be founded upon a bond, note, or other instrument, the original instrument shall be presented. If the claim be secured by a mortgage or other lien, such mortgage or other evidence of liens shall be attached to the claim, and filed therewith, unless the same be recorded in the office of the recorder of the county in which the land lies, in which case it shall be sufficient to describe the mortgage or lien, and refer to the date, volume and page of its record. In all cases the claimant may withdraw his claim from file on leaving a certified copy, with a receipt endorsed thereon by himself or agent.

After a claim is rejected, suit must be brought thereon within three months or it is forever barred ; if it be not then due, suit must be brought within three months from the time it falls due. An outlawed claim must not be allowed.

When a judgment has been rendered against the testator or intestate in his life-time, no execution shall issue thereon after his death ; but a certified copy of such judgment shall be presented to the executor or administrator, and be allowed, and filed and rejected, as any other claim, but need not be supported by the affidavit of the claimant; and if justly due and unsatisfied, shall be paid in due course of administration : *provided*, however, that if the execution shall have been actually levied upon any property of the deceased, the same may be sold for the satisfaction thereof, and the officer making the sale shall account to the executor or administrator for any surplus in his hands. The executor or administrator may, however, require the affidavit of the claimant, or other satisfactory proof, that the judgment, or any portion thereof, is justly due and unsatisfied.

Chapter XII.

AFFIDAVITS AND DEPOSITIONS.

An affidavit taken in another State or Territory, to be used in this Territory, shall be taken before a commissioner appointed by the Governor of this Territory to take affidavits and depositions in such State or Territory, or before any judge, or notary public, or clerk of a Court having a seal; when taken before a judge the genuineness of the judge's signature, the existence of the Court, and the fact that such judge is a member thereof, shall be certified by the clerk of the Court under the seal thereof.

The deposition of a witness out of the Territory may be taken in an action at any time after the service of the summons or the appearance of the defendant. It shall be taken under a commission issued from the Court under the seal of such Court. It shall be issued to a person agreed upon by the parties, or if they do not agree, to any judge or justice of the peace selected by the officer granting the commission, or to a commissioner appointed by the Governor of this Territory to take affidavits and depositions. The deposition must be returned in a sealed envelope, directed to the clerk or other person designated or agreed upon, by mail or other usual channel of conveyance.

Chapter XIII.

ACKNOWLEDGMENTS.

The proof or acknowledgment of every conveyance affecting any real estate shall be taken by some one of the following officers:

1. If acknowledged or proved within this Territory, by some

judge or clerk of a Court having a seal, or some notary public, or justice of the peace of the proper county.

2. If acknowledged or proved without this Territory, and within the United States, by some judge or clerk of any Court of the United States, or of any State or Territory having a seal, or by any commissioner appointed by the Governor of this Territory for that purpose.

3. If acknowledged or proved without the United States, by some judge or clerk of any Court of any State, Kingdom, or Empire having a seal, or by any notary public therein, or by any minister, commissioner, or consul of the United States appointed to reside therein.

Every officer who shall take the proof or acknowledgment of any conveyance affecting any real estate, shall grant a certificate thereof, and cause such certificate to be indorsed or annexed to such conveyance. Such certificate shall be :

1. When granted by any judge or clerk—under the hand of such judge or clerk.

2. When granted by an officer who has a seal of office—under the hand and official seal of such officer.

The certificate of such acknowledgment shall state the fact of acknowledgment, and that the person making the same was personally known to the officer granting the certificate to be the person whose name is subscribed to the conveyance as a party thereto, or was proved to be such by the oath or affirmation of a credible witness, whose name shall be inserted in the certificate.

A married woman may convey her real estate, her husband joining in the conveyance. No acknowledgment to be made by a married woman unless she be personally known to the officer taking the same to be the person whose name is subscribed to such conveyance as a party thereto, or shall be proved to be such by a credible witness ; nor unless such married woman shall be made acquainted with the contents of such conveyance, and shall acknowledge on an examination, apart from and without the hearing of her husband, that she executed the same freely and voluntarily, without fear or compulsion, or undue influence of her husband, and that she does not wish to retract the execution of the same.

CHAPTER XIV.

MARRIED WOMEN.

All property, both real and personal, of the wife, owned by her before marriage, and that acquired afterwards by gift, bequest, devise, or descent, shall be her separate property, and is not subject to the debts of her husband.

All property acquired after marriage, by either husband or wife, except such as may be acquired by gift, bequest, devise, or descent, shall be common property.

The separate property of the husband is not liable for the debts of the wife contracted before marriage, but the separate property of the wife shall be and continue liable for all such debts.

CHAPTER XV.

CHATTEL MORTGAGES.

Chattel mortgages may be made on the following property, viz :
Upholstery and furniture used in hotels and public boarding houses, when mortgaged to secure the purchase money of the identical articles mortgaged, and not otherwise ; saw mill, grist mill, and steamboat machinery ; tools and machinery used by machinists, foundry men, and other mechanics ; steam boilers, steam engines, locomotives, engines, and the rolling stock of railroads ; printing presses and other printing material ; instruments and chests of a surgeon, physician, or dentist ; libraries of all persons ;

19

machinery and apparatus for mining purposes; growing crops, grain in store or field; teams and implements pertaining to farming; stock of all kinds on farm.

No chattel mortgage made shall have any legal force or effect, (except between the parties thereto) unless the residence of the mortgagor and mortgagee, their profession, trade, or occupation, the sum to be secured, the rate of interest to be paid, when and where payable, shall be set out in the mortgage; and the mortgagor and mortgagee shall make affidavit that the mortgage is *bona fide*, and without any design to defraud or delay creditors, which affidavit shall be attached to such mortgage.

Mortgage not valid as to third parties, unless duly recorded, or unless the mortgagee receives and retains the actual possession of the property.'

CHAPTER XVI.

INTEREST.

When there is no express agreement fixing a different rate of interest, interest shall be allowed at the rate of ten per cent. per annum, on all moneys after they become due on any bond, bill, promissory note, or other instrument of writing, or any judgment recovered before any Court in this Territory for money lent, for money due on the settlement of accounts from the day on which the balance is ascertained, and for money received for the use of another.

Parties may agree, in writing, for the payment of any rate of interest whatever on money due or to become due on any contract; any judgment rendered on such contract shall conform thereto, and shall bear the interest agreed upon by the parties, and which shall be specified in the judgment.

Parties may agree, in writing, to compound interest.

CHAPTER XVII.

BILLS OF EXCHANGE.

Three days' grace allowed on notes and bills, except sight drafts.

The rate of damages to be allowed and paid upon the usual protest for the non-payment of bills of exchange, drawn or negotiated within this Territory, shall be as follows :

1. If such bill shall have been drawn upon any person or persons in any of the United States or Territories east of the Rocky Mountains, fifteen dollars upon the hundred upon the principal sum specified in such bill.

2. If such bill shall have been drawn on any person or persons in any port or place in Europe or any foreign country, twenty dollars upon the hundred upon the principal sum specified in such bill.

Such damages shall be in lieu of interest, charges of protest, and all other charges incurred previous to and at the time of giving notice of non-payment ; but the holder of such bill shall be entitled to demand and recover lawful interest upon the aggregate amount of the principal sum specified in such bill and of the damages thereon, from the time notice of protest for non-payment shall have been given, and payment of such principal sum shall have been demanded.

PART XII.

BRITISH COLUMBIA.

PREPARED EXPRESSLY FOR THIS WORK BY M. W. T. DRAKE, VICTORIA.

CHAPTER I.

COURTS—THEIR JURISDICTION AND TERMS.

The Supreme Court is presided over by a chief justice and two pusne judges. This Court exercises a legal and equitable jurisdiction in all matters. It has sole control over the estate of infants, lunatics and deceased persons, and claims a jurisdiction in divorce and matrimonial causes. The admiralty jurisdiction of the Province is vested in the chief justice alone. It is the Court of Appeal from all inferior tribunals, and from it there is an appeal to the Supreme Court of Canada and Privy Council of England.

The judges also sit as judges of assize for the trial of criminals.

The Court holds three terms annually for the purpose of disposing of law points reserved at trials, for hearing motions for new trials, appeals, special cases, etc., etc. These sittings are held at Victoria, and the terms are held in February, April, and November.

For matters of procedure the judges sit constantly.

The Assize Courts are held three times a year, for the trial of prisoners and civil causes with a jury. The Assize Courts are held all through the Province, the judges going on circuit for the purpose.

All matters not jury cases are disposed of by the Court on application.

The County Court is held for the trial of actions of debt or damage up to $500. Actions of ejectment, libel, false imprisonment, and some others, are excluded from the cognizance of these courts.

This Court is held every month, and disposes of the cases brought before it without pleadings, and in a summary and expeditious manner. The province is divided into six districts for this purpose.

The justices of the peace have no civil jurisdiction. All prisoners have to be committed by the justices before they can be tried. At the assizes, and after committal, the case goes before the grand jury, and if a true bill is found the prisoner is put on his trial; if no bill is found he is at once discharged.

The municipalities have also a limited jurisdiction for enforcing their by-laws.

Chapter II.

COMMENCEMENT OF SUITS.

Civil suits in the Supreme Court are commenced by writ of summons, to which the defendant has to appear in eight days; if he fails to appear after due service, the plaintiff signs judgment for his debt; if he appears, the plaintiff proceeds to state his cause of action in a pleading called a declaration, to which the defendant replies by a plea, and in the majority of cases the action being thus

put in issue is set down for trial ; but any neglect of the defendant to proceed according to the rule, subjects him to the penalty
of having judgment signed against him.   In some cases the pleadings extend considerably beyond this, until at last they arrive at
issue and are then ripe for trial.

Sometimes, by consent, a special case is stated and tried by the
judge without a jury.   In any case, if both parties consent, the
judge alone can dispose of the case without a jury.

In actions on bills of exchange and promissory notes, if brought
within six months of the due date of the bill or note, the defendants
are not allowed to defend except on special ground shown in affidavits.

All writs must be personally served, unless the defendant is keeping out of the way to avoid service, and then the Court allows substituted service.   If the defendant is abroad, whether a foreigner
or not, special forms of writ are provided, but the service must be
personal.

In equity cases proceedings are commenced by bill of complaint,
being a narrative of the circumstances on which the plaintiff relies
for relief.   The defendant has a month to answer, and after answer
there are several different modes of bringing the suit to a hearing.
The evidence is generally taken on affidavit, but may be *viva voce*.
A single judge disposes of equity cases without a jury.

Equity suits can be disposed of at any place the plaintiff fixes ;
liable to be changed on good cause shown.

CHAPTER III.

LIMITATIONS OF ACTIONS.

Six years is the limitation for all simple contract debts ; twenty
years for all specialty debts.   In case the cause of action arose in
a foreign country, the defendant may plead the statute of limita-

tions of such country as a bar. A foreign judgment is placed on
the same footing as a simple contract debt, and has to be sued
within the same time.

CHAPTER IV.

ATTACHMENTS—ARREST IN CIVIL ACTIONS.

Attachments are not allowed except under the Insolvency Act,
and then it practically binds the property for the benefit of all
creditors.

Arrest in civil actions is in practice only resorted to for the purpose of compelling a defendant who is about to leave the jurisdiction to give security for the alleged debt.   The sheriff keeps him
in charge until he has put in security, or until the trial of the
writ.   There is no imprisonment for debt.   But the County Court
judges have power of committal for disobedience of orders for payment of money.

CHAPTER V.

JUDGMENTS AND JUDGMENT LIENS.

A judgment binds the lands of a debtor when registered.   It
also enables a creditor to seize the goods of his debtor, or to compel payment of debts due to the debtor, to himself, under what are

called garnishee proceedings ; but a judgment does not bind the personal property of the debtor until the writ of execution is in the hands of the sheriff.

CHAPTER VI.

EXECUTIONS, EXEMPTIONS, REDEMPTION, SALE.

Executions are enforced against the land and personalty of the debtor.

The debtor is entitled to an exemption of five hundred dollars in personalty.

For homestead exemption, see " Homesteads."

The debtor may redeem his property at any time before sale. Personal property has to be sold without any delay, and by public auction.   Real property is advertised thirty days.

CHAPTER VII.

SECURITY FOR COSTS

Is always required when the plaintiff is resident out of the jurisdiction of the Court, in an amount of five hundred dollars ; but if within the jurisdiction, he may commence actions in *forma pauperis*, if he is not in a position to pay fees.

CHAPTER VIII.

APPEALS

Are allowed from the County Courts to the Supreme Court, if made within forty-eight hours after the decision is objected to ; from the Police and Magistrate Courts to the Supreme Court, if applied for in four days; from the Supreme Court to the Privy Council of England, or the Supreme Court of Canada, if the amount in dispute is over fifteen hundred dollars.   Security required is five hundred dollars.

CHAPTER IX.

ESTATES OF DECEASED PERSONS.

Intestate estates, where there is no next of kin or creditor who desires administration, are managed by the registrar of the Supreme Court as official administrator.   There is no statuteable time for sending in claims, but every estate is advertised and a time fixed. The claims have to be sworn to—if from a foreign country, before a notary public, attested by the British ambassador, consul, or charge d'affaires.   Twelve months is the time allowed to settle the estate, whether the deceased died intestate or not.   If the deceased left a will legally executed, his executors manage the estate without filing any security, and only file accounts at the end of the twelve months.   If they neglect their duty, the devisees have a legal remedy, but the Court does not control them.

CHAPTER X.

HOMESTEADS.

Land to the value of twenty-five hundred dollars may be home
stead, if duly registered as such at a time when the owner was free
from debt.

CHAPTER XI.

DEPOSITIONS.

For matters in civil suits, evidence abroad is generally taken by
commissioners appointed by a judge of the Supreme Court. In
other matters, affidavits can be taken before any minister, ambassador, consul, vice-consul, or consular agent, and if there is no one
representing these functionaries, then before a notary public duly
certified to be such by the Governor or Secretary of State.

CHAPTER XII.

JUDICIAL RECORDS—ACKNOWLEDGMENTS.

Judicial records of foreign States can be proved by examined
copies, sealed with the seal of the State if relating to State documents, or the seal of the Court if relating to judicial records.

Acknowledgments of deeds can be taken before a notary public, duly certified to be such by the British consul.

Chapter XIII.

LIMITED PARTNERSHIPS.

Joint stock companies can limit the liability of their shareholders to the amount subscribed for by each, by registering under the statute.

The law of private partnerships now allows a person to invest money in a business concern and receive a share of the profits, without being liable as a partner.

Chapter XIV.

MARRIED WOMEN

Can invest the money earned by any trade or occupation, and the same is free from the debts, control or engagements of the husband; and landed property, held before marriage or acquired subsequent thereto, can be dealt with by a married woman as if she were a *femme sole*.

CHAPTER XV.

MORTGAGES.

[: Chattel mortgages must be registered within twenty-one days after execution, and an affidavit filed of the day and date of execution, in order to protect the property from execution creditors of the grantor. A mortgage unregistered is good between the parties, and if the mortgagee take the property into his own custody an execution creditor cannot seize it. Furniture, goods, merchandise, etc., can be mortgaged. Farming stock and crops are not subject to the Act.

MORTGAGES OF LAND.

A mortgagee of land is a specialty creditor; he can sue his debtor for the amount due, sell the mortgage property, or foreclose the mortgage; if he sells the mortgage property, it is doubtful whether his remedy against the mortgagor has not gone, in case the sale fails to realize the whole amount due.

CHAPTER XVI.

INTEREST AND USURY.

The legal rate of interest is twelve per cent. per annum. All judgments carry this rate; so do accounts, after notice that interest will be charged; but any higher rate of interest is perfectly legal, as there are no usury laws in force.

Chapter XVII.

LAND LAWS.

Persons can acquire land (three hundred and twenty acres) by pre-emption, and on a survey being made, a grant in fee simple is issued without charge.

INDEX.

INDEX.

ARIZONA.

PART XI.

20

ATTORNEYS.

PART I.

BRITISH COLUMBIA.

PART XII.

CALIFÓRNIA.

PART III.

IDAHO.

PART VII.

JURISDICTION OF U. S. COURTS AND BANKRUPTCY.

PART II.

MONTANA.

PART IX.

NEVADA.

PART IV.

21

OREGON.

PART V.

UTAH.

PART VI.

WASHINGTON TERRITORY.

PART X.

WYOMING.

Part VIII.

318

INDEX.

www.ingramcontent.com/pod-product-compliance
Lightning Source LLC
Chambersburg PA
CBHW021218270326
41929CB00010B/1176